Sunnyside Gardens

SUNNYSIDE GARDENS

Planning and Preservation in a Historic Garden Suburb

Jeffrey A. Kroessler

With architectural illustrations
by Laura Heim

EMPIRE
STATE
EDITIONS

AN IMPRINT OF FORDHAM UNIVERSITY PRESS

NEW YORK 2021

Fordham University Press has no responsibility for the persistence or accuracy of URLs for external or third-party Internet websites referred to in this publication and does not guarantee that any content on such websites is, or will remain, accurate or appropriate.

Fordham University Press also publishes its books in a variety of electronic formats. Some content that appears in print may not be available in electronic books.

Visit us online at www.fordhampress.com/empire-state-editions.

Library of Congress Cataloging-in-Publication Data

Names: Kroessler, Jeffrey A, author.
Title: Sunnyside Gardens : planning and preservation in a historic garden
    suburb / Jeffrey A Kroessler.
Description: Empire state editions. | New York, New York : Fordham
    University Press, 2021. | Includes bibliographical references and index.
Identifiers: LCCN 2021001961 | ISBN 9780823293810 (hardback) | ISBN
    9780823293803 (trade paperback) | ISBN 9780823293827 (epub)
Subjects: LCSH: City planning—New York (State)—New York—Sunnyside
    Gardens—History. | Historic districts—New York (State)—New
    York—Sunnyside Gardens. | Landscape protection—New York (State)—New
    York—Sunnyside Gardens. | City beautiful movement—New York
    (State)—New York—Sunnyside Gardens—History. | Sunnyside Gardens (New
    York, N.Y.)—History—20th century.
Classification: LCC HT168.S88 K764 2021 | DDC 307.1/21609747243—dc23
LC record available at https://lccn.loc.gov/2021001961

Printed in the United States of America

23 22 21   5 4 3 2 1

First edition

CONTENTS

PREFACE

THIS BOOK HAS HAD a very long gestation period. As an undergraduate history major at Hobart College, I developed an interest in utopias and dystopias, and then I was fortunate to later take Frank E. Manuel's course in utopian thought while pursuing an MA at New York University. I first researched Sunnyside Gardens when I was studying with Richard C. Wade at the CUNY Graduate School, and it formed a chapter in my dissertation on the urbanization of Queens. How do utopian aspirations play out in practice? Historically, not well.

While a graduate student researching Queens, I became involved with local historical societies and preservation groups. In that way I met the individuals who had formed the Sunnyside Foundation to bring Sunnyside Gardens back to the form its designers intended. I have remained active in citywide preservation organizations—the Historic Districts Council, the Municipal Art Society, the City Club of New York—and have sought to bring a historian's insights into preservation controversies of the moment. That experience certainly contributed to the making of this book.

After history and preservation, architecture is the third dimension. Many of my observations and insights were facilitated by architect Laura Heim, my wife. We bought a house in Sunnyside Gardens in 2004, just in time for the fight over whether it should be designated a historic district. During the sometimes unpleasant disputes that ensued, we countered the inaccurate statements of the opponents of designation, I with historical facts, and she with architectural analysis. We had fun. At a key moment of the struggle, she put together images of what could happen to the little brick houses under the present rules—vinyl siding and stucco affixed to facades, Palladian windows, garish paint schemes. It was a turning point. The Landmarks Preservation Commission designated Sunnyside Gardens and Phipps Garden Apartments a historic district in 2007. I shudder to think what could have happened to this historic planned community had it not been designated, and worse, what would have been the fate of the landmarks law had misinformation and unwarranted fears torpedoed this designation.

Since opening her practice here in 2006, Laura has worked on dozens of homes in Sunnyside, bringing a contemporary sensibility into the protected brick buildings. Her process has involved analyzing the surprisingly numerous housing types, which revealed how they evolved over the five years of construction. She drafted plans for each court to highlight key features and generated drawings of each block. This book proves the benefits of a marriage of history and architecture, each incomplete without the other.

Sunnyside Gardens: Planning and Preservation in a Historic Garden Suburb brought together the many strands of my life, and in a sense it was inevitable: I grew up on Long Island, in Garden City.

SUNNYSIDE GARDENS CHRONOLOGY

1898   Ebenezer Howard self-published *To-morrow: A Peaceful Path to Real Reform*, reprinted in 1902 as *Garden Cities of To-morrow*.

1903   Howard formed the Garden City Association with the aim of achieving the ends outlined in his book, with local chapters created across Britain.

1903   Howard and associates formed First Garden City, Limited, and purchased 3,818 acres about thirty-five miles north of London for their initial endeavor, Letchworth Garden City. Raymond Unwin and Barry Parker were appointed the architects.

1906   Dame Henrietta Barnett began developing Hampstead Garden Suburb outside London. Raymond Unwin and Barry Parker laid out the original plan; Edwin Lutyens planned the Suburb's formal center and designed the two churches, St. Jude's and the Free Church.

1909   The Russell Sage Foundation Homes Company began building Forest Hills Gardens in the borough of Queens; Grosvenor Atterbury was the lead architect, and Frederick Law Olmsted, Jr., the landscape architect. The garden suburb has about 890 freestanding and attached houses, and 11 apartment buildings. Protective covenants covering the open space and the buildings instituted at the start remain in effect.

1911   The Queensboro Corporation began building Jackson Heights; Andrew J. Thomas designed the earliest buildings.

1912   Raymond Unwin published "Nothing Gained by Overcrowding!: How the Garden City Type of Development May Benefit Both Owner and Occupier."

1913   The Garden City Association became the International Garden Cities and Town Planning Association, with Ebenezer Howard as president.

1914–1918   During the First World War, Raymond Unwin worked with the British government to build new housing for war workers along garden city principles.

1917–1919   The U.S. government funded new housing for war workers through the Emergency Fleet Corporation of the U.S. Shipping Board and the U.S. Housing Corporation. Frederick L. Ackerman was chief of Housing and Town Planning under Robert Kohn; Henry Wright designed Colonial Terraces in Newburgh, New York.

1919   Howard and associates began the second Garden City, Welwyn. Louis de Soissons was appointed architect and planner.

April 18, 1923   Clarence Stein, Henry Wright, Lewis Mumford, Frederick L. Ackerman, Benton MacKaye, Alexander Bing, Charles Whittaker, Stuart Chase, and Robert Kohn formed the Regional Planning Association of America (RPAA).

March 14, 1924   Members of the RPAA organized the City Housing Corporation as a limited dividend corporation to build a garden suburb; by June they had acquired seventy-seven acres in Long Island City adjacent to the Sunnyside rail yards. Construction of Sunnyside Gardens began within months. Stein and Wright were the primary architects, with additional designs from F. L. Ackerman; Marjorie Sewell Cautley was the landscape architect.

1924–1936   Lewis Mumford and his family lived in Sunnyside Gardens, first in a co-operative apartment on 48th Street and then in a private house in a mews on 44th Street.

April 1925   The International Federation of Town and Country Planning and Garden Cities met in New York City. The gathering featured a visit to Sunnyside Gardens and Jackson Heights. Howard, Raymond Unwin, Barry Parker, and Ernst May attended. Lewis Mumford edited the May 1925 issue of *Survey Graphic*, with contributions from Stein, Wright, Bing, MacKaye, Chase, and Ackerman.

1928 Sunnyside Gardens was completed, with a total of 563 homes (293 one-family, 224 two-family, and 46 three-family houses) and 322 units in apartment buildings.

1929–1931 The City Housing Corporation built the first section of Radburn, a "town for the motor age," with a total of 430 one-family and 44 two-family houses, 90 row houses, and 92 units in two apartment buildings. The Great Depression brought construction to a halt by 1933.

1931 Phipps Garden Apartments, designed by Clarence Stein with landscaping by Marjorie Cautley, was completed adjacent to Sunnyside Gardens. The first set of buildings had 344 units for tenants of modest means. In 1935, Phipps Houses built a second block of garden apartments immediately behind the first.

1931–1936 Residents of Sunnyside Gardens launched a mortgage strike and banded together to resist foreclosures and evictions; more than half of the residents lost their homes.

1932–1935 Stein and Wright were the site planners and consulting architects for Chatham Village, a garden suburb of 197 homes in Pittsburgh.

1933 Stein and Wright dissolved their partnership of ten years.

1934 The City Housing Corporation filed for bankruptcy.

1934 Henry Wright joined the faculty at Columbia University in the new program in town planning and housing studies.

June 29, 1935 Governor Herbert Lehman dedicated Hillside Homes in the Bronx, funded by the Public Works Administration. Clarence Stein designed the five-block complex of five-story garden apartments with landscape architect Marjorie Sewell Cautley.

1935 Henry Wright published *Rehousing Urban America*.

1935 Stein and Wright consulted on the planning of Greenbelt, Maryland, for the Resettlement Administration, a New Deal agency. The community was completed in 1937, incorporating elements of Radburn.

July 10, 1936 Henry Wright died at age fifty-eight.

1939 "The City" premiered at the New York World's Fair, highlighting the ideas of the RPAA and featuring scenes of Radburn and Greenbelt. Clarence Stein had created Civic Films, Inc., to produce the film. Lewis Mumford prepared the script with Pare Lorentz; Aaron Copeland composed the music; Ralph Steiner and Willard Van Dyke were the cinematographers.

1957 Clarence Stein published *Toward New Towns for America.*

1962 Concerned about increasing speculation and the loosening of design controls, residents of Hampstead formed the Hampstead Garden Suburb Protection Society.

1964–1968 The forty-year easements regulating the open spaces and architectural features of Sunnyside Gardens expired; some residents erected previously forbidden fences along their property lines into the common courtyards, paved over front yards for driveways, and built rooftop additions.

1968 Hampstead Garden Suburb was designated a conservation area, and the reconstituted Hampstead Garden Suburb Trust began enforcing strong preservation controls as the ground landlord.

July 18, 1974 The New York City Department of City Planning voted to designate Sunnyside Gardens a Special Planned Community Preservation District, a new zoning classification that also applied to the Harlem River Houses, Parkchester, and Fresh Meadows.

February 7, 1975 Clarence Stein died at age ninety-two.

1975 Radburn was listed on the National Register of Historic Places.

1981 Sunnysiders formed the Sunnyside Gardens Conservancy to preserve the historic character of the community and foster restoration. This became the Sunnyside Foundation for Community Planning. They offered technical assistance on facade maintenance, obtained public funding to upgrade the commercial blocks of Skillman Avenue, and initiated a preservation easement program.

September 7, 1984 Sunnyside Gardens was listed on the National Register of Historic Places through the efforts of the Sunnyside Foundation.

January 26, 1990 Lewis Mumford died at age ninety-four.

2003 Residents organized the Sunnyside Gardens Preservation Alliance to gain designation as a historic district by the city.

2005   Radburn was designated a National Historic Landmark.

2007   The Landmarks Preservation Commission designated Sunnyside Gardens and Phipps Garden Apartments a historic district.

2008   City Planning removed the Special Planned Community Preservation District designation from Sunnyside Gardens; henceforward, only the Landmarks Preservation Commission would regulate.

2013   The Landmarks Preservation Commission rejected an application to locate the 1931 Aluminaire House, designed by Albert Frey, in the Sunnyside Gardens Historic District, but it granted tentative approval to building eight units of housing on the lot, a former playground. In 2016, the City Council allocated funds to purchase the site for a public park.

2016   Phipps Houses proposed a ten-story, 209-unit affordable housing building for the parking lot between the Phipps Garden Apartments and the railroad, but they withdrew the plan in the face of opposition from residents and the local councilman.

2020   The School Construction Authority demolished the parking garage designed by Clarence Stein to make way for a new middle school. The structure was included in the National Register historic district, but it was excluded from the historic district designated by the Landmarks Preservation Commission.

Sunnyside Gardens

⦙⦙⦙

Sunnyside Gardens and the Garden City Idea

A Cityscape for Urban Reform

SUNNYSIDE GARDENS HAS BEEN an icon of urbanism and planning from its inception in the 1920s. Urban historians, architects, and planners still study this distinctive community, and given the chance, they eagerly make a pilgrimage to experience firsthand its verdant landscaped courts and modest brick row houses.

This garden suburb was both the culmination of a generation of Progressive Era housing reform and an experiment in social engineering. Not the most beautiful planned community, perhaps, nor the most elegant, and certainly not the most perfectly preserved, Sunnyside Gardens nevertheless remains significant both in terms of the planning principles that inspired its creators and in its subsequent history. More than any other garden suburb, its builders were self-consciously following the garden city ideal first expressed in England in the last decade of the nineteenth century and given concrete form in the first decade of the twentieth.

The architects of Sunnyside were motivated by a reformist impulse. They asked how we might reshape our cities to foster more equitable communities and create a more livable urban environment. Remarkably, they also had the confidence to believe that they could do exactly that through enlightened planning and design. To a degree, that motivation continues to animate urban planning a century later, and the persistence of those ideals explains why Sunnyside Gardens remains as relevant today as when it was built.

There is no place quite like Sunnyside Gardens. That statement is not descriptive hyperbole; it is quite literally true. For all the interest in the place among academics and architects over the decades, it is unique. There have been hundreds of garden suburbs, planned communities, and model housing experiments in the United States, but no place follows the Sunny-side plan exactly.[1] What, then, accounts for its enduring appeal, and why is it still held up as an important example of enlightened urban design?

Why this garden suburb was built when and where it was, as well as how it has fared over its first century, is the heart of this book. The story of Sunnyside Gardens is more than a story of housing reform, because the builders sought also to offer an alternative design for urban living. This is a story of planning history, architecture, social history, and historic preservation, all played out within the grand narrative of Greater New York.

Utopia

The idea that the city could and should be remade has persisted from the Victorian Age into the present. Reform-minded architects and planners in England and the United States knew too well the social and environmental ills of the cities around them at the turn of the century. Lewis Mumford and other social critics emphasized the dehumanizing aspects of the contemporary city, with its "mechanization and regimentation," and how its forms, from overcrowded tenements to alienating towers in the park and sprawling suburbs, contributed to the unraveling of the social fabric.[2] Indeed, that generation of visionaries introduced the very idea of the livable city. In the early decades of the twentieth century, this meant reimagining how city dwellers could live, how the buildings and spaces of the city might produce happier, healthier, and more fully realized human beings. "No form of industry and no type of city are tolerable that take the joy out of life," wrote Mumford. This was not a matter of merely altering the form of the built environment, for "the task of city design involves the vaster task of rebuilding our civilization," of coordinating "on the basis of more essential human values than the will-to-power and the will-to-profits, a host of social functions and processes that we have hitherto misused in the building of cities and polities, or of which we have never rationally taken advantage."[3] It was an ambitious, even utopian aspiration.

No one, perhaps, was more influential in advancing this line of thought than Ebenezer Howard (1850–1928). Neither an architect nor a planner, Howard might be termed a Victorian utopian.[4] He was in fact a great admirer of Edward Bellamy's utopian novel *Looking Backward* (1888), and he arranged for the printing of that book in England.[5] Mumford, too, admired the book, calling it "one of the most important political pamphlets" of its time, a work illustrating how a community must prioritize the common good and tame the chaotic impulses of the individual. Furthermore, Bellamy understood that "socialization in one department was incompatible with unlimited individualism in every other."[6] It was a principle Mumford found appealing. The physical ordering of society would mold the people, and the people would shape its physical forms.

In 1898, Howard self-published *To-morrow: A Peaceful Path to Real Reform*. Reissued in 1902 under its more familiar title, *Garden Cities of To-Morrow*, that slim volume outlined his vision of an urban future, drawing upon various strains of English socialist thought. In contrast with the unregulated and uncoordinated free market development that then characterized urban growth, Howard proposed building entirely new garden cities beyond the confines of the existing metropolis. For a tract by an unknown, marginal figure, the book had a surprisingly immediate and widespread impact. Within a year of its publication, Howard was leading the newly formed Garden City Association, with local chapters springing up across Britain.

Such was the optimism and confidence of the age. The garden city idea gained traction across the Atlantic before the Great War, and for much of the twentieth century its principles, modified by American pragmatism to fit American conditions, were applied almost as a matter of faith by urban planners. The garden city as defined by Howard—a self-contained community with a limited population size, a mix of homes and industry, and surrounded by a greenbelt—would never be fully realized in the United States.

Mumford certainly embraced the utopian aspects of the garden city movement. This was an attempt "to build up a more exhilarating kind of environment—not as a temporary haven of refuge but as a permanent seat of life and culture, urban in its advantages and permanently rural in its situation." This was nothing less than "a movement towards a higher type of civilization than that which has created our present congested centers."[7]

As much as its physical form, the underlying economic and social arrangements of Howard's idea held great appeal to the generation that came of age during the Progressive Era. Frederic C. Howe recognized the fundamental difference between the ordinary city and the garden city: "The former is left to the unrestrained license of speculators, builders, owners, to a constant conflict of public and private interests; the latter treats the community as a unit, with rights superior to those of any of its individual members. One is a city of unrelated and, for the most part, uncontrolled private property rights; the other is a community intelligently planned and harmoniously adjusted, with the emphasis always on the rights of the community rather than on the rights of the individual property owner."[8]

Theories of ideal communities, innovative design, and urbanism were insufficient by themselves to transform cities. Even after a century of model tenements and planned communities, urban renewal and social engineering, the problems of urban America in the mid–twentieth century seemed as intractable as ever. Poverty and inequality, crime and vice, racial and ethnic tensions, and educational systems of limited effectiveness continue to bedevil cities. One aspect of life that has improved over the last century, at least in the developed world, is the urban environment. The air is cleaner; rivers, lakes, and oceans are far less polluted; streets are better lit and have less debris; and living conditions are far healthier and more comfortable for even the poorest citizens. Housing laws generated during the Progressive Era proved to be remarkably effective in mandating minimum standards of light, air, heat, and sanitation. The era also introduced zoning to regulate use and scale; New York passed its first zoning resolution in 1916.[9] Population densities dropped dramatically since the turn of the century, and the age of frighteningly overcrowded tenements all but faded from popular memory in the United States and Britain.

At the same time, however, we seem to have lost faith in the idea that motivated those urban visionaries: that by remaking the physical city, by providing new homes in a healthy and wholesome setting, we will not only improve people's lives, but actually foster the elevation of the human condition. For that generation, elimination of inferior housing and the building of well-designed new homes in a rational context became an imperative for the betterment of society, and no one doubted that the betterment of society should be our common goal.

Over the course of the twentieth century, many acclaimed housing experiments and planned communities were built in and around London and the city of New York based on those idealistic principles. Each embodied the faith that better housing would produce better people, that social ills were the result of the conditions of life rather than moral failings of the individual. Remove slum dwellers from the slums, the thinking went, and we will eliminate the social pathologies associated with the slum, and it was widely recognized that the slums were infecting the body politic.[10] In 1944, New York mayor Fiorello La Guardia exhorted, "Tear down the old. Build up the new. Down with rotten, antiquated rat holes. Down with hovels. Down with disease. Down with crime. Down with firecraft. Let in the sun. Let in the sky. A new day is dawning. A new life. A new America."[11]

Only later, after too many solid residential neighborhoods had been demolished in the name of urban renewal, did the question arise as to whether it was indeed necessary to wipe the slate clean, to demolish the old completely and build anew under supposedly enlightened planning principles.[12] Adding to the civic pushback was the banality of much of the new construction that replaced the familiar, human-scaled city, and certainly very little of the new housing embodied any of the ideals of the garden suburb.

By the middle of the twentieth century, urban planners and the government agencies that enabled them had embraced ideas of urbanism antithetical to the principles espoused by Howard and his followers. Rather than fostering community, economic and social diversity, and density, the ascendant standards emphasized the separation of land uses; a rejection of the street and street life; a rejection of traditional elements like squares and public plazas; the treatment of individual buildings as objects in space, not integrated into a complex urban fabric; and the primacy of the automobile, as evidenced by the construction of high-speed expressways through urban neighborhoods. As a result, compact and thriving urban neighborhoods were wiped away to make way for clean modernist spaces. Outside the city, the misinterpretation of garden city principles yielded suburban sprawl.[13] With the embrace of those anti-urban design principles by the federal bureaucracy came mandates for their universal application in all projects receiving federal funding.

Lewis Mumford thought that with urban renewal the city was only exchanging slums for super-slums. The design—elevator buildings, long anonymous corridors destined to become breeding grounds for crime (as indeed happened), dysfunctional open spaces—ordained that outcome. Yes, the real estate industry was profiting from urban renewal, but more damning was that they were not creating environments designed to foster community, but places seemingly designed to stifle human potential.[14] Nathan Glazer offered a particularly sharp critique of the result. Contrasting the cold and uniform public housing projects that replaced a vibrant, if run-down tenement neighborhood in East Harlem, the very neighborhood where he had grown up, in fact, he suggested that it "reflects what the housing reformers in league with the early modernists wanted." Examining the resulting social landscape, he wondered whether the established principles of housing reform actually benefited their intended beneficiaries.[15] What they represented was a perversion of the goals and design principles of Progressive Era urban reformers rather than a faithful application of them.

Austere, cold, and anonymous public housing projects of the mid-twentieth century may have been the unfortunate end, but unhappiness with that outcome ought not to negate the hopeful idealism of that first generation of urban planners. No doubt they, too, would gasp at Corbusier-inspired towers situated within superblocks, and nowhere more so than in the postwar public housing projects. As Mumford remarked, "There is nothing wrong with these buildings except that, humanly speaking, they stink."[16] The misappropriation of an idea does not necessarily invalidate it. The wonder is that alternatives had been built in and around New York decades earlier—Forest Hills Gardens, Jackson Heights, Sunnyside Gardens, Phipps Garden Apartments, and Radburn. Why, we must ask, did the builders of cities and suburbs turn away from those successful, human-scale precedents?

Jane Jacobs Doesn't Like Queens

The Death and Life of Great American Cities (1961) is a masterpiece of urban criticism. In that eye-opening book, Jane Jacobs not only provided a new perspective on the recent past, but also a prescription for future urban living. From transportation policy to zoning, historic preservation to urban planning, Jane Jacobs has been invoked as a guide and an authority. Voiced or unvoiced, "What would Jane do?" is the question floating above urban policy issues great and small.

No one can doubt that the values espoused by Jacobs have largely benefited our nation's cities. Diversity of scale; diversity of economic activity; urban density sufficient to promote a vibrant street life; small, locally owned shops; solid housing stock of generally modest scale; a city accommodating pedestrians rather than automobiles; local input on policy issues affecting neighborhoods—these are the bedrock principles of the livable city today, accepted and applied from New York to Seattle. But should all of these ideas be uncritically applied everywhere and under all circumstances? Are those families choosing to live in suburban neighborhoods, places antithetical to Jacobs's vision, simply wrong?

Jane Jacobs famously began her iconoclastic work with a forthright declaration of war: "This book is an attack on city planning and rebuilding." Her attack was "not based on quibbles about rebuilding methods or hair-splitting about fashions in design," but rather "on the principles and aims that have shaped modern, orthodox city planning and rebuilding."[17] At the time she was writing, federal urban renewal and highway construction programs had been eviscerating entire neighborhoods in cities across the United States for a generation. Her book was a reaction to the uncompromising destruction of what she saw as viable residential and commercial places to make way for multilane expressways and superblocks sprouting forbidding towers in the park.

But she went further than simply critiquing and condemning the planning practices of her time. She traced their origin to the urban thinkers of the early twentieth century who sought to reform cities. In fact, there was much to reform in their day, from overcrowding and poor sanitation to the absence of greenery and spaces for recreation. Jacobs, however, characterizes their critique as simply an anti-city, pro-suburban agenda. The targets of her criticism were the very designers and critics who provided the intellectual capital for the creation of Sunnyside Gardens. It is quite a leap to blame the planners of Sunnyside Gardens and Radburn for suburban sprawl and the monstrous postwar public housing projects, but that is what she does.

For all the history in *Death and Life*, it is ahistorical in that it ignores the main current of New York City's growth and, not incidentally, the way the majority of New Yorkers lived. When Jacobs published her book in 1961, Manhattan had been losing population for half a century. From a peak of 2.3 million residents in 1910, the number had dropped to 1.7 million by 1960, and Manhattan's population continued to fall into the 1980s.[18] Looking only at Manhattan, one would have to conclude that New York was a city in decline. No city losing a quarter of its population could be called a success. And yet, this is precisely when New York became the largest and richest city in the world, the capital of the arts and the capital of capital.

As Manhattan lost residents, the outer boroughs grew at a fantastic pace. In the decade of the 1920s, Queens, Brooklyn, and the Bronx each added more than half a million residents, a transformation that simultaneously lowered population density in Manhattan. This was the avowed goal of the planners Jane Jacobs criticizes, and as the intention was to improve the quality of life for the majority of residents who had few housing options beyond the tenement, it was undeniably a great public good. Much of the new housing beyond Manhattan was of a decidedly suburban character—detached one-family houses, low-rise two-family houses, and garden apartments. This was the antithesis of the tenement districts of the Lower East Side, Hell's Kitchen, Yorkville, and Jacobs's own neighborhood of Greenwich Village. Given the chance, many thousands of families willingly fled the environment Jacobs would praise so uncritically decades later.

Lewis Mumford reviewed *Death and Life* in the *New Yorker*, a piece dismissively titled "Mother Jacobs' Home Remedies for Urban Cancer." "Strangely," he wrote, "the city that so insistently drives its population into the suburbs is the very same city that Mrs. Jacobs describes as 'vital.'" The movement "into the vast, curdled Milky Ways of suburbia," as he put it, was a century old process, attracting "millions of quite ordinary people who cherish such suburban desires, not a few fanatical haters of the city, sunk in bucolic dreams."[19] Having written about cities and planning and architecture for forty years, Mumford gave no ground to this interloper. Moreover, she was attacking him personally, for he was a lifelong adherent to the ideas she was condemning.

Jane Jacobs wrote in response to the urban renewal of the 1940s and 1950s that erased still vital neighborhoods. But this was also when the outer boroughs of New York City steadily grew. Queens alone added nearly half a million new residents between 1950 and 1970, even as Manhattan lost another quarter million people. And where did those new residents live? Many of them moved into one-family houses and garden apartments made possible by automobile ownership. Thousands of families moved into Stuyvesant Town, Parkchester, and other high-rise neighborhoods inspired by Le Corbusier's vision of towers in the park, and by all accounts the new residents enjoyed living there. In sum, people were choosing to live in places Jane Jacobs did not approve of at all—places that did not resemble Hudson Street in Greenwich Village in the least. Despite the "grandiloquent title," commented Mumford, "her great American city has as its sole background the humble life of a very special, almost unique historic quarter . . . a backwater whose lack of dynamism accounts for such pleasant features as it has successfully retained."[20]

Jacobs began *Death and Life* with a critique of Ebenezer Howard and his garden city ideal, asserting that he hated not only "the wrongs and mistakes of the city," but the city itself as "an outright evil and an affront to nature." To save the people, she wrote, Howard would "do the city in." His garden city would be neither a dormitory suburb nor a city, but a self-sufficient town—in a word, a kind of utopia. She did not mean that as a compliment. In a remark similar to the intellectuals' dismissal of postwar suburbia, Jacobs summarized Howard's concept as "really very nice towns if you were docile and had no plans of your own and did not mind spending your life among others with no plans of their own."[21]

Far from wanting to "do the city in," the advocates of the Garden City idea sought to create an environment where the best attributes and advantages of urban life could flourish, in a setting offering ample open space and greenery. Furthermore, they intended their new communities to provide more healthy and humane living conditions for the working poor who had no option beyond slum housing. Their hope was that with the process of decentralization and the thinning out of urban populations, the ills of the city would be cured and a renewed sense of community would be engendered in the efficient, verdant, and self-contained garden city.[22]

In Jacobs's reading, Howard's spirit infused the "conceptions underlying all American city planning today." In particular, she objected to "the sorting and sifting of simple uses; the provision of wholesome housing as the central problem, to which everything else was subsidiary." Furthermore, she rejected his defining "wholesome housing in terms only of suburban physical qualities and small-town social qualities."[23] Howard, of course, was one of Mumford's heroes, and Mumford strenuously countered her assault upon a man who "devoted the last quarter of his life to the improvement of cities, seeking to find by actual experiment the right form and size, and the right balance between urban needs and purposes and those of the rural environment."[24]

In the United States, Howard's ideas immediately found a receptive audience among a new generation of planners, architects, and urbanists— among them Clarence Stein, Henry Wright, Frederick L. Ackerman, and Catherine Bauer. Bauer became involved with the Regional Planning Association of America (RPAA) through Mumford, whom she met through the literary circles of Greenwich Village (she and Mumford were soon lovers). In 1934 she published *Modern Housing*, which advocated nonspeculative workers housing such as had been built in Europe. Bauer called their group "Decentrists" because they sought "to decentralize great cities, thin them out, and disperse their enterprises and populations."[25] But for Jacobs, decentralization was a city-destroying idea responsible for the wounded state of contemporary cities.[26]

Roberta Gratz knew and admired Jane Jacobs.[27] She was a member of the Landmarks Preservation Commission when the agency designated the Sunnyside Gardens Historic District. Her immediate reaction on visiting the place for the first time was, "Your problem here is too little density."[28] True, Sunnyside, with its small brick houses and landscaped courtyards, was not as dense as a block in Manhattan, but that was the point. For Sunnyside's planners, low-rise housing and lower density was the solution, not the problem. It was the reform impulse made manifest.

As a practical matter, had the city not expanded beyond Manhattan it would have surely choked on its own success. Decentralization was not the threat Jacobs saw, but a necessary outcome, and during the first three decades of the twentieth century that is exactly what happened. The question, therefore, was not whether the city would thin out; indeed, that was greatly desired in terms of both the quality of life for those crowded into the tenements and the economic growth of the city as a whole. The question was what shape the new city would take. With options ranging from suburban one-family houses to high-rise apartment buildings, one thing was certain—no one wanted to replicate conditions in the slums.

It was not so much the physical city itself that troubled Mumford and his colleagues as it was its negative effects upon its inhabitants. They looked at the early-twentieth-century city and saw failure. The new garden suburbs, they believed, would unleash human potential as much as tenement life stifled it. Ada Louise Huxtable, architecture critic of the *New York Times*, saw in their "humane physical planning" an understanding of "the relationship between the built world and people's physical and spiritual needs" and a belief that "the answer to many of the ills of society seemed to be a better place to live."[29]

Again, Jacobs disagreed with such assumptions and simply dismissed the garden suburb as profoundly anti-urban. Speaking at the Conference on Urban Design at Harvard University in 1956, Jacobs said, "We are greatly misled by talk about bringing the suburb into the city. The city has its own peculiar virtues and we will do it no service by trying to beat it into some inadequate imitation of the non-city."[30] (When one considers Charlotte Gardens, the neighborhood of one-family houses built in the South Bronx in the early 1980s, one must concede that she had a point.) The cure, in Jacobs's view, was worse than the disease. "Model housing schemes by Stein and Wright, built mainly in suburban settings or at the fringes of cities, together with the writings and the diagrams, sketches and photographs presented by Mumford and Bauer, demonstrated and popularized ideas" now ingrained among urban planners: The street is bad; houses should turn inward to green spaces; a plan with frequent streets is bad; the superblock is good.[31] She was explicitly damning the planning principles successfully applied at Sunnyside Gardens and its sibling, Radburn.

Mumford, of course, took Jacobs's critique as a personal affront, as indeed it was. She was tearing down a belief structure that he had, in part, erected in the 1920s and then defended for the rest of his life. "For ten years I lived in Sunnyside Gardens," he wrote in his review of her book, "the kind of well-planned neighborhood Mrs. Jacobs despises: modestly conceived for people of low incomes, but composed of one-, two-, and three-family houses and flats, with private gardens and public open spaces. . . . Not utopia, but better than any existing New York neighborhood, even Mrs. Jacobs' backwater in Greenwich Village." Against the "well-planned, visibly homogeneous" communities Stein and Wright designed, Jacobs held to "her belief, unshaken by irrefutable counter-evidence, that congestion and disorder are the normal, indeed the most desirable, conditions of life in cities." Most damning for Mumford was the absence of beauty in the city Jacobs championed. "That beauty, order, spaciousness, clarity of purpose may be worth having for their direct effect on the human spirit even if they do not promote dynamism, increase the turnover of goods, or reduce criminal violence seems not to occur to Mrs. Jacobs. This is esthetic philistinism with a vengeance."[32] Mumford and Jacobs agreed that dehumanizing spaces had a deadening effect upon the human spirit, but they found little common ground as to what characterized such spaces.

Jacobs's second villain was Le Corbusier and his Radiant City. While the Decentrists advocated the low-rise, lower-density, spread out city, Le Corbusier envisioned the city of the future as towers in the park, what he called the "vertical garden city" rising within a superblock. Ever arrogant, he claimed he did not have to justify his vision in either "humane or city-functional terms." Jacobs thought that Corbusier's ideal, like the Garden City, was "nothing but lies."[33]

Having established the villains of her story, Jacobs champions the actual, lived-in, historic city first ignored and then bludgeoned by the planners. "Unstudied, unrespected, cities have served as sacrificial victims," she wrote.[34] Her plea is understandable in the context of the time she was writing—a historical moment when cities had few champions and did, in fact, need saving from big government, from the automobile, and from aesthetically inferior and alienating architecture. And her voice was not a solitary one. In the September 1964 issue of *Fortune*, Richard J. Whalen published an angry essay about his home town: "A City Destroying Itself." The next year he expanded the essay into a book-length jeremiad subtitled *An Angry View of New York*. Looking at his city, he saw only "tragic deprivation and massive failure," calling out especially the banality of most of the new construction.[35]

The application of present-day certainties to events and conditions in the past generally results in a bizarre misreading of history, and in this instance is nothing less than the evisceration of a century of urban reform. It was the dismal conditions in British cities and the depopulation of the countryside in the late nineteenth century that gave rise to Ebenezer Howard's ideas. Overcrowding, the absence of clean water, poor to nonexistent sanitation, the disease environment, and the prevalence of crime and vice in slums compelled Howard and other reformers to envision an alternative. Far from a tactic in a war on the poor, the garden city was to be the future of urban living for all classes.

We may critique some of the solutions offered by those reformers, but we ought not to mischaracterize their intentions. They sincerely believed that by improving the urban environment, by providing healthier, sunnier, and more verdant neighborhoods, we would also alleviate the social ills afflicting cities. Whether such a belief animates urban reform today is a worthy question.

Acolytes of Jane Jacobs would slavishly apply her ideas to the contemporary city at all times and in all circumstances and, in so doing, would misread urban history, misdirect contemporary urban planning, and erase from memory generations of housing reform.[36] Nevertheless, what remains is a multidimensional historic city, offering a wide range of housing choices. Urban historian Robert Fishman saw no reason why the urban virtues Jacobs championed had to be limited to older neighborhoods like her treasured Greenwich Village, as those virtues "might be achieved at many points in the region that combine the pedestrian scale and vitality of the best urban neighborhoods with rapid, efficient transit ties to the urban core."[37] There is no inherent contradiction between low-rise, low-density neighborhoods and the livable city, but reconciling our admiration for Jane Jacobs with the fact that millions of New Yorkers live in the kind of places she claims have neither vibrancy nor validity is certainly a challenge.

The Suburban City

No single set of characteristics defines the livable city. For some, it is a neighborhood of tenements, with small shops on the ground floor and apartments above. Since New York's low point in the 1970s, blocks once shunned as decrepit and threatening have rebounded through gentrification. Many young families, however, understandably seek a more suburban setting. Lower density means more green spaces for the children, greater privacy, and a quieter environment. No one but an ideologue or a radical leveler would argue that a city cannot accommodate both forms of urban living.

In actuality, suburban areas of the city possess many of the attributes Jane Jacobs attributes to healthy neighborhoods. While there may not be a mix of commercial and residential properties within each block, streets lined with shops are within walking distance of many homes. Rather than the vertical diversity Jacobs praised, neighborhoods like Forest Hills and Kew Gardens possess horizontal diversity.

Sunnyside Gardens was one experiment in recrafting the twentieth century city. The designers modified a ubiquitous urban form, the row house, to incorporate generous landscaping and combined the privacy of the one-family home with communal open spaces. It was a housing experiment in the city, but not of the city. Rather, it was a self-conscious alternative to common urban forms. Has the experiment succeeded? Indeed, how would success be measured? After a hundred years, the question is ripe for reassessment.

If it is a matter of emulation of specific form, then we have to accept that the specific plan of Sunnyside Gardens has fostered few imitators. But the founders intended to build a community, not simply houses, and that goal still inspires. While the social motives of the planners of Sunnyside and Radburn may have gone into eclipse over the decades, the design principles endure to a surprising degree. Reston, Virginia (1964), and Columbia, Maryland (1967), both follow in the garden city tradition. Indeed, Robert E. Simon, the developer of Reston, was the son of Robert E. Simon, who served on the board of the City Housing Corporation (CHC); as he planned his new community, he received a personal tour of Radburn by Charles S. Ascher, who had been counsel to the CHC.[38]

New Urbanism, the movement sparked by Andreas Duany and Elizabeth Plater-Zyberk's Seaside, the community built on the Florida panhandle in 1981, consciously sought to apply traditional architectural forms and planning principles to foster greater social cohesion among residents. In essence, that movement rediscovered the virtues of the garden city. Writing about Celebration, the New Urbanist community developed by the Disney Corporation in the 1990s, Witold Rybczynski noted that the design was infused with the ideal of supporting a sense of community. An executive with Disney Imagineering explained, "We understand that community is not something that we can engineer, but we think that it's something we can foster." Indeed, Celebration's website proclaims it is "not a town, but a community in every positive sense of the word."[39] The builders of Sunnyside Gardens said that a century ago.

Each of these successor places—Reston, Columbia, Seaside, and Celebration—shares with Sunnyside Gardens a desire for a more human-scaled environment. Each was the result of a single, unified vision, and from the start each was governed by strict zoning controls and design standards. In the early twentieth century, garden city advocates were reacting against unhealthy and congested urban environments. The New Urbanists of the late twentieth century reacted against pervasive suburban sprawl. That the New Urbanists struck a nerve with their throwback design principles only demonstrates how far we had diverged from the garden city ideal.[40] Interestingly, both the garden suburb advocates and the New Urbanists reached similar conclusions.

This book is divided into two parts. Part 1, "Planning," addresses the garden suburb idea as it was realized in London and New York in the early 1900s, and how Sunnyside Gardens itself was built, with an analysis of the housing types and landscape. It continues with the story of Radburn and Phipps Garden Apartments, and then the tragedy of the Great Depression, when more than half of that first generation of residents lost their homes to foreclosure. The section concludes with the persistence of these ideas in the New Deal. Part 2, "Preservation," discusses how garden suburbs have been regulated and preserved, concluding with the designation of Sunnyside Gardens as a historic district by the city of New York in 2007. The last chapter chronicles a controversial proposal to install the 1931 Aluminaire House, an experimental housing prototype, on the only vacant site in Sunnyside Gardens.

Sunnyside Gardens is a small neighborhood in the borough of Queens, but its story is of national, even international importance. That it endures is a testament first, to the ideas of its founders, then to the city of New York's recognition of its historic significance, and finally to the commitment of its residents to the hopeful ideals embodied in the design.

PART I

PLANNING

1

‡‡‡

The Garden City and the Garden Suburb in Great Britain

SUNNYSIDE GARDENS DID NOT ARISE in a vacuum. The ideas inspiring its creation developed at a time when cities in Europe and the United States were crowded, unhealthy places, and reform-minded citizens sought ways to ameliorate, or even transcend, those social ills. If we recognize that condition as a societal problem, and if we have the means to rectify it, reasoned housing reformers, then clearly we have the obligation to do so. The earliest steps called for improving specific conditions by mandating minimum standards of light, air, and sanitation. Too often, of course, the minimum became the maximum. Dissatisfied with the limited results of such an approach, urban critics began to reenvision the city entirely. What would we build if we could start anew, they asked.

In both London and New York, two truths were unavoidable. First, living conditions for a large number of city dwellers were abhorrent. Working-class and immigrant neighborhoods were overcrowded, with poor sanitation and a disease environment producing alarming rates of infant mortality and communicable diseases. "The mass of the people live in hovels and slums and our children grow up far from the sight and pleasure of green fields," wrote Raymond Unwin, the architect of Hampstead Garden Suburb. Second, Unwin saw that undeveloped land at the edge of the city was rapidly being built upon without any discernable plan. "Our land is laid out solely to serve the interests of individual owners, without regard to the common needs," he observed.[1] For him, designing and building for the common good was the essence of urban planning, but unless that principle was installed as municipal policy, cities would continue to grow in a haphazard, destructive fashion.

In the early 1900s, however, there was no mechanism whereby cities could control or guide growth. "Governing bodies have looked on helplessly while estate after estate around their towns has been covered with buildings without any provision having been made for open spaces, school sites, or any other public needs," wrote Unwin. "The owner's interest, too often his only one, has been to produce the maximum increase of value or of ground rent possible for himself by crowding upon the land as much building as it would hold."[2]

In addition to those capitalist imperatives, there was the banality or even ugliness of what was being built. It should not be surprising that aesthetics would remain a low priority where maximizing profit was the primary motivation of builders. Adapting construction to the specifics of site was not a consideration either and that resulted in the obliteration of the natural features and irregularities in the landscape. "Instead," complained Unwin in dismay, "some stock plan of a house which is thought to be economical is reproduced in row after row without regard to levels, aspect, or anything but just one point: Can the building be done so cheaply that it can be made to yield a good return on the outlay? Is it any wonder, then, that our towns and suburbs express by their ugliness the passion for individual gain which so largely dominates their creation?"[3] In a word, what is lost in such unplanned sprawl is charm. The question was whether the expanding metropolis would bulldoze natural features in favor of undifferentiated sprawl and congestion, or whether we could envision and realize an alternative, an environment that might unite town and country and encourage the happiness and potential of its residents. Building on the Arts and Crafts movement, which sought to bring beauty to everyday objects and so improve the conditions of industrial workers, housing reformers asserted that no one should be ineligible for the enjoyment of an environment of beauty and charm on account of social class.

In 1898, Ebenezer Howard published *To-morrow: A Peaceful Path to Real Reform*, reprinted in 1902 under its now familiar title, *Garden Cities of To-Morrow*.[4] This slim tract, with its schematic diagrams of the "Town-Country Magnet," would seem the very model of Edwardian Era eccentricity, but almost at once Howard's concept captured the imagination of both professional architects and planners and the general public, and launched the garden city movement.

Howard opened with the observation that while there was great over-crowding in the cities, at the same time rural areas were being depop-ulated. This imbalance only worsened the quality of life in both places. Central to his idea was the dispersal of industry rather than accepting as inevitable its concentration in congested cities. As current development trends only accentuated the differences between urban and rural living, Howard envisioned the best attributes of each combined into a new config-uration, the garden city. These new towns should not be permitted to grow in a haphazard fashion, he contended, and the best way to assure that end would be to build according to a rational plan and to surround the city with a greenbelt.[5] As it was unlikely that the British government would ever finance such a venture, it would be the responsibility of private citizens to invest in that future.[6]

Garden Cities of To-Morrow provided an attractive ideological frame-work, but suburbanization and a lowering of population densities in Lon-don and New York would have occurred in any event as new rapid transit systems opened up previously distant precincts to residential construction. The question was whether the expanding metropolis would bulldoze the landscape in favor of undifferentiated sprawl and congestion or whether it was possible to envision and realize an alternative—an environment that might unite town and country and encourage the happiness and full po-tential of its residents.

Another question was whether rearranging the spatial arrangements of society made it possible to also transform its economic basis. Howard asked, following the arguments of Henry George: What if, instead of the profit from housing going into the pockets of distant owners, it flowed back to the community? A new community simply incorporating the prevailing economic arrangements could not be the goal. C. B. Purdom, the finan-cial director of Welwyn, explained that the land values had to be "socially enjoyed." A garden city would have to be developed "on the economic basis provided by the systematic and deliberate creation of land values, the profits on which form part of the town's revenues." The idea of the land "being in public ownership, or held in trust for the community," was an essential feature.[7]

To prove his theory, Howard organized a private company to build a garden city outside London. In 1903 work began on what was called First Garden City, Letchworth, and in 1919 construction of the second com-munity, Welwyn, was underway. While not directly connected to Howard, Hampstead Garden Suburb, which launched three years after Letchworth, embodied many of his ideas and was the work of the same architects, Raymond Unwin and Barry Parker.

Lewis Mumford saw the garden city as a rebuke to the increasing regimentation and mechanization of contemporary society. What concerned Mumford was not so much architecture in and of itself—though he certainly embraced the principle that aesthetics is never irrelevant—but the impact of the built environment upon the human spirit. He championed Howard because "he returned to the human scale, and he conceived of a means of increasing the size and complexity of social relations without destroying this scale." Furthermore, by planning regionally and establishing controls for area, density, and population, new towns would offer an outlet for future growth without repeating the mistakes of the past.[8]

Many of Ebenezer Howard's ideas were simply impractical and, given the economic realities of suburban development, unlikely ever to be followed exactly. His interest was not so much in the form of the new community—the plan and architecture—as its potential for economic and social change. He envisioned the garden city "as a vehicle of fundamental transformation . . . the path to a higher plane of living." The result would be "not only a new balance of town and country but harmonization of human society with nature and reconciliation of individualism and socialism."[9] Howard's followers embraced that spirit of idealism and optimism and shared with him a desire to transform society.

Howard's garden city ideal inspired generations of planners and urban critics who embraced his underlying principles and goals while adapting their own designs to specific conditions. As much as Howard intended his little book to be prescriptive, in practice it remained largely inspirational. Housing reformers would work toward his ideal, never fully attaining its complete realization but holding ever true to its aspirations.

How deeply the garden city idea resonated with the public and the speed with which it spread across Europe and the United States is remarkable. A year after his book appeared, Howard and a few admirers organized the Garden City Association with the ultimate goal of bringing his ideas to fruition. Predictably, the movement initially attracted a variety of socialists and land reformers; Howard himself was sympathetic to socialist solutions to societal ills. But for his ideals to be realized, practical men of business and standing would be required, and there was a surprising degree of sympathy with his ideas among Britain's industrialists.

Not all industrialists blithely consigned their workforce to urban slums. In 1888, W. H. Lever began building Port Sunlight for his workers, a garden suburb named for the popular Lever Brothers soap. Located across the Mersey River from Liverpool, it represented "the first effective large-scale integration of nineteenth-century social reform with picturesque town design. For the first time, the utilitarianism of social-minded town planning, with rows of narrow houses on straight bye-law [sic] streets, gave way to a new sensibility of the garden village." In Birmingham a few years later, chocolate manufacturer George Cadbury developed his own workers' village, Bournville, with the avowed purpose "of alleviating the evils which arise from the insanitary and insufficient accommodation supplied to large numbers of the working classes, and of securing to workers in factories some of the advantages of the outdoor village life, with opportunities for the natural and healthful occupation of cultivating the soil."[10]

Clarence Stein visited Bournville in 1908 during a break from his studies at the École des Beaux-Arts. In a letter to his brother, Stein expressed his sympathy with the plight of the urban masses in England and his dismay over their living conditions. "The poor of the big cities here seem quite as badly off as at home, perhaps worse," he wrote. "The streets are full of ragged, dirty children, and plenty of the grown-ups are no better kept. . . . They seem to be crowded together in tenements facing on narrow lanes or alleys." Bournville, by contrast, was a revelation, a parklike setting where the residents benefited from a direct connection with greenery, with tree-lined streets and front and rear gardens planted with fruit trees. He adds that the planting preceded occupancy of the homes, "so they have the initial care of a good gardener." He took lessons from the siting and design of the houses, as well. The homes, rather than "being built in solid, monotonous rows, as they are in most workingmen's villages, are made for two to four families each. And then they are of an endless variety of design." He enthusiastically declared that it was "the most inspiring thing I had seen in England." He came away with the lesson that "utopian dreams can be made realities, if we only go about it in a practical, sane way."[11]

Port Sunlight and Bournville were essentially suburbs, extensions of an adjacent city. What set *Garden Cities of To-Morrow* apart from those industrial precedents was the idea of building a new, self-sustaining city entirely separate from the existing metropolis. Howard had the audacity to insist upon building such a place altogether and all at once.

Letchworth Garden City

In 1902, investors formed the Garden City Pioneer Company "to promote and further the distribution of the industrial population on the land on the lines suggested in Mr. Ebenezer Howard's book entitled *Garden Cities*

The home of Ebenezer Howard, Letchworth Garden City, 2012. (Author's photograph.)

of To-morrow, and to examine, test, and obtain information, advice, and assistance with regard to the matters therein contained, with the view of forming in any part of the United Kingdom *Garden Cities . . .* in accordance with Mr. Howard's scheme, or any modifications thereof." Within a year the company fixed on a site about thirty-five miles north of London and organized First Garden City, Ltd. They easily raised the initial capital of £300,000, and in keeping with the philanthropic and reformist spirit of the enterprise, investors agreed to limit their dividends to 5 percent. To assure success and secure their investment, they had to act all at once to realize gains from rising property values. Once the venture was complete, the investors would yield control to the residents and only then receive their 5 percent return. As the company's prospectus stated, "The inhabitants will have the satisfaction of knowing that the increment of value of the land created by themselves will be devoted to their own benefit." Not for twenty years, however, did shareholders receive that modest dividend.[12]

Work began immediately on First Garden City, soon renamed Letchworth. Architects Raymond Unwin and Barry Parker were charged with transforming Howard's grand vision into physical form. But they did not interpret their mandate as exclusively forward looking. Quite sensibly, they looked to the past for inspiration, specifically Christopher Wren's 1666 plan for rebuilding London. But Unwin and Parker also had an affinity for new approaches to community building. Both men were followers of the Arts and Crafts movement, and the writings of John Ruskin and William Morris in particular influenced Unwin, who understood that good design had a beneficial impact beyond simply aesthetic appreciation. Unwin's reputation as a leader in this area was cemented with the publication of *Town Planning in Practice* in 1909 and *Nothing Gained by Overcrowding* in 1912.[13] Unwin and Parker's unlikely combination of traditional, even nostalgic, designs with the modernist garden city ideal accounts for a good deal of the charm in the outcome.

As planned, Letchworth would house 30,000 inhabitants over 6,000 acres. As built, however, it covered only 1,250 acres, buffered by a 2,500-acre greenbelt. The community featured a range of housing types, from one-family homes to attached row houses, some grouped around interior gardens, others lining cul-de-sacs. Throughout, the houses were arranged so as to enhance the sense of a more intimate scale and to ward off any prospect of a monotonous streetscape. To prevent a plague of lower

Attached single-family cottages, Letchworth Garden City, 2012. (Author's photograph.)

quality, contractor-built houses, Unwin created a set of regulations governing design, *General Suggestions and Instructions Regulating Buildings Other Than Factories in the Garden City Estate* (1904). Though Unwin moved on to oversee the planning and construction of Hampstead Garden Suburb, Barry Parker remained a consultant at Letchworth until 1943.[14]

Welwyn Garden City

Howard and his associates had to wait until after the First World War to embark on Welwyn, their second undertaking. As he initiated that venture, he remarked, "A city will arise as superior in its beauty and magnificence to our first crude attempt as the finished canvas of a great artist to the rough and untaught attempts of a schoolboy."[15] In 1919, he took it upon himself to purchase about 2,400 acres twenty miles north of the King's Cross Station; Letchworth was another thirteen miles distant along the same rail line.

The board of this new enterprise intended that their work would provide "a convincing demonstration of the garden city principle of town development . . . in time to influence the national housing programme. . . ." In 1918, Frederic Osborn, who was involved with Second Garden City from the start, published *New Towns After the War*, arguing for the building of one hundred towns, each with a population of 40,000 to 50,000. That was not to be, but in 1946, after the Second World War, Britain passed the New Towns Act. By 1950, fourteen new towns were under construction, and by 1968, nearly a million people were living in twenty-two postwar new towns designed around garden city lines.[16]

Welwyn would be a true garden city. The statement of purpose explained that "healthy and well-equipped factories will be grouped in scientific relation to transport facilities, and will be equally accessible from the new houses of the workers." This would be "a self-contained town, with a vigorous life of its own independent of London." In terms of management, the company would retain "the freehold of the estate . . . (except in so far as parts thereof may be required for public purposes) in trust for the future community." But the plan was as concerned with aesthetic issues as with social and economic matters, stating that "preservation of the beauty of the district, and the securing of architectural harmony in the new buildings, will be among the first considerations of the Company."[17]

Construction began almost at once, with architect Louis de Soissons preparing the plans. Like Letchworth, Welwyn would fit the existing topography rather than being randomly imposed upon it. The houses were

Welwyn Garden City, 2012. (Author's photograph.)

grouped around curving roads, greens, and cul-de-sacs. The infrastructure was in place—gas, electricity, water, sewerage—and there were shops, churches, and a theater. Building a garden city required a great deal of capital up front, and only with rapid construction could the developers hope to recoup their investment. Within twelve years, a community of 9,000 inhabitants occupying 2,500 homes arose, and forty industries had opened. Still, it grew slowly and was never fully built out. Planned for 50,000 residents, by 1948 its population was only 18,000.[18]

Mumford was rather more impressed by Welwyn than Letchworth, perhaps because "the Georgian revival was in full swing, and the planner, Louis de Soissons, achieved greater charm and coherence." Even so, he thought Welwyn seemed to lack the social mission that he believed essential in a planned community. The scale was too sprawling, privileging "private functions and traditional forms and ample greenery" rather than a focus "on association and intercourse, on public functions, on focal meeting places and social intermixture, all of which call for the pedestrian scale and a more close-textured design."[19]

Ultimately, both Letchworth and Welwyn fell short of Howard's garden city ideal. Alexander Garvin suggests that while Letchworth and Welwyn may have been planned under garden city principles, there was little to distinguish them from other "less-ambitious dormitory suburbs" built around greater London at the same time. Even Mumford thought the design "uninspired." He understood that mechanically applying Howard's idea was impractical and inadvisable, but "in leaning backward to avoid the stark simplicity of Howard's diagrams, the planners managed to avoid any positive visual expression of the idea itself. And though much of the domestic architecture was more fresh and vigorous than anything of comparable cost being built at the time . . . the total architectural effect was mediocre, and as far as the idea went, esthetically unconvincing. Neither the plan nor the structures articulated the differentiated but balanced structure of the new city. Visually, the garden displaced the city."[20] Such a judgment is too harsh. Both Letchworth and Welwyn exude considerable charm and provide significantly more green space and a more generous public realm than typical suburbs.

However inspired the public may have been by Ebenezer Howard's ideas, his two garden cities were only modest successes. His idea "soon became an anachronism, resting as it did on notions of a transformed society" based on the union of town and country and communitarian principles. "Even at Letchworth and Welwyn . . . the social aspects [were] almost completely ignored."[21]

The planning principles and design elements Unwin, Parker, and de Soissons applied were increasingly in evidence in suburban developments on both sides of the Atlantic. However short they may have fallen from Howard's vision, Letchworth and Welwyn inspired a generation of American planners, and none more so than the architects of Sunnyside Gardens.

Hampstead Garden Suburb

In 1907, four years after work began at Letchworth, Dame Henrietta Octavia Barnett dug the first spade of earth for Hampstead Garden Suburb. It was her vision that brought the Suburb to life, and it grew more directly out of a traditional reform impulse than did Letchworth and Welwyn. For years she and her husband, Canon Samuel Augustus Barnett, tended the parish of St. Jude's Whitechapel in London's working class East End, but they also had a cottage near Hampstead Heath, a bucolic and unspoiled expanse north of the city. After learning of plans for the extension of the underground to Hampstead, Dame Henrietta formed a syndicate to purchase an extensive open tract to control future development. When Eton College, the owner, informed her they would not sell to a woman unless she had the support of men of substance, she lined up an impressive list of backers, and in May 1906 they purchased the open land. What resulted was, in the words of architectural historian Nicholas Pevsner, "the most perfect example of that English invention and speciality, the Garden Suburb."[22]

The Hampstead Garden Suburb Act (1906) limited the number of houses that might be built on the estate and exempted the Suburb Trust from certain local building ordinances, specifically regarding the width of roads and open space requirements, enabling them to provide "wide grass margins and wayside greens, so as to preserve the natural beauty of the estate." This governing legislation also proved a strong selling point, because the act would "prevent the *possibility* of their ever being surrounded by crowded buildings or mean streets, and thereby depreciated in value, as so often happens in ordinary estates."[23]

For the undertaking to be successful in the way they envisioned, Dame Henrietta and her backers recognized the need to break from the common pattern of urban growth, which flowed from the decisions, beneficial or harmful, of individual builders. The 243-acre site adjoining the Hampstead Heath Extension was twenty-five minutes from Charing Cross by a new transit line. Sheltered from the "smoke and fogs of London," the site possessed "a frontage of some 6,500 feet to open country." It was the perfect landscape for Henrietta Barnett's "pursuit of an ideal." "The Hampstead Garden Suburb was not created as a commercial speculation: the intention of its founders was to preserve for London, unspoiled by vulgar houses and mean streets, the foreground of the beautiful country that forms the western boundary of Hampstead Heath, and to create a residential quarter for Londoners, where the comfort of the inhabitants and the beauty of their surroundings should not be sacrificed to the greed of the landowner or the necessities of the speculative builder."[24] The Suburb Trust knew what they did not want. "Our aim is that the new suburb may be *laid out as a whole* on an orderly plan. When various plots are disposed of to different builders, and each builder considers only his own interest, the result is what may be seen in the unsightly modern streets. Our hope is that every road may have its own characteristic, that small open spaces may be within reach of every child and old person, that no house may darken or offend a neighbour's house, that the whole may be so grouped round central features and central buildings, and that from every part there shall be good views or glimpses of distant country."[25]

With those principles in mind they created the Garden Suburb Development Company (Hampstead) Ltd. Even by controlling the architectural quality of what would be built by private parties, they could not assure "symmetry and architectural beauty." They determined that the houses "should not only themselves be examples of the best work that could be

Single-family houses facing green, Hampstead Garden Suburb, 2012. (Author's photograph.)

obtained, but also should be designed and grouped in proper relation to one another, so that each should form part of a well-considered scheme for making the streets, as well as the houses, beautiful." To control costs, the Company built many groups of homes at the same time.[26]

The Development Company selected Raymond Unwin to plan the garden suburb and guide its construction. Having spent three years working on Letchworth, Unwin was the perfect man for the job. He recognized that however innovative and attractive a scheme might be, it would be tarnished if control over design was yielded to individual builders. In that case, "each architect will think only of the one house and plot and of developing his own particular fancies upon it, with little or no regard for the total effect of the street. The designs may be good, but, for want of any co-ordination, the result will be little more than an inharmonious jumble. At worst the site will fall into the hands of that type of speculative builder who employs no architect, and who, being intent merely on making all he can out of the ground and houses, is fairly sure to spoil any scheme the designer of the site plan may have had."[27]

To prevent that unhappy outcome, Unwin tasked individual architects with groups of houses. Economies of scale would result from "a reasonable amount of repetition of work without doing injury to the whole scheme, or producing monotony of effect." Underlying this approach was a concentration upon the ultimate beneficiary of the work—the new residents. "It is quite wrong to suppose that the best can be made of all the plots by considering the interest of each alone," wrote Unwin. "Frequently some quite minor gain, or supposed gain, to one may seriously injure the outlook of many others. It is only by considering them together, and developing each with regard to the whole, that the best result can be obtained."[28]

Edwin Luytens designed the three monumental structures around the formal squares at the center of Hampstead: St. Jude-on-the-Hill parish church, the Free Church, and the Institute, each in a distinctive interpretation of a historical style. The section of Hampstead Garden Suburb closest to the tube station was largely built out by the time of the Great War. With increased automobile ownership after the war, construction of more distant sections proceeded with dispatch. The Suburb was essentially completed by the mid-1930s.[29]

War Housing

The beginning of the Great War in 1914 meant not only the mobilization of Britain's naval and military forces, but also the nation's industrial capacity. Almost overnight, industry had to build new armament and munitions factories—facilities that employed thousands. As workers flocked to these expanding enterprises, the question of where they would live became a pressing concern. The government embarked on a large-scale program but broke with past practices and embraced a more enlightened model for working-class housing.[30]

In 1917, Charles Harris Whitaker, editor of the *Journal of the American Institute of Architects*, dispatched architect Frederick L. Ackerman to England to study the new war housing. What he found was that the British, rather than erecting temporary houses or barracks, built solid homes and charged the worker "a reasonable rental based upon pre-war conditions." Expenditures above returns were to be written off as the cost of war. The British seemed to understand that the prewar methods of financing housing were inadequate, so the government shouldered the costs of construction and management.[31] In the architecture and community plan, they were determined not to mindlessly replicate the inadequate housing found in older working-class neighborhoods, but to develop new communities along the lines of the garden city. The result was "a creative synthesis: it was both modern and yet oriented to vernacular designs based on an appreciation of the diversity of picturesque styles found in local villages."[32]

As director of the housing branch of the Department of Explosives Supply, Raymond Unwin was directly involved in that effort. He supervised several projects and personally designed Eastriggs and Gretna,

Cottages for munitions workers at Gretna; Raymond Unwin, architect, 1915. (Published in *Journal of the American Institute of Architects*, February 1917.)

two new communities near a massive munitions plant employing 30,000 workers along the Scottish border. He prepared the plan, and Courtenay Crickmer, who had worked at both Letchworth and Welwyn, supervised the design of the housing. Construction was underway within months of the start of the war, and by 1916 Gretna housed 20,000 residents in solid, red brick houses with provisions for active community life. Eastriggs was built along similar lines between 1916 and 1918. Scottish architect Robert Lorimer thought Unwin had succeeded at Gretna, for "all is plain, practical, straightforward, of pleasant and reasonable proportion, and mercifully devoid of ornament or pettiness. A satisfying feeling of variety is achieved, not so much in an artificial attempt to get variety in the individual houses as by a happy scheme of plan. . . ."[33]

During his tour, Ackerman visited Gretna and was greatly impressed. "To witness an enormous industrial community in which law, order, and arrangement prevailed; to see no slums and to realize that in this community there would be no slums; to sense the balance which it is possible to maintain between intensive industry and the normal life of the worker—is to feel a thrill such as one seldom experiences," he wrote. "To realize that this great war is the impulse which brought this thought into being gives to us an added significance, for we know now, long before the end, that it has not been in vain." Beyond the quality of the design and construction, however, he took away deeper lessons. English war housing clearly demonstrated "that high social, moral, and physical standards are essential to a nation's well-being in war or during peace." Further, the examples he saw reinforced his belief that the private sector could never be expected to provide quality, affordable housing for the masses. He understood that these new industrial garden cities would serve "as a permanent exhibit of what the State can do when it acts with the full power of its rightful authority and with a broad enlightened conception of its aim and purpose. It is an exhibit of what may be accomplished by delegating to imaginative men the necessary power and authority; and it is also an example of what any enlightened community can achieve by surrendering its burden of fallacies regarding super-individual rights and the rights of property."[34] Ackerman enthusiastically applied these lessons to his work in New York after the war, though he never did witness the American government exercise the "full power of its rightful authority" in the realm of housing.

Ninety years later, the Glasgow architectural firm charged with developing a new master plan for Gretna expressed admiration for the way Unwin "was able to turn principle into practice." The architects marveled that his "winding picturesque pattern of streets . . . set very comfortable in the 21st century—they are safe, walkable, they keep traffic in check, they have generous private and public open spaces together with well-placed centres and focal points."[35]

American planners had certainly attempted to apply the garden city idea in the years before the war, but it was the war housing that demonstrated how it could be applied to homes for workers of modest means. The English example pointed the way for the United States to build housing for war workers, and that experience resonated deeply after the war. Louis Pink, a member of New York State's Board of Housing, visited England in the mid-1920s and understood that the early garden cities were not intended to house the masses. Rather, "they are the laboratory of the housing movement—the pathfinders. They experiment and point the way. All the world is in debt to Letchworth—not because it houses a few thousand people—but because it has transformed the architecture of workers' cottages and has vastly improved the layout of low-cost developments elsewhere."[36]

After the war, New York City would experience an unprecedented housing boom. Large, undeveloped tracts in Brooklyn, the Bronx, and Queens provided quality housing for hundreds of thousands of families. This was also a moment for housing reformers to step forward.

2

░░░

The Garden Suburb in New York

THE SUCCESSFUL APPLICATION of the garden city idea outside London offered a timely inspiration to architects and planners in the United States. In New York City, the borough of Queens proved especially fertile ground for such housing experiments. In Queens there was room to build innovative planned communities and model tenements, and there was certainly demand for new housing of any kind. There the major goals of Howard's garden city ideal could be realized—"improved housing at lower cost through the availability of inexpensive land, and increased productivity and happiness of the residents through isolation from the evils of urban environments."[1]

At the end of the nineteenth century, the Tenth Ward on the Lower East Side of Manhattan was reputedly the most densely populated place on earth. In 1890 in that tenement district, 334,080 people were jammed into a square mile, or 522 per acre. As a whole, the population density in Manhattan was a comparatively comfortable 63,119 per square mile, or 114.53 per acre. Manhattan's population peaked at over 2.33 million in 1910, and density had increased to 102,146 per square mile. By comparison, in 2010 Manhattan's population stood at 1.6 million, a mere 69,000 per square mile. That figure is even more stunning when we consider how many people reside in high-rise buildings today; in the immigrant city of 1910, people were jammed into low-rise tenements. To take one particular example, a four-story tenement at 94 Orchard Street was home to 66 persons in that year; a century later, it was home to only 15.[2]

Jacob A. Riis published *How the Other Half Lives* in 1890, featuring his photographs of the city's immigrant and working-class neighborhoods, some of the most impoverished to be found anywhere. At the time, reformers had achieved but limited success in passing legislation aimed at improving the quality of life in the tenements. The Tenement House Law of 1901 mandated side courts and a rear yard, and limited a building's footprint to no more than 72 percent of a lot.[3] These were modest successes in mitigating the worst conditions, but the tenements remained—overcrowded, unhealthy, and, in the view of some, a breeding ground for immorality and crime. They remained because many New Yorkers had no choice.

An alternative to urban crowding was life in a distant suburb. Riis settled his family in Richmond Hill, Queens, a gracious community of suburban homes along the line of the Long Island Railroad. In his autobiography, *The Making of an American*, he described the sense of comfort provided by the "ridge of hills, the 'backbone of Long Island,' between New York and us. The very lights of the city were shut out. So was the slum, and I could sleep." There is no question that Riis identified the ultimate victory over the slum with a suburban future. Each year, he and his wife welcomed to their home children from the crowded tenement districts of the Lower East Side, certain that their deprived visitors could only benefit from a day in that wholesome suburban environment: "Even as I write the little ones from Cherry Street are playing under my trees. The time is at hand when we shall bring to them in their slum the things which we must now bring them to see, and then their slum will be no more."[4]

The welding of the five boroughs into Greater New York in 1898 presented a singular opportunity to remake the city. New transportation links soon opened the outer boroughs to real estate development, and for the first time in the city's history a building boom supplied in abundance new, quality homes for working-class and middle-class families. No longer would three rooms in a walk-up tenement be their only option.

In a sense, this was a specifically New York problem. While there was inadequate housing for the poor and marginal in all cities, few places had congested tenement districts on the scale of New York. Indeed, the tenement itself was largely a New York artifact. In other American cities the poor were housed in small homes, and in the early decades of the twentieth century, fully two-thirds of the housing starts in cities were one-family homes.[5] It was the dramatic situation in New York that informed the critiques of architects, planners, and housing reformers, however, and the solutions they offered came out of that very Manhattan-centered perspective.

Suburban Growth in Queens

The opening of the Williamsburg Bridge in 1903 and the Queensboro Bridge in 1909 forged essential physical links with the city and made possible a migration from the tenements to new housing in Brooklyn and Queens. In 1913, the Dual Subway System combined the Interborough Rapid Transit Company and the Brooklyn Rapid Transit Company and made possible the extension of service into Queens. Completion of the Flushing line along Queens Boulevard (1917) and the Astoria line (1917) sparked a decade of unprecedented growth. New transit links also opened up the outer sections of Brooklyn and the Bronx, as well as upper Manhattan, lowering the city's population density overall.[6]

Between the end of the First World War, during which housing construction had been limited, and the onset of the Great Depression in 1929, the city's demographic profile changed dramatically. Manhattan lost nearly half a million residents during those years, while Brooklyn grew by almost a million and the Bronx by more than 800,000. Queens, the largest of the five boroughs in area, saw its population explode from barely 150,000 in 1900 to 1.1 million in 1930, with more than 600,000 arriving during the 1920s alone. Only eight cities in the country—Chicago, Philadelphia, Detroit, Cleveland, St. Louis, Boston, Baltimore, and Pittsburgh—had a population greater than the number of residents Queens gained in the twenties. In a remarkably brief time, previously distant rural and suburban precincts were integrated into a modern metropolis. Between 1924 and 1929, the city issued 73,656 permits for one- and two-family homes in Queens, providing housing for 93,000 families, or an estimated 400,000 persons. The erection of 4,400 apartment buildings provided homes for another 53,464 families, or an estimated 213,000 persons. The assessed valuation in the borough had also skyrocketed in the decade after 1918.[7]

Manhattan may have been losing population, but during those decades it gained its distinctive skyline, with skyscrapers rising downtown in the Financial District and in the new midtown business district around Grand Central Terminal. In Brooklyn and Queens, much of the new development was characterized by low-rise, low-density neighborhoods, some with attached row houses, others where one-family homes predominated. Those fleeing the tenements found new homes with indoor plumbing, central heating, hot water, electricity, and generous light and air—all within walking distance of transit lines.

Table 1. Population Change in New York City, 1890–1930

	Manhattan	Brooklyn	Bronx	Queens	Staten Island	Total NYC
Population in the Five Boroughs, 1890–1930						
1890	1,441,216	838,547	88,908	87,050	51,693	2,507,414
1900	1,850,093	1,166,582	200,507	153,999	67,021	3,438,202
1910	2,331,542	1,634,351	430,890	284,041	85,969	4,766,793
1920	2,284,103	2,018,356	732,016	469,042	116,531	5,620,048
1930	1,867,312	2,560,401	1,265,258	1,079,129	158,346	6,930,446
Decennial Change, Number and Percent						
1890–1900	408,877	328,035	111,599	66,949	15,328	930,788
	28.4%	39.1%	125.6%	76.9%	29.7%	37.1%
1900–1910	481,449	467,769	230,383	130,042	18,948	1,328,591
	26.0%	40.1%	114.9%	84.4%	28.3%	38.6%
1910–1920	–47,439	384,005	301,126	185,001	30,562	853,255
	–2.0%	23.5%	69.9%	65.1%	35.6%	17.9%
1920–1930	–416,791	542,045	533,242	610,087	41,815	1,310,398
	–18.2%	26.9%	72.8%	130.1%	35.9%	23.3%
Percent of New York City's Population in Each Borough						
1900	53.81	33.93	5.83	4.48	1.95	
1910	48.91	34.29	9.04	5.96	1.80	
1920	40.64	35.91	13.03	8.35	2.07	
1930	26.94	36.94	18.26	15.57	2.28	
Population Density: Persons Per Square Mile						
1890	63,119	11,847	2,114	802	891	8,284
1900	81,034	16,478	4,774	1,410	1,148	11,059
1910	102,146	23,073	10,238	2,617	1,473	15,751
1920	100,044	28,495	17,387	4,321	2,004	18,570
1930	81,778	36,148	30,048	9,942	2,707	22,898

High demand, easy credit for builders and buyers, and tax incentives spurred the building boom in Queens. Much of the new construction was speculative, with homes and apartments fitting into the regular blocks of the street grid imposed over the western half of the borough. Whether free-standing one-family homes, as in Rego Park, or attached one- and two-family homes, as in Astoria, or modest apartment buildings or larger apartment blocks, all were built to a uniformly high standard. And with demand outpacing supply, new units were occupied as soon as the paint was dry.

Beyond providing quality housing, this surge also contributed to an increase in home ownership. More than any other municipality, New York was a city of renters, with only 12.7 percent of its inhabitants owning their homes. Noting a downward trend in home ownership nationwide, Secretary of Commerce Herbert Hoover commented, "Nothing is worse than increased tenancy and landlordism." Reversing that trend would improve the health of the body politic. Writing in the *Times*, J. Charles Laue pointed out that "simple, modest dwellings suitable for the man of average earnings can be bought for rent money." At Sunnyside Gardens, for example, an $8,630 home could be had for only a 10 percent down payment and total monthly payments of $66.75.[8] Laue himself purchased a home in Sunnyside on those terms, and ironically, lost it to foreclosure ten years later during the Great Depression.

While much of the new housing was speculative and conventional, Queens was also the site of several important housing experiments, ranging from garden suburbs to model tenements. More than merely offering modern amenities, each of these places was specifically designed so as to prevent the possibility that they would deteriorate into slums.

From 1904 into the 1930s, the G. X. Mathews Company erected hundreds of three-story multi-unit buildings in Ridgewood, Astoria, Woodside, Elmhurst, and Sunnyside. With their distinctive yellow and orange brick facades (the brick came from the Kreischer brickworks on Staten Island), Mathews Model Flats provided new apartments at affordable rents. In 1915, the company exhibited their model flats at the Panama-Pacific Exposition in San Francisco to great acclaim.[9] The six-unit buildings were attractive and solidly built, but they were still railroad flats, and lacked any connection to open space or greenery.

Queens offered an opportunity to remake the city, not only by reducing density, but also by demonstrating an alternative vision of urban living. These exemplary developments included Forest Hills Gardens (1909), arguably the finest expression of the suburban ideal, Jackson Heights (1911–1920s), the first garden apartment community, and Sunnyside Gardens.[10] Forest Hills Gardens was conceived as a railroad suburb, while Jackson Heights and Sunnyside Gardens were built along the new subway lines, a difference reflected in the overall design and density of each community.

Forest Hills Gardens

Architect Robert A. M. Stern has called Forest Hills Gardens the "most complex and finely articulated" expression of the railroad suburb, "both a pinnacle and an end."[11] The Russell Sage Foundation Homes Company began building this gracious community in 1909, utilizing the talents of architect Grosvenor Atterbury and the Olmsted Brothers (as Frederick Law Olmsted's landscaping firm was known after his death). The site was adjacent to the new electrified main line of the Long Island Railroad running into Pennsylvania Station. Mrs. Russell Sage admired the English garden cities and hoped to incorporate their most attractive features in a new community constructed at no greater cost than less attractive housing developments planted on a repetitive grid. In the earliest promotional pamphlet, company president Robert W. de Forest elucidated the social, economic, educational, and aesthetic qualities of the undertaking: "Mrs. Russell Sage, and those whom she has associated with her in the foundation, have been profoundly impressed with the need of better and more attractive housing facilities in the suburbs for persons of modest means who could pay from twenty-five dollars a month upward in the purchase of a home. They have thought that homes could be supplied like those in the garden cities of England, with some greenery and flowers around them, with accessible playgrounds and recreation facilities, and at no appreciably greater cost than is now paid for the same roof room in bare streets. They have abhorred the constant repetition of the rectangular block in suburban localities where land contours invite other street lines. They have thought, too, that buildings of tasteful design, constructed of brick, cement or other permanent material, even though of somewhat greater initial cost, were really more economical in their durability and lesser repair bills than the repulsive, cheaply built structures which are too often the type of New York's outlying districts. They have hoped that people of moderate income and good taste, who appreciate sympathetic surroundings, but are tied close to the city by the nature of their occupation, might find some country air and country life within striking distance of the active centers of New York."[12]

The Sage Foundation sought to create a living example of an ideal suburb, but central as this educational aspect was to the plan, the company remained "a business investment conducted on strictly business principles for a fair profit." While a reform enterprise, it was hardly a philanthropic one; still, profits would be limited to 5 percent, "far less," according to a contemporary real estate journal, "than that aimed at by the average tract or subdivision developer." This difference represented what the foundation was "willing to expend out of its own pocket in giving the home owner surroundings and advantages which cannot be obtained where the developer takes the higher profit."[13]

Because the Sage Foundation expressed such lofty ideals, it is often mistakenly assumed that the original intention was to build affordable, high-quality housing for working-class families. In his introduction to Clarence S. Stein's *Toward New Towns for America*, Mumford repeated this misconception, stating that Forest Hills was "meant to serve as a working-class community, but destined by the very generosity of its housing to become an entirely middle-class, indeed upper middle class, community." Housing reformer Louis H. Pink, who was appointed to the state's Board of Housing by Governor Al Smith in 1926, was even more bluntly critical. He called the Sage Foundation's effort "a tragic failure," as it offered extravagant design but nothing for the workingman.[14]

From the very start of construction, it was clear that the homes would be priced far above what families of modest means could afford. Proximity to the city pushed land values so high as to render one-family detached homes on generous lots affordable only to upper-middle-class families. The mandated open space and the quality of construction also dictated the final cost. In the "Declaration of Restrictions" published in 1913, the company stipulated that "no dwelling houses shall be erected or maintained which shall cost less than the amounts to be specified by the Homes Company in the several deeds." The same restrictions also barred buildings or rows longer than 250 feet, a restriction aimed at eliminating deadening blocks of tenements and row houses. As de Forest explained, "The Sage Foundation has not forgotten the laboring man. It may be ready to announce something for his benefit later on, but the cost of the land at Forest Hills Gardens, and the character of its surroundings, preclude provision there for the day laborer." All plans and designs pointed to the exclusive nature of this suburb. It was never intended to be a model for multi-class communities. In contrast with other suburban places, the Sage Foundation built and retained possession of the streets, public spaces, and lighting, and then assessed maintenance charges on all property owners. To achieve its end, the company established an exclusive and completely private enclave.[15]

The Olmsted plan simply delights. According to Frederick Law Olmsted, Jr., the goal was to respond to the topography rather than imposing a street grid that would obliterate it. "The monotony of endless, straight, windswept thoroughfares which represent the New York conception of streets will give place to short, quiet, self-contained and garden-like neighborhoods," he wrote. In fact, Forest Hills Gardens was the first violation of the street grid in Queens, and perhaps the entire city.[16] Its once innovative features—the curving, tree-lined streets, the homes set back on lawns, uniform architectural scale and language—are now so common as to have become "an ever-present suburban cliché," in the words of Alexander

Mackwood Road, Forest Hills Gardens, circa 1915. (Courtesy of the Queens Borough Public Library, Archives, Illustrations Collection.)

Garvin. But that in no way diminishes the effect at Forest Hills Gardens, where "one wanders along the curving roads, never sure where they will end, constantly surprised and entertained by some aspect of the design."[17]

The reform aspect was thus limited to the design; the company did not aspire to social engineering. The subsequent construction of thousands of working-class homes and apartments in Queens shows that the Sage Foundation could have attempted such a housing venture, but the result would not have been the ideal realized in Forest Hills Gardens.

As a financial undertaking, however, Forest Hills Gardens was a failure. The Sage Foundation terminated their involvement in 1922, having accumulated losses totaling $360,800. Speaking for the foundation, Clarence Perry explained, "The cost of preparing the land, grading, electrical conduits, sewer systems, street lighting, paving, and landscaping, while contributing greatly to the attractiveness of the development, was nevertheless unpredictably high."[18] Responsibility for completing the garden suburb and enforcing the design standards fell to the Forest Hills Gardens Corporation, an organization of property owners that persists into the present.

Jackson Heights

While Forest Hills Gardens represented the highest expression of the rail-road suburb, Jackson Heights set a standard for urban housing along new rapid transit lines. The Queensboro Corporation, named for the recently completed Queensboro Bridge, was founded in August 1909. William F. Wyckoff, descendant of one of Brooklyn's oldest families and president of the Homestead Bank and the Woodhaven Bank, headed the enterprise, but the driving force was the thirty-five-year-old general manager, Edward Archibald MacDougall, an experienced real estate man who had already been involved in several other suburban developments in Queens—Kissena Park North and Kissena Park South, Terminal Heights in Wood-side, and Elmhurst Square.[19] The Queensboro Corporation dwarfed those earlier ventures, both in scale and execution.

In 1914, the Queensboro Corporation commenced construction of blocks of elegant apartment buildings for middle-class families. The early ones went up near Northern Boulevard, which had trolley lines running to the bridge. Plans for the new Dual Subway System were well advanced, though it would be three years before the elevated line was in operation. Even so, the corporation's advertisements touted the subway as a prime attraction. Until then, the buses of the Fifth Avenue Coach Company provided a direct commute over the bridge into Manhattan.

The architects of Forest Hills Gardens planned their suburb to be set apart from the city and consciously rejected all urban forms. The curving streets, the spacious lawns, the emphasis on privacy, and the restrictive covenants combined to reinforce the distinctiveness of the place. Jackson Heights, on the other hand, fit comfortably into the urban grid, and the buildings seemingly embraced those constraints. Although the Queensboro Corporation would erect a few blocks of one-family homes, the predominant form was the apartment building. Unlike Manhattan, where the buildings went up without any consistent design, covering as much as 80 percent of the lot and crowded together to utilize every inch of street front, the apartment buildings in Jackson Heights adapted some of the most innovative features of the English garden cities and pioneered the concept of the garden apartment in the United States. The buildings were set back from the street to create a small garden in front, and the rear yards were treated as landscaped parks for residents. This arrangement guaranteed ample light and air, far more, in fact, than the tenement laws mandated.

The Queensboro Corporation erected only a few buildings before the war, which brought most residential construction to a halt. Construction

Interior garden of The Towers, Jackson Heights (Andrew Thomas, architect, 1924), circa 1940. The Chateau is visible beyond. (Courtesy of the Queens Borough Public Library, Archives, Thomas Langan Collection.)

resumed in 1919, and a year later the *Newtown Register* estimated that one tenth of the 3,862 apartments then under construction in the city were being built in Jackson Heights.[20] Jackson Heights was soon recognized as offering the most innovative residences in the city, with extraordinarily high standards of design and materials.

Nothing articulated the distinction between Jackson Heights and Manhattan more than the introduction of free-standing apartment buildings and the generously landscaped inner courtyards extending the entire length of the block. Even the most expensive new buildings along Fifth Avenue or Park Avenue lacked such features. To further enhance the appeal of Jackson Heights for the urban middle class, the corporation built tennis courts and set aside eight square blocks for a golf course; residents could even putter in their own garden plots. This was a creative exercise in land-banking, as each of these amenities was eliminated over time to make way for new construction. Integral to the success of Jackson Heights was the introduction of a co-operative ownership plan, presenting families with the opportunity to own rather than rent, and thus combining a defining feature of suburbia with urban living. These were among the first co-ops in the city. During the Great Depression, however, many apartment owners fell into foreclosure and the units became rentals; they remained rentals until the first wave of co-op conversions began in the 1970s.[21]

Spurring New Construction

Innovative and attractive as they were, neither Forest Hills Gardens nor Jackson Heights offered housing to the wage earner of modest means. That became a pressing concern after the war when the city faced a severe housing shortage. Writing in the *New York Times* in early 1920, Walter Stabler, Controller of the Metropolitan Life Insurance Company, described how state and federal tax laws were pushing investors to municipal bonds which, while they may have had a lower rate of return than real estate investment, were not taxed. Investors "surely cannot be expected to leave their money in highly taxed mortgages or make new investments of this kind when there are many other perfectly safe securities which will pay twice as much because of tax exemption." The solution, he argued, was legislative action to relieve "this best of all investments from income taxes for a period of years long enough to enable us to build what we must have and what we cannot get without this relief."[22]

New York Governor Al Smith was well aware of the housing situation. In 1919 he created a Reconstruction Commission to examine a range of economic and social issues, particularly housing. This was not political pandering on Smith's part, for he was genuinely concerned with the limitations facing the state's poorest citizens. He was, after all, a child of the tenements. Smith expressed that commitment in his introduction to housing advocate

Louis H. Pink's 1928 book, *The New Day in Housing*. "What could be of more vital concern to all public spirited citizens than the subject of decent, adequate housing," he wrote. "Children are still being brought up in dark, ill-ventilated, over-crowded, unsafe tenement houses. . . . The social ills and moral dangers consequent upon our neglect of housing have been ably presented by the courts dealing with juvenile offenders, by church, social and civic bodies of every kind." Unless remedied, the government ultimately would have to bear the cost of that neglect.[23]

Architect Clarence S. Stein volunteered to serve as the secretary of the Housing Committee of the Reconstruction Commission. Educated at the École des Beaux-Arts in Paris, he had worked for a time in the office of Bertram Goodhue.[24] Addressing the question of providing quality homes for families of modest means defined Stein's career for the rest of his life.

In the committee's report for 1920, Stein wrote: "It is economically un-profitable now, it has been economically impossible for many years past to provide a large part of the population of this State with decent homes according to American standards of living. Decent homes and wholesome environments in which to bring up children cost more than most workers can afford." The solution was to obtain cheap land where it would "be possible to build apartments far less congested than existing apartments." Furthermore, such sites would increase in value as development com-menced, enabling the funding of additional housing. It was essential, he believed, that any such program had "to permit conservation of the incre-ment of land values for the benefit of the community."[25] Given his mildly socialist tendencies and his dedication to Ebenezer Howard's garden city idea, Stein could not accept that speculators would be allowed to capture that inevitable rise in land values.

Stein was also secretary of the City Planning Committee of the City Club of New York, which submitted a memorandum discussing Stein's own report. They endorsed the idea of using tax exemptions to encourage new construction, arguing that rent regulations alone would do nothing to stim-ulate building. At the same time, Stein suggested that "temporary relief of taxation of buildings or mortgages will only help the speculating system that has created our slums." The private sector could not possibly solve the housing problem on its own, he concluded, but neither should the public sector be absolved of responsibility, for "the provision of adequate housing in decent surroundings for all people is a public service." From that guiding principle, Stein introduced the possibility of municipal hous-ing, arguing that as "speculative building cannot, under the most favorable conditions, supply us with sufficient homes," cities should be empowered "to build and operate housing."[26] Stein and his associates at the City Club could only advance such proposals and hope to influence public policy, recognizing, of course, that such a scheme of publicly built housing was unprecedented in American cities.

From the perspective of Stein and his City Club associates, thus far all efforts at solving the housing problem had been defensive, that is, enforcing restrictive law to redress unhealthy and undesirable living conditions. They wanted New York State to take the offensive, proactively funding or even erecting new housing built to higher and more generous standards.[27] As much as Stein may have desired government leadership and investment in this problem—and he and his circle certainly had great faith in the capacity of government to solve social problems—he recognized that this idea was not practical in the current climate. The solution would have to come from the private sector and philanthropy.

What Stein termed "investment housing" was already established in New York. The City and Suburban Homes Company of New York was formed in 1896 to erect model tenements on the East Side of Manhattan. Rents were fixed so as to yield a 5 percent return to investors representing the cream of New York society, including Bayard Cutting, Caroline and Olivia Stokes, Cornelius Vanderbilt, and Darius Ogden Mills. Elgin R. L. Gould, author of *The Housing of the Working People*, was appointed president. "The broad underlying principle on which the company is founded," he wrote, "is that the housing problem can only be solved by economic methods. Philanthropy is powerless to do much, because the field is altogether too vast. But there is a middle ground between philanthropy and pure business. We may call it investment philanthropy; that is, a philanthropy made seductive by co-ordination with a reasonable commercial dividend."[28]

In September 1920, Governor Al Smith called a special session of the legislature to address the housing crisis. In that brief session, the legislature passed several measures for "the relief of housing evils," including new protections for tenants and a ten-year exemption from local property taxes for new houses and tenements. That enabling legislation required action from the city, but not until the following February did the Board of Aldermen finally act. Republican Fiorello La Guardia, president of the body, led the opposition, arguing that the bill was nothing more than a gift to the real estate men. Rather than lose $8 million in tax revenue, he argued, the city should embark on a program of municipal housing.[29] Such publicly built and publicly managed housing for workers was being advanced in Vienna, Frankfurt, Berlin, and Amsterdam, but that idea had very little traction in the United States at the time.

The Metropolitan Life Insurance Company had strenuously lobbied in Albany for that tax-exemption bill, and it had a provision inserted permitting insurance companies to invest up to 10 percent of their assets in real estate. In 1922, the company began building model tenements for working-class families on that basis, financing construction of several thousand apartments and investing in other construction companies, including the Rickert-Brown Company and the Queensboro Corporation. By 1924, only two years after Governor Al Smith signed the law, Met Life had built apartments for 2,125 working-class families in Sunnyside, Woodside, and Astoria, sites selected because the land was relatively inexpensive. For their architect, the company tapped Andrew J. Thomas, who had designed the first buildings in Jackson Heights. During the war, Thomas worked with the Emergency Fleet Corporation, as did Frederick L. Ackerman, Henry Wright, and Robert D. Kohn. He generated a plan almost identical in outline to Linden Court, the garden apartments he designed in 1919 in Jackson Heights, but on a less generous scale and with more Spartan appointments, of course.[30]

The fifty-four identical U-shaped buildings featured modern kitchens, central heating, hot water, and excellent ventilation, with windows in every room opening onto either the street or the landscaped courtyard. Separate entry stairways opened to only two apartments per floor, an arrangement affording greater privacy to residents while also eliminating public corridors, a waste of nonrevenue generating space. Repeating the same design kept the costs low, as did the uniform fixtures and trim. The design also demonstrated the "advantages gained by big scale planning of the city block as a whole—the highest point which housing economies can reach." The rents, $9 a room by law, were still sufficient to cover the operating expenses and provide a 6 percent return on investment.[31]

The hopeful spirit of this enterprise was expressed best by seven-year-old Alberta Glenn, daughter of the project's construction foreman. At the groundbreaking ceremony in July 1922, the little girl stepped from the flag-draped bucket of a steam shovel and, presenting a shovel to Haley Fiske, president of Metropolitan Life, said: "We the children of New York want to thank you ever so much for these beautiful homes. Now we needn't be shut up in the dark old tenements where we haven't any place to play; but we will come here to live in sunshine and see the wonderful garden and flowers all day. We hope that every little child in New York may have as fine a home as these."[32]

Forest Hills Gardens, Jackson Heights, and the Met Life Houses may have been worthy examples of the application of the garden suburb ideal in Queens, but they were nonetheless exceptions. It was in this context that Clarence Stein, Henry Wright, and their colleagues launched their own enterprise.

3

###

Planning and Building Sunnyside Gardens

THE 1920S WAS A TIME of economic expansion and feverish real estate development in New York City, and nowhere was this more evident than in Queens. The pace of new construction was staggering, as the borough added 610,000 new residents during that decade. But with few exceptions, the resulting housing was undistinguished, without any thought to larger questions of urbanism or quality of life. Sunnyside Gardens was an exception, and one that captured the imagination of both professional planners and the public.

War Housing

The men who conceived of and built Sunnyside Gardens came together after the First World War, several having worked on planning and housing for the federal government during the war. The war years provided an unprecedented opportunity to put into practice ideas that had been percolating over the preceding decades. For the first time, the government sponsored the construction of entire communities, and that program brought together a remarkable group of like-minded architects and planners, each of them committed to building homes of high quality in a gracious, respectful setting, an approach certainly lacking in most housing for industrial workers.

After the United States entered the war in 1917, Frederick L. Ackerman journeyed to Britain specifically to visit the new war housing and reported his impressions in the *Journal of the American Institute of Architects*. He returned an enthusiastic advocate of the British model, convinced that such an approach was needed in the United States, even if it was without precedent. There was then no government body with the authority to acquire land and to finance, build, and manage housing. Furthermore, there was the question of what would happen to the new communities after the war. Ackerman suggested that the properties be turned over to a nonprofit organization that could then save "the appreciation of land values for the benefit of the community as a whole," an idea that came straight from Ebenezer Howard.[1]

"Designed and constructed under the handicap of tremendous speed," these homes would not be "the last word," wrote Ackerman, but would "mark a milestone in our progress." He saw a parallel with the impact of the 1893 World's Columbian Exposition. "But the reaction will be of another sort," he thought, "for instead of focusing our concept of town planning upon the magnificent, the planning of a community will come to be conceived in more rational and humble terms. The benefits to be derived from orderliness of arrangement and forehanded planning will be measured in better conditions of living." And again indirectly referencing Howard, Ackerman wrote that by building such workers housing, the nation was "actually preparing for the physical conditions for a better peace."[2]

Upon his return from England, Ackerman was appointed the chief of Housing and Town Planning for the Emergency Fleet Corporation, created by the U.S. Shipping Board to build housing for shipyard workers. In that capacity, he had the chance to apply the lessons he had learned from British war housing. Working under Robert D. Kohn (later head of the Public Works Administration during the New Deal), Ackerman's role was similar to Unwin's in England. Mumford credited Ackerman with "the remarkable quality of the work that the Shipping Board so promptly turned out."[3]

What was especially notable in the housing built by the Emergency Fleet Corporation was that for the first time in the United States the best practices of garden suburb design were being applied to housing for the working class, not the rising middle class.[4] The housing reformers saw this as an unprecedented opportunity to improve physical conditions for industrial workers; the shipbuilders hoped that by providing quality homes they could temper labor militancy. The resulting homes were far superior to any private housing available in the vicinity. That program was the first instance of government financed and constructed housing in the United

States. The homes were well-built and affordable, but then profit was not a consideration.

Behind the design of the new developments lay a very clear set of values and assumptions. Frederick Law Olmsted, Jr., manager of the Town Planning Division of the U.S. Housing Corporation, recognized that while the housing was built to address "a war-time emergency . . . that emergency developed from acute local situations which even in peace times were becoming widespread and were steadily growing worse." The deterioration of urban dwellings into slums was "unfavorable to that self-respecting home life upon which the security of our democracy rests." No other factor, thought Olmsted, "does more to fix the conditions that determine the health and mould the character of our people than housing." He expected that after the war, private builders would learn from these "intelligent, if hurried, experiments."[5]

The program was intended to attract "the most skilled and steady, self-respecting men, generally married men with families, the strength of American industrial life," men "willing to pay for decent and comfortable living conditions, schooling and play opportunities for their children, and all reasonable essentials of civilized life." At the same time, they declined to address the "more difficult problem of satisfactory and economical housing for families of unskilled and relatively low-paid workers." With this in mind, the war housing consisted overwhelmingly of single-family dwellings, "with their many social advantages to the community as compared with tenement houses, due to the favorable conditions they offer for sound family life."[6] This was not the imposition of middle-class values on industrial workers, but a recognition that those values were to be found among Americans of all classes.

Limited as it was, the program provided an opportunity to marry the housing reforms of the Progressive Era with the concept of the English garden city. This went beyond the architecture and plan to social aims and demonstrating that it was indeed possible to build quality homes for the working class. After the war, the British government sold the homes to the workers occupying them. Ackerman thought this was a crucial element of the program, for in this way the increase in property values would be returned to the community, not siphoned off by deep-pocketed investors. The costs should be written off as "the cost of war. . . . Why should we base our policy, as regards this phase of the war, upon the principle that the Government should not suffer a financial loss? It's stupid, it's tragic!" But the United States did not follow the British example. The federal

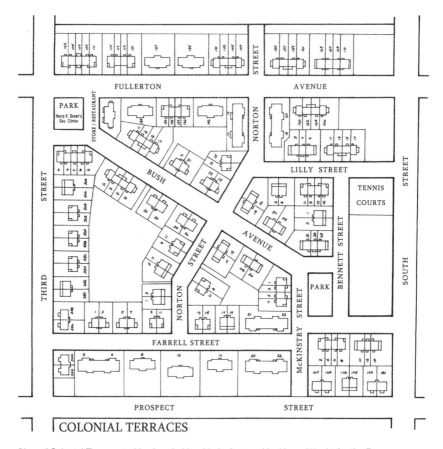

COLONIAL TERRACES

Plan of Colonial Terraces in Newburgh, New York, designed by Henry Wright for the Emergency Fleet Corporation, 1918. (Laura Heim Architect.)

government sold the properties at auction, and the shipyard workers could then purchase from the new owners.[7] Clearly, social engineering as undertaken in England was alien to the decision-makers in Washington.

Before the war, Henry Wright was designing homes for an upper-income suburban clientele, particularly in Brentmoor Park outside St. Louis, but the war gave him a new focus.[8] Working under Ackerman and Kohn, Wright designed Colonial Terraces for workers at the Newburgh Shipyard, about sixty miles up the Hudson from New York City. Like the other communities built through that program, Colonial Terraces drew inspiration from English examples. Colonial-style, semidetached one-family homes and row houses, some wood frame and others brick, many with porches, were grouped around undefined shared open space, almost immediately used for parking.[9]

Wright's plan for Colonial Terraces drew upon his memory of a visit to Ireland in 1902. In Waterford, he wrote, "I passed through an archway in a blank house wall on the street to a beautiful villa fronting upon spacious interior gardens. That archway was a passage to new ideas which have struggled up through the ensuing years. I learned then that the comforts and privacy of family life are not to be found in the detached dwelling, but rather in a house that judiciously relates living space to open space, the open space in turn being capable of enjoyment by many as well as by few." He and his colleagues developed a "theoretical scheme which reversed our awkward and irrational arrangement of house fronts on the street, where unpleasant things must take place, and the inconvenient placing of service doors on the rear or garden sides just where they ruin what should be a pleasant and quiet garden spot."[10]

Mumford thought that no one was more influential in this undertaking than Ackerman, for "without his work on the Shipping Board, it is safe to say that the housing and planning movement would have lost some of the main footings for the work done in the twenties and still more in the thirties." In particular, "Sunnyside Gardens, that experimental project . . . grew directly out of Government war housing."[11] According to planning historian Jon Peterson, the Emergency Fleet Corporation's worker villages

Row houses in Colonial Terraces designed by Henry Wright, 2015. (Author's photograph.)

were, on the whole, successful and "reflected the attention that had been lavished on model suburb design prior to the war by landscape architects, garden city admirers, and other reformers."[12]

Clarence Stein did not design workers housing during the war, but he gained valuable experience in 1915 while working in the office of Bertram Goodhue as the site supervisor for Tyrone, New Mexico, a company town designed for the Phelps Dodge Corporation. Constructed along a railroad line near a copper mine, Tyrone featured a central landscaped plaza, along which were positioned the company headquarters, a church, a library, and shops. Continuing the design language Goodhue established in his work at the 1915 Panama-California Exposition in San Diego, all homes were in the Spanish Colonial–style. And in keeping with the social standards of the time, there were separate neighborhoods for the American managers and the Mexican workers.[13]

The Regional Planning Association of America

Between 1915 and 1920, Stein was secretary of the City Planning Committee of the City Club of New York, and after the war he served as secretary of the Housing Committee of Governor Al Smith's Reconstruction Commission with men whom he would work with for decades to come—Robert Kohn, Andrew Thomas, and Fredrick L. Ackerman. He also was chairman of the Committee on Community Planning of the American Institute of Architects, with Henry Wright and Ackerman. Stein actively sought out like-minded individuals to generate new solutions to the housing problem, and through the City Club he met Charles Harris Whitaker, editor of the *Journal of the American Institute of Architects*. Whitaker, in turn, introduced him to Mumford and Benton MacKaye, originator of the idea for the Appalachian Trail. In 1923, that extraordinary collection of architects, planners, and urban critics formed themselves into the Regional Planning Association of America (RPAA). Their avowed purpose was to reimagine city living along more enlightened lines, that is, how cities might be redesigned to foster a more humanistic environment. In Stein's words, the purpose was "to improve living and working conditions through comprehensive planning of regions including urban and rural communities and particularly through the decentralization of vast urban populations by the creation of garden cities."[14]

The founding group included Stein, Wright, Ackerman, Kohn, Mumford, MacKaye, real estate developer Alexander Bing, John Irwin Bright, and Frederick Bigger. Others joined later—Edith Elmer Wood, Catherine

Bauer, Robert Bruére, Joseph K. Hart, Stuart Chase, and Clarence Perry. Whitaker initially brought the group together, but it was Stein who provided much of the intellectual and organizational energy. This group, combining a remarkable breadth of experience and insight with a strong sense of civic obligation, met at least twice a week to discuss housing reform, urban planning, and urbanism.[15]

Many of these individuals were also connected through the Ethical Culture Society. Dr. Felix Adler founded the organization in 1876 with adherents of Reform Judaism at Temple Emanu-El. He opened a kindergarten, and within a few years added elementary grades, then in 1900 a high school. The Society's early motto was "Deed, not Creed," and Adler certainly lived up to that. He was appointed to the Tenement House Commission, and in 1885 he organized the Tenement House Building Company to erect model tenements. The company soon raised $150,000 (6,000 shares at $25 a share), with dividends capped at 4 percent, all additional profit to become a reserve fund. They purchased a lot at 338–344 Cherry Street on the Lower East Side for $29,500, and a row of four connected buildings, built at a cost of $123,215.13, was ready for occupancy in December 1887.[16]

Bing, Stein, and Kohn were all associated with the Ethical Culture Society, and Stein and Kohn later designed the school's Fieldston campus (1926) and the new Temple Emanu-El at Fifth Avenue and Sixty-Fifth Street (1927). Stein's apartment on West Sixty-Fourth Street overlooked Kohn's Ethical Culture Society building. Charles Ascher, later counsel to the City Housing Corporation (CHC), attended the high school. He was "brought up to be a do-gooder," he said, and saw his involvement in that light, that he was doing "something of a civic purpose."[17]

What unified this circle was a critical attitude toward the contemporary city and a commitment to solving the housing problem—specifically, how to provide quality homes for families of modest means. From their admiration for the garden city movement, they understood that only a regional approach could successfully address those issues. Their discussions revealed a shared understanding that they were addressing social questions as much as matters of architecture, planning, and economics.

Ackerman had been considering these questions for several years before associating himself with Stein and Wright. Speaking before the national Conference on City Planning in 1915, he outlined the principles and assumptions that later underlay the RPAA. "Our battle," he said, "is not so much against a definite or an established order of things as it is against chaos. Chaos is our problem. To go on in an endeavor to express chaos more adequately is about as futile in developing a better civic architecture as is the attempt to sound a bell in a vacuum." City planning must be more than simply a set of material components, he contended. It was rather "the act of providing a more adequate physical expression for the composite ideals of groups of people thrown together by social and economic forces in our communities." Above all, it had to be "a conscious effort to transform our vague ideals of community living into forms which will accurately express such ideals."[18]

For Ackerman, the only legitimate purpose of city planning was "to engage in the operation of giving conscious direction to the development of our material environment so that it will better serve the common good." To achieve that end, it would never be enough to merely "attempt to modify existing conditions" because it was necessary first to eliminate "the causes which gave rise to existing mal-adjustments." Ackerman decried "the right of the individual to use the community as a machine for procuring profits and benefits, without regard to what happens to the community."[19] As the profit motive had created the urban housing problem, it was unreasonable to expect that the solution would come from the same impulse. Reform, in other words, needed to address the financing of urban housing.

Over the decades the individuals involved in the RPAA remained steadfast in their advocacy of the principles that underlay their plans, designs, and critiques. Testifying before a congressional committee in 1967, when the United States was belatedly facing up to what came to be known as the "Urban Crisis," Lewis Mumford referred to the founding of the RPAA. He described "a group of men whose human vision and practical judgment, had they been heeded in any large way, could have transformed American housing and planning. If their basic proposals had been carried further, we might have averted the grim conditions you now face."[20] Mumford never wavered from his belief that the ideas he and his colleagues generated in the 1920s offered an enlightened corrective to the chaos and banality of the free market, with its attendant diminishment of the human experience.

The City Housing Corporation

The private sector, naturally seeking to maximize profit on investments, simply could not build housing that would be affordable to a family of modest means. As chairman of the New York State Housing and Regional Planning Commission in 1924, Stein observed that "the standard that the public has required for its own protection has gradually risen. The ability of the individual to pay for that standard has diminished," an "ominous parting of the ways" between the adequate house and the inadequate incomes of those who cannot afford to live there.[21] Under prevailing conditions, the most practical solution was not to press the government to undertake the construction of affordable housing, but to modify how the private sector built.

In 1924, the visionaries put their ideas into practice, just as Ebenezer Howard had at Letchworth. Out of the stimulating and wide-ranging discussions of the RPAA came plans for the City Housing Corporation (CHC). Stein had prepared a report, unpublished, the previous year in which he advocated a large-scale, planned development inspired by Unwin's planning principles. Alexander M. Bing, who made his fortune developing apartment houses along Park Avenue, agreed to head the enterprise. The stated purpose was to address "New York's housing difficulties" by building a modern model community, melding as far as practicable the concerns of American housing reformers with the ideals of the English garden city movement. The building of such a garden community would "demonstrate the social and economic advantages of developing self-contained communities in which industry and business will be within walking distance of homes." The enterprise would further demonstrate "that philanthropic funds can be utilized in financially sound investment in good housing in such a way as to gradually release the original funds so that they may be used again in similar or other constructive measures for social betterment."[22]

The endeavor was truly ambitious. They intended to provide an "ideal home of good taste and design, sound construction and with sunlight, air, a garden outlook and lawns for the children to play in safety." In sum, they sought to bring those positive attributes of the upper-class suburb to an urban neighborhood of affordable housing. At the same time, the plan addressed "the civic and social need for a scientific attack on the problem of providing better homes for families of moderate income."[23]

Although the founders of the CHC were not primarily motivated by profits, they could not ignore the example of the Metropolitan Life Insurance Company, which received rentals in excess of $1 million a year from their model tenements, an 8 percent return on their investment. Seeking to offer quality housing for wage earners as close to cost as possible, the CHC also embraced middle-class suburban values. Behind Sunnyside Gardens was the assumption that a community of homeowners was fundamentally more stable than a neighborhood where the majority of the residents rented.

Described by its incorporators as a "socialized business," the CHC was a limited dividend company that would "operate without profit—that is to say, its dividends will be limited to six percent." Shares sold for $100 and, according to the company's second annual report, 320 stockholders invested a total of $1.76 million. CHC President Alexander Bing brought in several high-profile investors. John D. Rockefeller invested $150,000; Herbert Hoover, $10,000; and the Sage Foundation purchased a block of second mortgage bonds. On their Advisory Board, the CHC counted Eleanor Roosevelt (appointed at the suggestion of Governor Al Smith's trusted advisor Belle Moskowitz); Dr. Felix Adler; William Sloane Coffin Sr., director of the W. & J. Sloane Company and a trustee of the Metropolitan Museum of Art; and V. Everit Macy, heir to an oil fortune and later president of Teachers College. Housing reformer Louis H. Pink commented, "It is 'quite the thing' to be connected to the City Housing Corporation."[24]

Construction costs, many of them essentially fixed, meant that under ordinary patterns of development it was simply not possible to build private homes for lower-income buyers. The CHC therefore "endeavored to supply a practical medium to finance, construct and sell a superior type of home at a reasonable cost." That was possible only because the CHC was organized as a limited dividend company, "where the investor seeking security and a fair return is willing to engage in an enterprise offering those advantages and which also is intended to contribute something toward public welfare." The undertaking was neither strictly philanthropic nor exclusively profit seeking. "We are trying to combine business with civic development," said Bing. The company's business model was to reinvest profits in new building after paying the annual 6 percent dividend to investors, and that arrangement proved remarkably successful. Within two years, the company had authorized capital of $5 million, outstanding stock of $1.2 million, and a surplus of $170,000, and they began to show a profit shortly before the last units were completed in 1928.[25]

The City Housing Corporation never intended to serve the lowest segment of the population, but sought to make home ownership possible for lower middle-class families otherwise priced out of the market. Initial payments ranged from $1,000 to $2,000, with monthly charges pegged at $10 a room per month.[26] A 1925 survey conducted by the New York University Bureau of Business found that half of the families in Queens had annual expenditures of about $3,000. Sunnyside Gardens was specifically designed for that income group, and to a large degree the planners succeeded; in 1926, the average income of the new residents was $3,000.

For Stein, an emphasis on "good management, low-cost land close to rapid transit, economical planning, and orderly large-scale building" all contributed to their success, as did, no doubt, the consistently high demand for moderate-priced housing.[27]

The directors understood that this first undertaking was in many ways experimental. Over the five years of construction at Sunnyside Gardens the designs evolved while still adhering to the original scale and materials. In 1926, the company set aside $50,000 to carry out experiments in housing design and construction. Bing was especially enthusiastic about this idea, having recently returned from Germany where he visited Romerstadt in Frankfurt am Main, a development of pre-cast concrete housing for workers designed by modernist architect Ernst May. He noted proudly that their achievement at Sunnyside had gone far toward advancing the problem of affordable housing and that the directors were "prepared to experiment with new materials and construction methods. We hope that by combining these savings with economies in other directions, particularly in financing costs, we will eventually arrive at a really cheap, substantial, well-constructed house. Building construction, like other major industries, should profit by the advances which applied science has made possible. Our houses are still handmade. We are certain that machine methods can be made applicable to small house construction, and feel that sooner or later this will be done successfully."[28] The *New York Times* considered this announcement sufficiently significant to warrant coverage.

Sunnyside Gardens

For their initial effort, the CHC looked for a cautious, safe investment because, according to Stein, they "required practice in large-scale planning, building, and community organization." The tract in Queens ideally suited their purposes, for it was situated within easy commuting distance of Manhattan, along the Dual Subway System elevated line on Queens Boulevard. On the northern edge of the property lay the mammoth Sunnyside Railroad Yard; immediately to the west was the industrial district of Long Island City. Another element which compromised the garden city ideal was the inability of the CHC to purchase all of the adjacent blocks, and housing of a similar, if less distinctive, character soon went up near the Gardens. A surrounding greenbelt in the manner of an English garden city was never possible. Sunnyside Gardens would rise in the midst of a stark urban landscape, "a new community in the midst of a dismal city," in the words of Henry Wright.[29]

Stein and Wright were the chief architects, joined midway through by Ackerman; Marjorie Sewell Cautley was brought in as the landscape architect. According to Mumford, Wright was "an able technician and a dreamer," possessing the "independence and freedom of the unfettered intellectual." A middle-class family man, Wright actually lived in Sunnyside for a time, as did Mumford. Stein, on the other hand, was an "artist and organizer; a man of fine taste, delicate discrimination, and a background of adequate means."[30] He came from a family of considerable wealth and lived in a penthouse on West Sixty-Fourth Street overlooking Central Park. For all of his disparaging of "dinosaur cities," he never left Manhattan.

Their plans went beyond building beautiful and functional blocks of houses to the creation of "a setting in which a democratic community might grow." The CHC's ambition was to build a place where the values of neighborliness and cooperation might take root and blossom. In design, appearance, and organization, Sunnyside Gardens would provide an alternative to contemporary urban life, a conscious rejection of the values, disorder, and confusion of the city in favor of the healthy environment of small-town America. Mumford called Sunnyside a "village," adding, "perhaps that was the best part of it." But the planners always understood that this was only an initial experiment, the first step toward the ultimate goal of the CHC, the development of a "complete, self-contained, regionally planned community."[31]

The enterprise moved quickly. In February 1924, the City Housing Corporation purchased 1,200 lots, a total of seventy-seven acres, from the Pennsylvania Railroad Company. The groundbreaking ceremony was on April 1, and the first units were ready for occupation in September. Stein and Wright, attending to all aspects of the design from the arrangement of the buildings to the layout of the individual units, consciously sought to apply Raymond Unwin's dictum, "Nothing gained by overcrowding." Indeed, soon after construction was underway, Stein and Wright traveled to England to meet with Howard and Unwin and to experience the garden suburbs firsthand.[32]

Unwin and Howard traveled to New York in April 1925 for the convention of the International Federation of Town and Country Planning and Garden Cities. The weeklong gathering featured an exhibition at the Grand Central Palace in conjunction with the American Institute of Architects, the Regional Plan of New York, the Russell Sage Foundation, and other architecture and planning organizations. For this event, *Survey Graphic* published a "Regional Planning Number," edited by Mumford, and featuring contributions by other members of the RPAA—Stein,

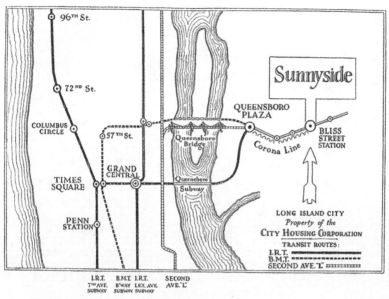

Times Square or Grand Central Station in fifteen minutes from Sunnyside. The service is continuous night and day. Three roads to Bliss Street Station—I. R. T., B. M. T., Second Avenue "L." And the fare each way is only five cents.

City Housing Corporation brochure showing the proximity of Sunnyside Gardens to Manhattan. (Clarence Stein Papers, Division of Rare and Manuscript Collections, Cornell University.)

Wright, Ackerman, MacKaye, Chase, Bruére, and Bing, with an essay on garden cities by C. B. Purdom, the finance director of Welwyn. On the eve of the gathering, the City Housing Corporation hosted a dinner at the Hotel Commodore, with remarks by Howard and Unwin. Robert Kohn presided over a joint gathering of planners and architects, with remarks by Unwin, Stein, and Mumford. On the last day, delegates visited Jackson Heights and Sunnyside Gardens. A year later, Alexander Bing was elected the organization's vice president, representing America.[33] Clearly, Stein, Wright, Mumford, and company had positioned their efforts at the center of a transatlantic movement.

The CHC believed in the superiority of their innovative plans and fully expected that to attract buyers, but, given the booming housing market and the willingness of banks to provide mortgage money, it is likely that any homes built in that location would have found buyers. The entire development, a total of 563 homes and apartments, was built out within five years.[34] In their monthly magazine, the Queens Chamber of Commerce boasted, "With this new community Queens becomes the setting for

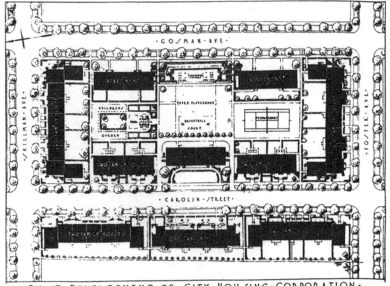

·FIRST·DEVELOPMENT·OF·CITY·HOUSING·CORPORATION·
·AT·SUNNYSIDE·LONG·ISLAND·CITY·

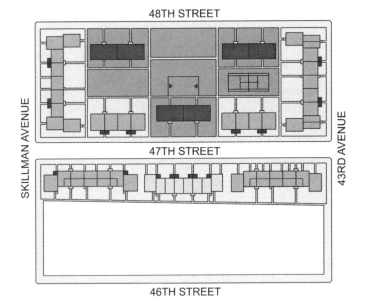

48TH STREET

SKILLMAN AVENUE

43RD AVENUE

47TH STREET

46TH STREET

Plan of Colonial Court, built in 1924, with two-family houses on each end and four-story apartment buildings mid-block; across Carolin Street two-family houses bracket a row of single-family houses. Lewis and Sophia Mumford moved into one of the apartment buildings in 1924. The central court originally featured a playground and a tennis court. (Top: published in Henry Wright, *Rehousing Urban America*, Columbia University Press, 1935; Bottom: Laura Heim Architect.)

another demonstration of model housing. Sunnyside is unique and its development will be closely watched by those interested in seeing substantial homes provided in the suburbs for people of moderate income."[35]

This pace was by no means extraordinary for Queens during the decade. In 1924 alone, developers submitted plans for 24,610 new buildings, and nearly 85,000 new homes went up between 1924 and 1928, three-fourths of them one-family or two-family houses. To take one example, the firm of Gross & Lemmerman purchased 700 lots near the Long Island Railroad's Hollis station; the land had been under tillage in 1923, but by early 1925 they had built 374 houses, with 142 more under construction. Like the CHC, these developers also installed the sidewalks, streets, curbs, and water mains. Queens developed a more pronounced suburban character than Brooklyn and the Bronx, which also grew exponentially during the twenties. The borough averaged only 1.7 families per dwelling unit, compared to the citywide average of 3.5 families per unit.[36]

The architects faced several constraints in achieving their dream of a garden suburb. In the first place, the streets were already laid out in a grid of standard city blocks 190 to 200 feet wide and 600 to 900 feet long. The borough engineer refused their request to create superblocks by closing certain streets, not even the dead end streets abutting the railroad yards, despite the fact that they existed on the map only. "We were forced to fit our buildings to the blocks rather than the blocks to the living conditions," commented Stein.[37]

The CHC did achieve a partial victory. They wanted to build a row of garages at the edge of the community against the Long Island Railroad embankment. The problem was that the street grid continued right up to the embankment, and before they could proceed they had to have those stub streets demapped. Bing sent CHC counsel Charles Ascher to see Belle Moscowitz, a member of Governor Al Smith's inner circle. She told him, "Go to the controller's office, tell him I sent you, and he'll do this for you." As Ascher later recalled, "She noticed a look on my face that led her to say to me rather bitterly, 'Too ethical, I suppose?'" Bing indeed visited the controller, and the city indeed agreed to issue a deed for the nonexistent streets for a nominal consideration of one hundred dollars.[38]

Architect Robert A. M. Stern has suggested that Sunnyside Gardens "does not strictly qualify as a suburb," but is "a uniquely successful example of how the garden suburb idea can be adapted to the grid typical of most American cities." Even so, their design was "one of the most ingenious adaptations of the New York City 200-foot block," according to Alexander Garvin.[39] The designers may have been disappointed that they could not break out of the grid, but the result was a distinctive urban form, at once similar to other city blocks—front entries, a consistent street wall—and unique in the way it is experienced—the verdant interior courts, the mid-block pathways, the modest scale. The result was more urban than Forest Hills Gardens, and more suburban than Jackson Heights.

Another constraint was the pressure to keep costs low. While the land itself at Sunnyside was inexpensive—about fifty cents a foot—it lacked sewers and sidewalks, and utilities ran only to the edge of the property. The CHC soon realized that it was more economical to install the sewers and pave the streets themselves than to wait for the city to do the work. In line with their emphasis on efficient construction methods, they installed utilities only as needed and completed each block without leaving any vacant lots, a practice which "saved greatly on carrying charges as compared with typical spotty methods of development."[40]

Further minimizing costs was the fact that the CHC had purchased the entire site at the same time and could build on the basis of those lower property values. That was indeed fortunate, because land values in Western Queens doubled during the time Sunnyside was under construction. This upturn also meant that the company could sell excess property at the edges of their development at a profit, the unearned increment easily paying the 6 percent dividend with the surplus funding future construction. The profitability of Sunnyside made Radburn possible.[41]

While the CHC was building its progressive garden suburb, the G. X. Mathews Company erected blocks of low-rent tenements nearby. Before the war the company had concentrated its efforts in Ridgewood, but after 1918 they constructed rows of three-story tenements in Astoria, Woodside, and Sunnyside. The flats were attractive, but differed little in design from other urban tenements, and lacked landscaping entirely. Mathews flats boasted steam heat and hot water, electric lights, modern kitchens and tiled baths, in short, "all modern comforts," but the primary attraction was the low price for buyers and the affordable rents for tenants. In their literature, the company explicitly compared their homes with the model development in Sunnyside, especially regarding the respective costs per room.

In actuality, the City Housing Corporation and the G. X. Mathews Company aimed their homes at different sectors of the housing market. The CHC had no interest in low-rental apartments for owner-occupied investment, and the Mathews Brothers did not then build one-, two-, or three-family houses for the middle class. The Mathews Company recognized their niche and excelled at filling it, as one of their brochures explained: "The safest of all real estate is that which caters to the masses—at lowest rents. This is the secret of the success of Mathews Model Apts. They supply an absolute necessity of life—shelter. Luxury buildings are a speculation—necessities are sure income producers."[42] A comparison of comparable rentals reveals that apartments in Sunnyside Gardens rented for between 18 percent and 30 percent more than units in the Mathews flats.

Despite the best efforts of the CHC, homes in Sunnyside Gardens were more expensive than comparable properties in the vicinity, $8,300 as compared to about $6,000. But it was in the distribution of costs that the difference was most pronounced. Expenditures for the building itself, including materials, fixtures, and labor, amounted to $5,212, as compared to only $2,450 in homes built nearby. Marketing and overhead, however, represented only 19 percent of the total cost at Sunnyside, compared to 45 percent for the typical builder. Writing in *Architecture* magazine in 1933, Henry Wright argued that to keep costs low, developers should improve the financing of their new homes rather than skimp on building costs. Better housing and "improved planning in terms of stable communities will decrease the risk of vacancies and obsolescence," he argued. In a breakdown of comparable costs, Wright demonstrated that a greater percentage of the final cost of a new home in Sunnyside went toward actual construction (63 percent versus 41 percent); even so, the houses cost about 28 percent more than other new homes in Queens.[43]

Mumford thought that the modest, if well-built, homes were not the primary attraction: "What the houses themselves lacked in imaginative design, the community as a whole made up for in open spaces, carefully reserved for public use, in playgrounds and gardens on a scale then unheard of anywhere else in the city, and in opportunities for spontaneous neighborliness. Something more than our isolation, something more than the fact that the rear gardens and lawns were not choked with asphalt pavements and garages, gave us the sense of a common purpose. Even those who were only grasping at a 'good buy' found themselves enjoying a good life."[44]

The buildings covered only a third of each block, the remaining two-thirds reserved for gardens, lawns, and walkways. Stein "counted on the spaciousness of the gardens to compensate for any undue tightness inside the houses." The houses were indeed small, only two rooms deep to ensure good ventilation. The first advertisement for Sunnyside Gardens in *Queensborough* listed among the features of the new development "built-in kitchen cabinets and bathtubs, clothes dryers that fold away

"Sunnyside: A Step Toward Better Housing," City Housing Corporation brochure, 1927. The mews units of Madison Court North are seen under construction in the lower left; the community's private park is at the top. (Clarence Stein Papers, Division of Rare and Manuscript Collections, Cornell University.)

compactly against the kitchen ceiling, [and] breakfast nooks." There was an eight-inch firewall between each building and, furthering their goal of maintaining higher aesthetic standards, underground wiring.[45]

The most innovative features of the plan were the landscaped court-yards. The attached row houses had token front yards, some providing only a couple of feet between the front entry and sidewalk, but they enclosed within a large green. Each home had a private backyard up to thirty feet deep; encircled by a path, the central courtyard was about sixty feet wide, and "although legally the property of the individual homeowners, they were to be used in common by all those in the surrounding houses under a 40-year easement agreement. These common greens were intended for restful gatherings or for quiet play of the very young."[46] The open spaces served to bring people together. Mumford understood that "when both private and public spaces *are* designed together, this mingling and meeting may take place, under the pleasantest possible conditions, in the neighborhood."[47] Stein and Wright achieved that in Sunnyside and later at Radburn.

Automobile ownership grew exponentially during the 1920s, and that presented a difficult design problem—where to place the garages.

According to Wright, "while the planners were scheming to group the garages in one way or another (all of which entails difficult lines of ownership and deeds) a fortunate decision lifted the garages bodily from the block interiors to isolated groups on the rim of the community. The resulting 'vacuum,' even in a New York block (only two hundred feet deep from street to street) suggested the *internal common park area* which became characteristic of the whole development."[48]

Stein reasoned that the "parklike courts more than compensated for the lengthy walk to the garages." Some of the homes built in the final phase of construction actually incorporated garages, and the last group of row houses included an alley lined with garages, but that was only because it was at the edge and backed upon homes built by other developers. In 1928, a two-story parking garage designed by Stein went up near the rail yard. The problem of the automobile was never satisfactorily solved, however, and after the easements lapsed in the 1960s a number of homeowners installed parking pads and curb cuts, disrupting the harmonious design so thoughtfully planned by the architects. The CHC's second enterprise, Radburn, New Jersey, was designed from inception as a "town for the motor age."[49]

By mid-1928, the last year of construction, only two of the final group of forty-nine homes remained unsold. But it was not merely the availability of new houses that attracted buyers. The *Times* noted, "As Sunnyside has grown and its many unusual features have become more generally known, the houses have become increasingly popular and many homes in the final unit were purchased before completion." By 1930, all the apartments in the development had been rented, more than three-quarters of them with three year leases, and there were very few vacancies in the two- and three-family houses. The on-site sales manager remarked, "This record has been due in part to provisions for sunlight and air through parks and gardens adjacent to apartments and homes. . . . Unsightly backyards have been eliminated."[50]

The experiment attracted attention from the start, from the design principles and the social aspirations of the organizers to the financing. That the City Housing Corporation seemed to successfully combine all three was something of a marvel. As early as 1926, Richard T. Ely of the Institute for Research in Land Economics and Public Utilities at the University of Wisconsin praised the intentions and accomplishment of the CHC. Although primarily concerned with the innovative economic arrangements, Ely also noted the superiority of the design "to other developments designed for people, not merely of similar resources, but even of far larger resources."[51]

Unlike Forest Hills Gardens, Sunnyside Gardens was indeed a financial success, and that permitted the City Housing Corporation to pay the 6 percent dividends, reinvest the surplus in Radburn, their second undertaking, and follow through on their commitment to their original philanthropic aims. In June 1930, eight months after the Wall Street crash but before the full impact of the Depression was felt, they created a $50,000 endowment fund administered by the New York Community Trust to support the park and other community projects. Here, the CHC was fulfilling its promise to return to the community any surplus not needed to safeguard their investment above the 6 percent dividend paid to investors.[52]

Housing advocate Louis H. Pink was an enthusiastic admirer. "No semi-philanthropic housing experiment here or abroad has had the financial success of Sunnyside," he commented. "While there is nothing very remarkable about the development itself, it is entirely creditable and intelligent. It may not have aimed very high, but few mistakes were made and it accomplished in double-quick time what it set out to do. Sunnyside must be regarded not as an end in itself but merely as a beginning."[53]

With an attractive design, a convenient location, and cooperation between the residents and the company that held their mortgages, Sunnyside Gardens was destined for success. Mumford was more than satisfied with his family's experience, and he frequently referred to the marvels of Sunnyside in his later writings, even long after he had moved away. "None of us pretended that Sunnyside wholly fulfilled our dreams," he wrote, "but the main outlines of the community were right." It was truly a garden suburb in the city: "Always there was a wide sweep of sky, though the air was sometimes polluted by the yellow-plumed effluvia of a chemical factory's chimney over toward Newtown Creek. When the snow fell on a winter night on the dark slate roofs, the skyline toward Manhattan emitted a rosy glow, and in spite of the nearby waste of railroad yards, the snow stayed white longer in Sunnyside than it did in the city. If we had to settle anywhere within a big city at the time Geddes was small, we are not sorry, at least on human grounds, that we chose Sunnyside. It had been framed to the human scale. A little boy could take it all in."[54]

4

Design and Community

Architecture and Landscape as a Social Good

THE *AIA GUIDE TO NEW YORK CITY* describes Sunnyside Gardens as "a great and successful experiment in urban housing design," but then dismissively notes that "the architecture is unimportant—even insipid." An earlier edition called it "pallid." ("That's what the younger architects think of it," remarked City Housing Corporation counsel Charles Ascher in his oral history).[1] The authors use the word "delight" to convey the experience of wandering through Sunnyside, but what exactly is the source of all this delight, especially if the architecture is "pallid" and "insipid"? The pleasure of walking through the courts derives from the innovative site plan, with its public, private, and quasi-public spaces; a consistency of materials applied throughout; a modest scale; and yes, a deceptively plain design language and architectural style. The composition exudes a modern feel while retaining the charm of an English garden city.

What set Sunnyside apart was not the architecture as such. Louis H. Pink suggested that the place "would not be noteworthy in Europe; but it is the most hopeful beginning of all attempts to found garden cities in the United States. We have accomplished so little! It has none of the artistry of Forest Hills or Mariemont. It has no Grosvenor Atterbury to ensure architectural beauty and mounting expenses. It lacks grace and charm. The flat roof predominates. There is little variety. The buildings are square boxes relieved only by good proportion. But for the tree and shrub planting and occasional windowboxes and awnings, Sunnyside would be somber as well as plain. What it lacks in art it makes up in intelligence."[2]

More than an assemblage of modest buildings of harmonious design and scale, Sunnyside was the expression of an idea—that is, combining a community plan and a simple architectural language to foster a sense of neighborliness. In garden suburbs, open spaces serve to bring people together. Mumford observed that at Sunnyside and Radburn, as at Hampstead, the interplay of public and private spaces designed together enhances and encourages the "mingling and meeting . . . under the pleasantest possible conditions."[3]

In *The Brown Decades*, published in 1931 when he was living in Sunnyside, Lewis Mumford wrote that "wherever the social and economic condition of society was faced realistically"—and here he was specifically referring to Bournville, Hampstead, and Letchworth in England and new housing in Germany—"the major problem became that of integrating a modern community, treating the individual building as a mere unit in the larger design." Mumford considered that to be the central problem facing the architects. "Sunlight, air, gardens, play-space, outlook: these are the main requirements of the modern house," he wrote. For such attributes to be denied in housing provided for the mass of industrial workers and city dwellers was a failing of modern society. The solution, he concluded, was to provide "these elements on a communal scale." The architect's "individual house will be a type-unit, adapted to the special whole in which it functions," requiring a "community plan, properly oriented toward sunlight, with publicly maintained open spaces and gardens and insulation from unnecessary traffic and movement." A "bare, severe interior, so necessary for simplified housework" completes the picture.[4]

The garden city idea had always been tinged with a socialist sensibility, and the economic crisis of the Great Depression only reinforced the impression that capitalism was collapsing. It was understandable, therefore, that urban design expressing communal ideas would seem attractive and, perhaps, inevitable. This certainly colored Mumford's thinking. "Once the new architecture becomes the medium, not of some individual's tastes and desires, but the informed, positive consensus of the community," he concluded, "form will cease to be a sporadic possibility and become instead the mark of our whole civilization." It should not be surprising that the old system should produce dysfunctional, dehumanizing housing. The change Mumford anticipated "implies a real revolution in our social and economic ideas; and no revolution would be worth working for if it did not imply, among other things, such concrete and comprehensive changes."[5]

Plan and Architecture

The City Housing Corporation set out to build affordable housing, and thus sought as many economies as possible to keep costs down. The architects, of course, believed beauty to be an essential aspect of any planned community. Of necessity, architectural ornament was kept to a minimum, though Stein and Wright would have rejected excessive ornament in any event. This is not to say that the simple buildings are bare or boring. Far from it. At first glance the houses look identical, but subtle differences on both the facades and the interior layout distinguished the homes in each court, and the plans evolved from year to year. The designers opted for charming, if subtle, variety over a uniform statement.

Stein and Wright always understood their first project to be an experiment, an opportunity to work out the practical problems of building a garden city. They incorporated different kinds of dwellings: "the individually owned house, the co-operative apartment, and the rented apartment; and these differences in function serve as the basis for differences in design." Behind the materiality of the project was an egalitarian principle. In the May 1925 issue of the *Survey Graphic*, the regional planning number edited by Mumford, Wright wrote, "Planned housing of this kind is able to achieve the sort of honest individuality that comes from performing adequately one's own part in a larger whole; each house is, as it were, a good private citizen, with its individual entrance, its individual porch, its individual drying green, its complete sense of privacy, and at the same time it performs its civic obligations," by which he meant supporting public spaces and amenities. "Above all," he asserted, "no house attempts to shout down its neighbor by reason of special size or style."[6]

The homes and apartment buildings employ the same kit of parts: common brick, slate, six-over-six wood windows, and an intentionally limited palette of paint colors—white, cream, and dark green. Within that simplified aesthetic there is remarkable variation, however. Some houses have enclosed porches in the front, others in the rear; some rows feature a hood above the entrance, others only a simple decorative element. Parapets and brickwork vary from one court to another. "Although the architectural effect at Sunnyside is on the whole harmonious and apparently homogenous," wrote Henry Wright, "it represents a continuous evolution of fundamental planning and planning theory."[7]

Clarence Stein justified using common Hudson River brick for both its aesthetic and social benefits, not to mention the long-term economic advantage. "Brick exteriors remain more harmonious than wood because they are not painted," he wrote. "Therefore, there is no danger of assertive souls expressing their individuality, to the dismay of their neighbors, by coloring their dwelling with an inharmonious pigment. The natural quality of the brick eliminates the need of one expensive item of upkeep."[8] In that way the materials contributed to the preservation of the aesthetic, while also serving to symbolically unify a distinct residential community.

Most of the row houses have flat roofs, but slate-clad pitched roofs are interspersed throughout. Even there the architects did not simply repeat a single design, but varied the shape and placement of the pitched roofs to add interest to what could have become a streetscape rendered in monotone. Like brick, slate required minimal maintenance. The life expectancy of a slate roof is about a century, and after nine decades some of the slate roofs in Sunnyside were in need of replacement. That has become an issue at the Landmarks Preservation Commission, as homeowners, citing cost, resist resurfacing in traditional slate and apply to use synthetic materials. In instances where the commission has permitted the use of synthetics, the integrity of the overall ensemble has been accordingly diminished.

The architects took as their mandate that all residents, including both renters, and homeowners, should have some connection to the gardens. This, too, reinforced the egalitarian nature of the design. Stein and Wright included porches on every home from the start, refining the design and placement with each subsequent block. The idea was to offer every resident a transition from the public exterior spaces to the private interiors. What they found was that almost immediately homeowners began to enclose the front porch, and as a result the architectural harmony of the street was compromised. In the next iteration of housing plans, the porches were all enclosed. Wright noted that the evolution from the first units, from the "living porch" on the street side to later plans where "the living porches were turned inward as was the entire outdoor life of the community,"[9] preserved the unity of the street facades. This also pointed the way to the "turned around house" they introduced in Radburn, where the public functions of the house faced the interior court and the private functions opened to the street.

Landscaping was an integral aspect of the plan. Cornell-trained landscape architect Marjorie Sewell Cautley became part of the team very early on. She likely met Stein through Robert Kohn when she was working on the Ethical Culture Fieldston School in the Bronx. Urban progressives understood that the environment shapes the character of the individual and impacts society for good or for ill, and Cautley brought that sensibility to her design for the courts and gardens. Her main concern was not nature in and of itself, but rather "bringing such landscapes into the daily lives of the working class, in particular women, mothers, and children."[10]

How well Cautley succeeded is evident in the reminiscences of a woman who grew up in Sunnyside in the 1940s and 1950s. "Overriding any other distinguishing feature of Sunnyside Gardens for me as a child were the sycamore trees that lined its streets," she wrote. "Something about their numbers and size, and the way their towering presence separated our neighborhood from the rest of Sunnyside immediately marked the place a special one—beyond the traffic, the heat, the noise—a refuge." Roaming the courtyard outside her back door gave her "a sense of adventure" as she entered her own "phantasy landscape, immediately becoming Peter Pan or Robin Hood or a girl on a horse. And children did just that in great numbers." When she was seven her family moved from Washington Court, where "the vegetation was unruly, dense and shady," to more man- icured Lincoln Court, with "its weeping willow trees gracing the far ends of a carefully tended center lawn enclosed by a wire fence. No children galloped about here. . . . At the far end of the courtyard stood a large per- gola covered in wisteria vines, the sweet scent of which drew me to quiet solitude. Two tall ginkgo trees in the alleyway, bright orangey-yellow in autumn, held my child attention. . . . This setting may not have provided the backdrop to wild imagination, but it did do much to fulfill my need for peace."[11] Today, that court is completely inaccessible, with fences along property lines creating private yards in place of the common.

Sunnyside Gardens was built in phases over five years, court by court, not street by street. Row houses facing each other across the street feature varying decorative elements. Each court also possesses its own rhythm as to setbacks and the location of porches, entries, and mid-block paths. Each block is broken up into smaller courts to provide a more intimate and private experience; that, more than any other single feature, contrib- utes to the charming sense of place. That Sunnyside was built in stages during a tight span of construction demonstrates how the optimal court configuration and house plans evolved. A chronological review reveals the experimental and dynamic nature of the design, with revisions and dele- tions marking each year.

Finally, many of the courts were named for historical figures—Washington, Hamilton, Roosevelt, Madison, Monroe, Harrison, and Wilson (the excep- tions being Colonial Court and Carolin Gardens), each with its own court association to maintain and monitor the common spaces.

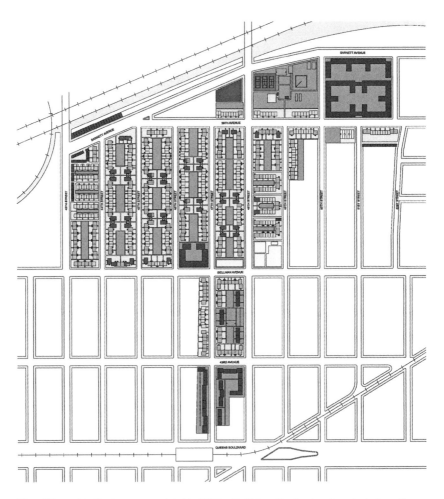

Plan of Sunnyside Gardens as completed in 1928, with Phipps Garden Apartments, designed by Clarence Stein and built between 1931 and 1935, upper right. Apartment buildings are shown in the darkest shade, then three-family, two-family, and one-family houses in progressively lighter shades. In the courtyards, the darker shade denotes common spaces, lighter the private yards. (Laura Heim Architect.)

1924

Colonial Court was experimental in every way, from the house plans to the common courtyard. A mix of two-story one- and two-family houses and four-floor co-operative apartment buildings, it reveals the growing pains of the Sunnyside idea. Stein and Wright were clearly feeling their way here, but they quickly understood what elements worked and which needed further development. But such was the enthusiasm that Lewis Mumford became one of the first residents, purchasing a co-operative apartment (41-12 Forty-Eighth Street).

The buildings were arranged around the perimeter of one entire block and half of the block facing. Here, the garden court opens directly to the street midblock, rather than being enclosed on all sides as in later configurations. The generous interior provided room for children's play equipment, private gardens, and landscaped sitting areas, but this arrangement, with an unclear allocation of public, private, and semi-public spaces, proved inefficient and, in terms of the evolving plan, a dead end. Because the City Housing Corporation owned only half of the block on the west side of Forth-Seventh Street, there was no way to create an interior greenspace, only private rear yards.

Forty of the forty-eight residences are two-family houses. The interior plans are rather eclectic, however, as the architects seem to have been experimenting with various plan types. There were five two-family and two one-family layouts in all. The two unusually large one-family houses on the ends of the block had four bedrooms and a carved-out side porch, a feature eliminated in later iterations. In layout, size, and porch configuration, the other one-families pointed toward the predominant building type in later courts. The two-family houses included large three-bedroom units, later eliminated, and two-bedroom units in three separate configurations: porch and side stair, side stair with a split entry, and central stair. Variations on two of these evolved into the basic building type in later courts, but models with an individual porch entry or shared front porch entries were not repeated.

1925

With the first court under construction, Stein and Wright traveled to England to consult with Raymond Unwin. That visit proved fruitful, as their second set of designs demonstrated an elevated degree of sophistication.

Carolin Gardens is a row of five three-story brick apartment buildings, presenting an understated streetscape with a linear garden behind. The City Housing Corporation originally marketed the flats as co-operative apartments, but sales were slow and the units were soon made available as rentals. Instead of a single, large building deadening the street, the massing was broken down into the five separate buildings, each with its own entrance. This yielded the kind of variety and intimacy the architects sought. Charming bay windows and prominent hoods in combination with creative brickwork enliven the facades, an advance over the austere apartments in

Colonial Court. Each building has a small planted yard in front, and the landscaped common space in the rear the full length. The landscaping and quiet sitting areas demonstrate how the Sunnyside plan could be applied to multi-unit buildings.

Roosevelt Court was the first section built with the courtyard configuration that came to characterize Sunnyside. Row houses line the perimeter of the block to enclose a landscaped common within. Rejecting the four-story apartment buildings as in Colonial Court, the architects inserted three-family houses, with the owner occupying the garden floor and two rental apartments above. Here the planners introduced the features that generated the sense of intimacy typical of Sunnyside Gardens. Where a tedious, unbroken row of attached houses running the length of the block was usual in other Queens neighborhoods, Stein and Wright cut walkways through the middle of the block to form three smaller, and thus more intimate interior courts.

The rhythm of the streetwall differs in each of the three sections of Roosevelt Court. Here they introduced the idea of setting back larger three-family houses to bracket the through-block paths. The middle court established the pattern followed in later courts—one-family houses in the

Roosevelt Court, with half-roof terraces, 1925. The City Housing Corporation installed the drying poles in the private yard of each home. Today few of the half-roof terraces remain in their original condition. (Clarence Stein papers, Division of Rare and Manuscript Collections, Cornell University Library.)

center of each row set back from the street bracketed by two-family and three-family houses facing the mid-block walkways.

Two years later, the homes at the northern end of the block were built; the southern end was left undeveloped, and the CHC, taking advantage of rising land values to fatten its balance sheet, later sold those lots. The apartment building erected later, while stolidly handsome and in a complimentary style, is not part of the historic district.

The mix of one-, two-, and three-family houses yielded a new sense of scale and massing. Still, the architects struggled, employing five variations on the two-family house. One design featured entries with three doors—one for each of the attached homes and a middle door used as a common coal corridor (a design utilized only here). Introduced on the one-family houses in this court is the paired grouping of front porches with separate entries. Rear porches are only found on the two-family houses. Flat roofs predominate; the half pitch introduced in Colonial Court is continued in the center court on the one-families, and the two-families bracketing the ends have pitched roofs.

Construction of Hamilton Court began with the mix of one-, two- and three-family houses. At 200 by 275 feet, the configuration of the middle court became the standard followed in later construction. The northern end is open to the street, with a low brick wall enclosing the private garden.

As with Roosevelt Court, the southernmost court has only two-family houses; the northern court groups one-family houses between two-families at the open end and three-families facing the mid-block walkway. The one-families in Hamilton Court are aligned to create a continuous face to both the street and the garden; pitched-roof houses bracket the ends. Paired porches with balconies above facing the courtyard on the two-family houses assured that all residents, homeowners, and renters alike had an outdoor space connecting with the garden.

1926

In Washington Court, the Sunnyside idea was fully refined and achieved its fullest expression. The two mid-block paths cutting through the clean rectangular block plan are offset so that they do not line up with those through courts across the street. Looking through the block, one glimpses a brick home in the distance, not a straightaway. This adds considerably to the charm of walking through Sunnyside.

The rhythm of the housing types was rationalized—two-family houses bracket a short row of one-family houses, with larger three-family houses

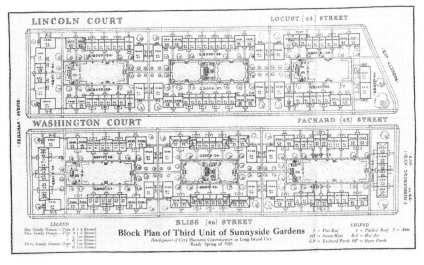

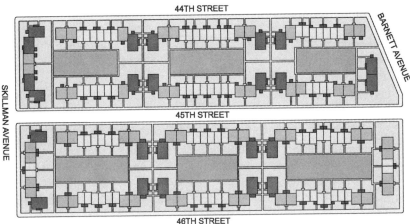

Block Plan of Third Unit of Sunnyside Gardens (Washington Court and Lincoln Court), City Housing Corporation, 1926. Through-block walkways divide the long city blocks into three courtyards, and are offset from block to block; note the location of porches on the front of the one-family houses and in the rear of the two-family houses. (Top: Clarence Stein papers, Division of Rare and Manuscript Collections, Cornell University Library; Bottom: Laura Heim Architect.)

facing the mid-block walkways. The buildings do not form a uniform row, but stagger, with some set closer to the street and others set further back, varying the size of the front and rear yards and introducing a subtle rhythm to the streetscape.

Interiors were also refined. At Washington Court, the architects fixed on an enclosed porch for all homes, finally setting on a uniform pattern

Two-family houses (facing street) and three-family houses (facing walkway) in Washington Court, 1926. Note the two-level iron porch on each three-family house. (Clarence Stein papers, Division of Rare and Manuscript Collections, Cornell University Library.)

and establishing a set design principle. Here they used a single design for one-family houses and two plans for the two-families. The one-families have front porches, the two-families have paired two-level rear porches. Bay windows on the three-family houses face the walkways, with a front entry into the living room and a side entry through the kitchen.

In plan, Lincoln Court is similar to Washington Court, but the architecture differs slightly. Here was a design used only once—a two-family with a pitched roof extending down the entire front facade. It was not even used on the opposite side of the court. The court's southern end and triangular northern end feature unique three-family configurations.

Begun in 1926, Jefferson Court was the first to introduce housing in a mews configuration, an idea introduced by Frederick Ackerman. The homes were arranged in a "U" opening onto the street. The common here is the front garden shared by all the residents. Only these mews groupings benefit from a permanent easement (obviously, a fence along property lines would prevent neighbors from accessing their property). Two more mews groupings and a traditional court with homes around the perimeter of the block completed Jefferson Court the next year.

Slightly raised above street level, the mews created extraordinarily quiet and intimate spaces in the front, but the rear proved to be a problem. As much as Stein and Wright decried the typical Queens block with an alley running behind, the mews houses back onto what is essentially

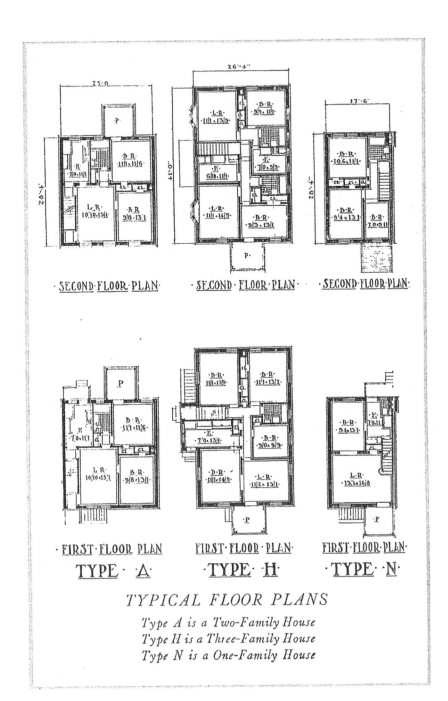

Typical floor plans, City Housing Corporation brochure, 1926. (Clarence Stein papers, Division of Rare and Manuscript Collections, Cornell University Library.)

a service alley necessary for emergency vehicles. At the back of the "U" facing Forty-Ninth/Hester Street they designed a few private garages, an uncommon solution but one later embraced at Madison Court. They also included larger two-family units which had an extra pair of bedrooms with a shared bathroom, a plan utilized only this once. As evidenced in Jefferson Court, the architects never did achieve a successful solution to the edge conditions. It seems as though they intentionally turned their back to context they could not control.

The mews configuration clearly points the way to the Radburn idea, the first iteration of the turned around house. The entry from the rear alley into the kitchen provides access to the private, functional area of the house, and the front door from the shared garden opens to the living area. At the northern end of the block was built a traditional court, with homes around the perimeter enclosing the common garden. All porches on two families face the interior, again anticipating Radburn.

1927

Completing Hamilton Court, a four-story apartment building with ground-floor commercial spaces was erected at the south end along Skillman Avenue. The buildings rise on the perimeter to enclose a landscaped garden opening to the adjacent courtyard lined with private houses (today fencing prevents passage from the apartment building to the other courtyards).

Located at the western edge of Sunnyside Gardens, Madison Court North consists of three mews groupings. All the mews groupings there have an open end facing west toward Manhattan, with stairs leading down to the street. These mews houses were wider and shorter than previous models, with an entry vestibule rather than a porch. Oddly enough, these houses had no back door on the ground floor; the yard could be accessed only from the cellar, reinforcing the utilitarian service functions of those spaces rather than their recreational potential. The northernmost row of houses was an exception. Here, at the edge, Stein and Wright introduced garages entered in the rear on the ground floor, with two residential floors above. The garages did not infringe upon the gardens in front of the homes, but did mean that those homes had no rear yards. This configuration, too, pointed toward Radburn.

Madison Court South is unusual in that the perimeter consists entirely of two-family houses with paired rear porches, reinforcing the idea that the common was the center of community life, not the street. Moving the wood porches to the rear also maintained a consistent row of brick facades

Mews houses in Madison Court North, 1927. Lewis and Sophia Mumford bought a home in this court in 1927 when their son, Geddes, was born. They left Sunnyside in 1936. (Clarence Stein papers, Division of Rare and Manuscript Collections, Cornell University Library.)

fronting the street and eliminated the possibility of jumbled renovations disrupting the ensemble.

Designed by Henry Wright, and his only solo contribution, Monroe Court went up adjacent to Carolin Gardens, and for several years Wright and his family rented there. The relatively plain buildings enclosed a landscaped rear yard, demonstrating how an apartment building could be incorporated into a garden suburb. With changes in ownership over the years, however, Monroe Court lost the garden aspect entirely, with the rear yards completely paved over and chain-link fences erected along property lines.

As Sunnyside Gardens neared completion, Clarence Stein designed a two-story brick garage at the northern edge of the community. As only a few homes accommodated the automobile, the garage proved to be an essential and popular amenity. But Stein gave this utilitarian structure a special grandeur through lively brickwork and a dignified tower, and oversized industrial style windows. In both scale and materials the garage fit into the community. Over time the structure suffered from many unfortunate changes, and despite its obvious pedigree and significance to the overall plan of Sunnyside, the Landmarks Preservation Commission excluded the garage from the historic district (it was likewise excluded from the special zoning district, though included in the National Register historic district). In 2020, over the objections of many residents, it was demolished to make way for a middle school.

Parking garage designed by Clarence Stein built at the edge of Sunnyside Gardens in 1927. The building lost much of its original detail over the years, and the Landmarks Preservation Commission omitted it from the historic district. It was demolished in 2020. (Published in *Architectural Record*, 1929.)

1928

At the edges of their garden suburb, the City Housing Corporation owned only parts of blocks, an unhappy circumstance inhibiting any attempt to build the courtyard configuration they had pioneered. As a result, Harrison Place both typified and deviated from the Sunnyside plan. Here were erected, if slightly wider, one-family houses, each with an entry vestibule rather than the characteristic front porch. One row backs onto the parking garage, but also has a common walkway running behind the houses, essentially a half-court. Two rows flank the entrance to the park, and another went up directly across the street. Homes in the final set built a block away have private rear yards, but rather than backing onto a landscaped common, there is a wide alley and a row of private garages. The automobile, so long pushed to the edges, was finally incorporated into Sunnyside Gardens.

The final piece of Sunnyside Gardens was Wilson Court, a handsome block of apartment buildings designed, fittingly, by Stein, with rather distinguished ornamental brickwork. Like the five buildings in Carolin Gardens across the street, these apartments offer an uninterrupted streetwall fronted by a continuous greenspace, with a landscaped court behind.

The New Community

When completed in 1928, Sunnyside Gardens provided homes for 1,200 families. A 1926 survey determined that half of the new residents had left tenements on the East Side of Manhattan. Two years later, a survey of 504 residents found 184 blue collar workers, including 116 mechanics, 50 chauffeurs, and 18 restaurant workers; there were also 355 white collar workers, including 99 professionals (teachers, social workers, lawyers, and doctors), 79 office workers, 55 small tradesmen, 49 salesmen, and 35 government employees. A great proportion of them were of German or Irish extraction, "with native Americans predominating," as well as a number of Jewish families, many attracted by the socialistic aspects of the plan. The newcomers chose the Gardens because of the facilities provided for the children, the quiet suburban atmosphere, the design and quality of the homes, and the community spirit, not to mention the convenient location.[12]

There were no black residents in the new community, but while Sunnyside Gardens was not integrated, it was not segregated either. Restricted covenants were in place, but they were only a "tool of property law" and had nothing to do with race. Quite intentionally, the founders did not take on racial integration. Charles Ascher recalled that they "were waging enough of a battle to get acceptance of our very advanced ideas in town planning without trying at the same time to settle every social problem." He pointed out that the covenants had no prohibitions against "a person of color from buying a house." Still, "they didn't enter the community and we didn't press it in the '20s."[13]

The CHC capitalized on the suburban appeal in their promotional literature: "For most of us the ideal home of good taste and design, sound construction and with sunlight, air, a garden outlook and lawns for the children to play in safety is associated with the outlying suburbs and prices the average family cannot afford. Within a 20 minute subway ride of Times Square [are] attractive, substantial brick homes with acres of gardens and park at prices no higher than the rents they had been paying for ordinary city flats."[14]

Lewis and Sophia Mumford were among the first residents. In 1924, they bought one of the co-operative apartments in the first set of buildings. In *Green Memories*, a poignant chronicle of his son, Geddes, who was killed in combat in 1944, Mumford stated that when he "had written in discreet praise of this development I never dreamed that we would presently test the handiwork of our friends Clarence Stein and Henry Wright by living in these quarters." Years later, Sophie recalled that was not to live out part of the great social experiment; rather, "it was the only place we could afford. Lewis was determined to be a writer, and I was determined he should. We had no backing, and were quite poor. He was involved with the City Housing Corporation from the start, but it was not an attempt to prove anything on our part." (They were being a bit self-deprecating.) After Geddes was born in 1927, they purchased a mews house in Madison Court at the western edge of the development (40-02 Locust/Forty-Fourth Street). From their back window they looked out over a landscaped court, and when he stepped out his front door, the author of the "Sky Line" column in the *New Yorker* could see the Queensboro Bridge and the Manhattan skyline to the west.[15]

Charles Ascher, then a young Wall Street attorney, was a neighbor of the Mumfords in Brooklyn Heights, and the families summered together on Martha's Vineyard. At his friend's suggestion, he "went over and looked at Sunnyside and decided that this was indeed a very good place to try to bring up two small children in New York." Ascher purchased a home on Carolin Street, and soon after he approached Alexander Bing about becoming counsel for the City Housing Corporation. His was certainly one of the few households there employing a maid. The Aschers moved to Croton-on-Hudson in 1928, though he remained as CHC counsel.[16]

This was an extraordinarily productive time for Mumford. He published four books—*The Golden Day* (1926), *Herman Melville* (1929), *The Brown Decades* (1931), and *Technics and Civilization* (1934)—and was working on a fifth, his acclaimed *Culture of Cities* (1938). He also continued writing for his "Sky Line" column in the *New Yorker* and publishing articles in other magazines. He and Ascher often went for extended walks around Queens, and one beautiful spring day, Ascher stopped by to suggest they head out. "I can't, Charles, I'm thinking," came the reply. "He's the only person I've ever known in my life from whom I would have accepted that," Ascher reminisced. "He had no book, no paper, no pencil. He was thinking and thank you, he couldn't be bothered."[17]

By design, Sunnyside Gardens was to be a mixed-income community. Mumford wrote that interacting "with a wide range of income groups (from twelve hundred to twelve thousand dollars a year) living side by side, has led me to believe that this is the best kind of community. In terms of education of the young and of making the institutions of democracy work, the arguments are entirely in favor of a mixed community."[18] The uniform scale and appearance of the houses certainly contributed to the blurring of class distinctions. At least in the beginning, the social experiment that was Sunnyside was a success.

As Stein had stated, their goal had been not merely to build moderately priced homes, but to create a community where democratic values and small town neighborliness might flourish. Sunnyside Gardens was thus an experiment in both home building and civics, and the common experience of home ownership, which was new to almost all of the residents, was key to that. To further those ends, the CHC created the Sunnyside Gardens Community Association (SGCA). Dues were initially $12 a year, and while membership was strictly voluntary, all residents were strongly urged to join. According to one company spokesman, the CHC made an effort "to interest all residents in belonging to clubs and the Community Association because it feels it would be beneficial to them and increase the usefulness of Sunnyside." The CHC had a representative on the SGCA, "not to influence the policies or the activities but to bring about consensus of opinion in community matters and to carry out the wishes of the majority." So constant a presence was the SGCA that Mumford described how his five-year-old son Geddes ended one of his childish verses with "Hoorah! Community Association!"[19]

As with any progressive housing project, the question of where the children would play was crucial. The courtyards, while appropriate for toddlers, could not accommodate the active games of older children. In response, the CHC in 1926 donated a three-and-a-half-acre tract, forty-five lots worth $45,000, for a playground, with an additional donation of $37,000 toward equipment, fencing, and construction of a heated, two-story cabin. In early 1929 the company donated an additional ten thousand square feet for the park; the New York Community Trust was empowered to ensure that the property would always be dedicated for civic purposes.[20]

The park embodied the idea of progressive education. The cabin had a piano, pool table, a meeting room, and a workroom furnished with tools; there was also an apartment upstairs for the park director. For that position the SGCA hired Ralph McClintock, a young man with a master's degree from New York University who had previously worked at a settlement house in Manhattan. The park soon became the center of community activities. Small children enjoyed handicraft classes and storytelling sessions; older boys and girls enjoyed athletic clubs and the Campfire Girls. Adults joined the Garden Club, the Bridge Club, the Little Theatre, and the Bowling Club. Other examples were the Attic Club, formed to "develop art appreciation in the community" and the Forum, a discussion group presenting programs on such topics as Negro education, Soviet Russia, birth control, and disarmament. "The Sunnyside News," begun in 1925 and published monthly by residents, listed all community events and boosted SGCA membership drives. The progressive climate of the place was bolstered by the weekly visits of a nurse from the Henry Street Settlement who conducted classes in childcare and examined and weighed each infant. Sophia Mumford and other residents, including Mrs. Charles Ascher, also organized the Sunnyside Progressive School, a day care center and nursery school serving about fifty children every day in space provided by the CHC. The purpose, Sophia recalled, was "to give some content to their lives."[21]

The mix of rental apartments, co-operative apartments, and private homes opened Sunnyside Gardens to families of varying income levels and yielded the social mixing the planners intended, while exuding a generally egalitarian air. The unifying elements of the modest design, together with the innovative plan, with its private, public, and semi-private areas, enhanced the egalitarian atmosphere and reinforced the social goals of the City Housing Corporation. Unanswered at the time was how this egalitarian environment could be maintained over the decades to come.

5

Building on Success

Radburn and Phipps Garden Apartments

WHETHER MEASURED IN terms of planning and architecture, social engineering, or profitability, Sunnyside Gardens was an unquestioned success. Certainly the City Housing Corporation could be pleased with their initial effort, having accomplished what they set out to do. Starting with an idea, they had built a community. Still, the men and women involved believed they could build upon what they learned and create even better places, where their ideas would not be confined to an urban street grid and subject to encroachment by market-rate housing and where they could come closer to realizing the garden city ideal.

With Sunnyside half complete, the CHC began planning its next venture. The company boasted 320 stockholders and a total investment of $1.76 million. In their second annual report in 1926, Alexander Bing wrote that "Sunnyside has been regarded from the first as a laboratory where all phases of the housing problem—structural, financial, and social—can be experimented with and studied." As that first experiment neared completion, the company would "look for another piece of property on which to commence our second development. With the experience and knowledge gained in the construction of Sunnyside Gardens and the development which is to follow, it is hoped we will be strongly enough organized, financially and otherwise, to achieve our ultimate goal—the building of a complete, self-contained, regionally planned community, modeled somewhat on the lines of the English garden cities."[1]

Radburn: A Town for the Motor Age

The second undertaking would be, in the words of Bing, "a new community recognizing modern traffic conditions." Where at Sunnyside they had accommodated the automobile as an afterthought, placing garages at the edge of the community, they would now "meet the needs of a completely new mode of living" by making the family car a primary consideration.[2] The result was Radburn, a "Town for the Motor Age."

CHC counsel Charles Ascher apparently originated the name, taking the nearby Saddle River as his inspiration. He "found a book on English place names which said 'Rad' meant 'saddle'; so I added 'burn'—and there we were." Further research determined that there was not already an existing place of that name, so it was not in the public domain. Ascher then filed Radburn as a registered trademark in New Jersey to head off "the inevitable developer who would trade on our success by promoting 'Radburn Manor' or 'Radburn Gardens.'"[3]

Plans were unveiled on January 25, 1928, and generated immediate interest and praise from the planners and critics; 222 approving editorials appeared in newspapers across the country, from the *New York Herald Tribune* and the *Brooklyn Eagle* to the *Saginaw Daily News*, the *Columbus Enquirer-Sun*, and the *Des Moines Register*. Writing in *Survey Graphic*, Patrick Geddes enthused about "a town turned outside-in—without any backdoors. A town where roads and parks fit together. . . . A town in which children never need dodge motor-trucks on their way to school. A new town—newer than the garden cities and the first major innovation in town-planning since they were built."[4]

Radburn would be one step closer to realizing Ebenezer Howard's ideal. The traditional pattern of urban growth was expansion of the city outward from the center, resulting in suburban sprawl and obliteration of the landscape. This was why Mumford, Stein, Wright, and the others objected to the approach of the Regional Plan of New York and Environs. It would result in "centralized traffic of such magnitude as to make present congestion look like a deserted city," wrote Wright.[5] The alternative was the creation of new urban centers, limited in size by a surrounding greenbelt.

The City Housing Corporation selected a site in rural Fair Lawn, New Jersey, where the fertile land had produced abundant crops of spinach for decades.[6] Ultimately, the CHC anticipated expending between $60 and $80 million to build a community of twenty-five thousand. Like Sunnyside, Radburn was also a limited dividend undertaking, and it attracted a number of wealthy investors—John D. Rockefeller, Jr., and Arthur Lehman among them. The remainder of the capital was raised through the sale of stock, with dividends limited to 6 percent.[7]

A seasoned corps of architects and planners got to work. Stein and Frederick L. Ackerman designed the houses, with contributions from Wright; Andrew J. Thomas, architect of Jackson Heights and the Metropolitan Life Apartments; and Robert D. Kohn. Again, Marjorie Sewell Cautley was brought in as the landscape architect. Raymond Unwin himself served as a consultant. The design was predicated upon an efficient and cost-effective building process. They fit the same number of houses onto the site as in ordinary suburban developments, but without a profusion of local streets, which demanded additional water and sewage pipes, utility lines, and paving. They also anticipated that their verdant, innovative plan would be more profitable. By the end of 1929, the City Housing Corporation had completed 170 one-family houses, 10 two-family houses, and 92 garden apartment units. Within a year, 202 families had moved to Radburn, and the company planned 115 additional houses.

Unlike Sunnyside, where the street grid constrained the planners by limiting options for design, Radburn offered a blank canvas on which the planners could demonstrate the practicality and superiority of their ideas. With Sunnyside only a year into construction, Stein outlined an alternative approach. "The size and shape of the individual plot should be determined by the best needs of the whole," he wrote. "Instead of fitting our houses to plots whose size and shape were determined purely on commercial grounds, community planning demands that the commercial arrangements shall be shaped to best serve the character of the whole development."[8] Again, economics must yield to social benefits. At Radburn, the architects could create the superblocks they had dreamed of and group the houses as the topography dictated rather than forcing them into a standard rectangular urban block.

An innovative feature of the "town for the motor age" was the separation of vehicular traffic from pedestrians, a concept Stein readily credited to Olmsted and Vaux and their plan for Central Park. Here, "the interior park of Sunnyside now expanded into a continuous parkway with all pedestrian ways safely segregated from traffic."[9] They designed an underpass to take people from their homes to the shops across the main road and allow every child to walk to school without crossing a single road. But as Alexander Garvin points out, Radburn has only one underpass, and it is far from the defining feature of the place. Far more influential for suburban planning in his estimation are the cul-de-sacs around which they grouped

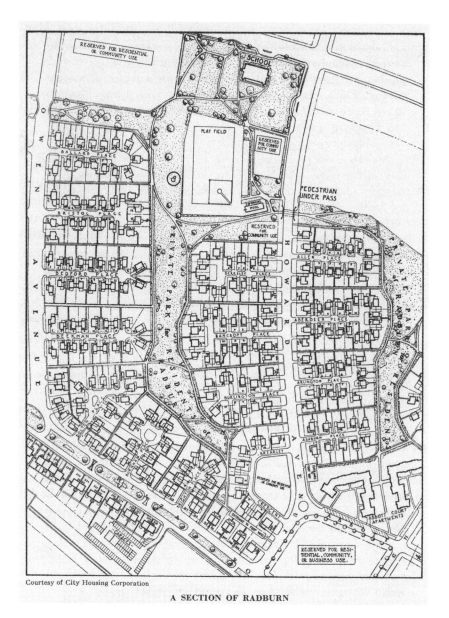

A SECTION OF RADBURN

A section of Radburn. (Marjorie Sewell Cautley Collection, Architectural Archives, University of Pennsylvania.)

the houses.[10] Still, the underpass was a central feature of Greenbelt, Maryland, the garden suburb built by the federal government during the New Deal on which Stein served as a consultant.[11]

Another defining characteristic was the turned-around house. Why should the primary facades face the busy street, with the garage and driveway dominating, Stein asked. The house of tomorrow would be "turned around so that the living rooms and porch will face toward the garden and the park," the kitchen, garage, and other service functions facing the cul-de-sac off the public way.[12] With this design, Stein and Wright developed the concept introduced in Sunnyside, with its hierarchy of private, semi-private, and public spaces. There, many homes had rear porches and opened onto an interior courtyard encircled by footpaths. At Radburn they carried that idea further. One might say that the houses had two front doors—one opening to the cul-de-sac, the other to the park running through interior of the superblock.

Marjorie Cautley's contribution to the success of this undertaking cannot be underestimated, for Radburn's interior greensward was far more dramatic than the tight courts of Sunnyside. Just as the community plan and home designs of the architects evolved from their initial undertaking, so did Cautley's approach to the landscape, building upon the separation of private and public spaces and assuring a connection to nature for each family. At Radburn, she explained, there were no backyards, but every porch offered "an extended view, across garden plots and flowering hedges, to the park beyond—a view which can never be spoiled by some neighbor's garage or service wing." The idea behind her design was "to preserve . . . a part of the beautiful natural landscape that is being destroyed so rapidly throughout northern New Jersey." She preserved a natural meadow and planted a grove of cedars so that "when Radburn is a city of twenty-five thousand souls there will still be an echo of the woods and meadows upon which it was built." Trees and shrubs were planted so as not to block views of the open space beyond, and fences could be no higher than two and a half feet.[13]

As at Sunnyside, the City Housing Corporation instituted a set of controls to assure the perpetuation of their scheme. Each new homeowner received a copy of "Radburn Protective Restrictions and Community Administration," which included the "Declaration of Restrictions." The Radburn Association was established before the first homes were sold in order to "convey the parks, swimming pools, and footpaths to an independent entity as assurance of their permanence to the prospective homebuyers." The "mutual covenants running with the land" empowered the association to

Radburn, Houses facing walks instead of streets. (Marjorie Sewell Cautley Collection, Architectural Archives, University of Pennsylvania.)

regulate all architectural matters and made it the beneficiary of an annual fee upon all properties. Ascher saw this as "an affirmative, constructive tool in community building." Because these private contracts relied upon "promise and consent, rather than legal regulation," such as zoning and building codes, they fostered a sense of common purpose among residents through self-government.[14]

Radburn began as a great success, and Clarence Stein fully expected it to serve as a model for all subsequent suburban development. Lewis Mumford, however, thought the place fell short. "Admirable as is the layout," he wrote, "no candid critic can pretend that the individual one-family houses in Radburn are particularly triumphant examples of modern architecture." The challenge of building affordable housing was almost insurmountable, "even with large-scale organization and limited dividends." Mumford returned to their first effort. Considered architecturally, the "studiously suburban types" at Radburn "fall down badly beside the finer rows and quadrangles of Sunnyside; and if anyone thinks he can do better with the cheap free-standing house, let him try it." He certainly thought that Radburn pointed toward a mistaken goal, the preservation of the one-family house. Again, Sunnyside was, for him, a superior model. No longer could architects think first of the individual unit. Instead, they had to re-direct the focus to "a whole neighborhood or community; and the place where collective economies are sought is not merely in factory production, but at every point in the layout or development."[15] On that last point, at least, Radburn did meet Mumford's high standard.

The planning profession readily acknowledged the significance of the undertaking, and it was held up as the standard for future suburban devel-opment. In 1932, Philip Johnson and Henry-Russell Hitchcock curated the first architecture exhibit at the Museum of Modern Art, and the Housing Section featured Sunnyside and Radburn alongside the modernist housing schemes in Europe. This was not entirely surprising, given that Mumford was a member of the committee and Alexander Bing was listed among the patrons of the exhibition.[16]

As Radburn was under construction, planner Tracy Auger, a recent member of the Regional Planning Association of America (RPAA), wrote, "Radburn stands out singly not because it is the biggest or best or most beautiful of cities but because it is the first tangible product of the new ur-ban science . . . that seeks to make the place of man's habitation and indus-try fit the healthy requirements of daily life. . . . Radburn is not a theory, it is a demonstration. Radburn cannot be a model for all types of a city, nor for all cities of the residential type; it stands in recognition of the varying functions cities serve, and in planning to serve one of the more common of them it points the way to the service of others." When he was charged with planning a new town for the Tennessee Valley Authority during the New Deal, Auger enthusiastically applied those design principles at Norris, the community built for workers building the Norris Dam. Another mark of its impact was that the Federal Housing Administration (FHA) incorporated many of the key features, including the use of restrictive covenants to pro-tect the architectural and aesthetic character of a new community, in its 1939 manual, *Planning Neighborhoods for Small Houses*.[17]

The grim realities of the Great Depression made complete realization of the plan impossible. In 1931 the company could build only sixteen units at Radburn, eleven in 1932, and ten more in 1933. Then construction ceased. In 1934 the City Housing Corporation declared bankruptcy, and the un-built parcels were eventually sold off. Inevitably, what this meant was that "the development of vacant land within the original layout of roads and streets departed from the Radburn Idea and followed the conventional pattern of American suburbs, where homes fronted on the street and were centrally sited on their lot with open lawns and private driveways."[18] The emphasis on architectural harmony and shared open space inherent in the Radburn idea was abandoned. Also in eclipse was the idea that developers should strive to build not just homes, but community.

Phipps Garden Apartments

Before the New Deal, municipal governments did not finance, build, or own affordable housing. At best, municipalities regulated housing, a power greatly enhanced during the Progressive Era. In the early 1900s, private philanthropic organizations took the lead in designing and building afford- able and well-appointed housing, most notably in New York's Russell Sage Foundation, the Society of Phipps Houses, and the City and Suburban Homes Corporation. The City Housing Corporation followed in that mold of investment philanthropy. To a significant degree, these organizations shared ideas and they shared architects.

Steel magnate Henry Phipps founded the Society of Phipps Houses in 1905 specifically to build model tenements. He and Andrew Carnegie had sold Carnegie Steel to J. P. Morgan for $500 million. Carnegie famously donated millions to build public libraries. Phipps, alarmed by tuberculosis endemic in tenement districts, devoted part of his fortune to improving housing conditions for the working poor. He put the first million dollars into the fund that became Phipps Houses, with the stated intention of receiving a modest 4 percent return (at the time, builders of tenements expected returns in the area of 15 to 20 percent a year). Once income from the new housing had accumulated it would be reinvested in similar projects.

The initial effort was an elegant row on East Thirty-First Street in Man- hattan designed by Grosvenor Atterbury, who went on to design homes in Forest Hills Gardens for the Sage Foundation.[19] In 1911, Phipps Houses built a block of model tenements on West Sixty-Third Street, a section known as San Juan Hill and home to a sizable black population. A year later another group of apartments went up immediately behind on West Sixty-Fourth Street, also for black tenants. The *AIA Guide* notes that "they offer little as urban design, but their interior planning was an esteemed prototype for efforts to improve working-class housing." In the 1950s, the East Thirty-First Street complex was demolished to make way for Kips Bay Plaza, and the West Side buildings were sold and converted to market-rate rentals.[20]

In 1930, using $400,000 generated by rents from the Manhattan buildings, Phipps Houses embarked on their third undertaking, a model

Aerial view of Phipps Garden Apartments, completed in 1931, with the second group of buildings in the rear nearing completion, 1935. The Phipps Playground is in the lower left corner; part of Harrison Place, the final section of Sunnyside Gardens, is at the lower right. (Courtesy of the Queens Borough Public Library, Archives, Illustrations Collection.)

housing complex immediately adjacent to Sunnyside Gardens. In keeping with the reform-minded spirit of Sunnyside, the City Housing Corporation sold the two-acre site to the Society of Phipps Houses specifically for the construction of low-income housing. The anticipated rental income would net a modest 5½ percent return. Phipps planned the 344-unit complex in cooperation with the City Housing Corporation to "conform to the general architectural character of the community."[21] Clarence Stein was selected as architect, and Marjorie Sewell Cautley the landscape architect.

The 6 six-story elevator buildings and 16 four-story walk-ups covered two full blocks and enclosed almost two acres of landscaped courtyards; the buildings occupied only 43 percent of the site, with gardens, walkways, and sitting areas covering 57 percent. The four-story walk-up buildings were designed in an "I" configuration; the six-story elevator buildings were in a "T" form. Isadore Rosenfield, the architect in Stein's office who worked on Phipps, explained that "a simple perimeter for so large a plot would have created a rather monotonous inner court. Thanks to the projection of the 'T' stems, the court assumes a great deal of interest, and at the same time the effectiveness of the perspective of distances is not destroyed."[22] The effect was to foster a sense of intimacy within the larger space.

To interrupt the massing of these twenty-two buildings, Stein designed a separate entry for each, an idea first applied a few years before in Carolin Gardens. This also limited noise and gave a greater sense of privacy. Furthermore, having the individual units open directly onto the stairway kept costs down by eliminating wasteful interior corridors. Some ground floor units had private gardens, much like the homes in Sunnyside Gardens. For the courtyard, Cautley insisted on planting mature trees rather than waiting years for saplings to grow. Phipps Houses embraced the design because it "makes possible abundant sunshine and air and a pleasing outlook from every apartment." Monthly rents ranged from $40 to $100, relatively low but sufficient to generate a 4 percent return on the investment, just as Phipps's earlier projects in Manhattan had.[23]

A second set of four-story buildings went up immediately behind the first in 1935 on lots that had been used for tennis courts. Rosenfield essentially replicated the original plan, reduced by two-thirds. This fit the

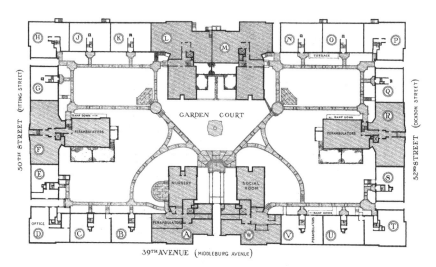

PLOT PLAN

Locating the various buildings and showing their
street frontages and garden exposure.

Plot Plan for the Phipps Garden Apartments, with walks leading to separate entrances for each building. This eliminated wasteful corridors and provided residents with additional privacy. (Marjorie Sewell Cautley Collection, Architectural Archives, University of Pennsylvania.)

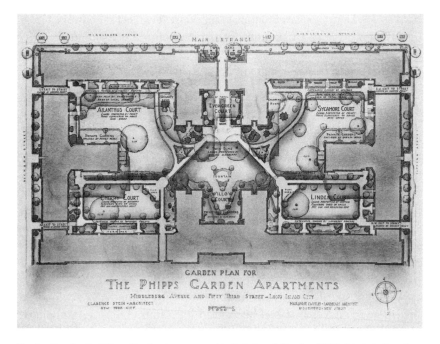

Garden Plan for the Phipps Garden Apartments, Marjorie Sewell Cautley, 1930. (Marjorie Sewell Cautley Collection, Architectural Archives, University of Pennsylvania.)

housing into the available space, but yielded a less generous courtyard, and the architectural brickwork was less exuberant. Still, it successfully maintained the spirit of the original.

The complex received the Medal of Honor from the New York Chapter of the AIA for large-scale planning. "This apartment group shows what can be done in the way of commodious planning when the unit of design is no longer a few buildings on the regulation street layout," the award stated. "The enormous inner court is landscaped with trees and shrubs that have plenty of sunlight for growth; here Mrs. Marjorie Cautley has done an excellent job."[24]

The *AIA Guide to New York City* praises Phipps Garden Apartments as an "apartment incunabulum surrounding a 2-square-block lush, green, private, center-courted world." Oddly enough, the authors dismiss the design: "The architecture here is clearly secondary to a sense of place."[25] The sense of place is certainly profound, but the architecture—the creative brickwork and the rhythm of the buildings—is significant in its own right. The quality of the design is even more impressive since this complex was built as affordable housing, and remains so today.

The Courtyard of Phipps Garden Apartments, June 1932. As at Radburn, Cautley insisted on planting mature trees rather than saplings. (Marjorie Sewell Cautley Collection, Architectural Archives, University of Pennsylvania.)

Phipps Houses was not the only philanthropic organization to build model tenements in Sunnyside. In 1931, the City and Suburban Homes Company, well-known for their model tenements on the East Side of Manhattan, completed the first of twelve apartment buildings on what had been Celtic Park, home of the Irish-American Athletic Club. Ernest Flagg designed the first four units of the complex of affordable apartments, grouping them around a landscaped courtyard, much as Andrew Thomas did with the Metropolitan Life Apartments, and as Stein did with Phipps. The firm of Springsteen & Goldhammer designed eight others. The units ranged from two and a half to five rooms and rented for between $44 and $81 a month.[26]

Taken together, these projects comprise a remarkable ensemble of model tenements, affordable housing, and housing reform in western Queens. Whether built by a private company seeking a profitable return, as the Mathews Model Flats, a limited dividend enterprise, such as the City Housing Corporation, or a philanthropic undertaking, like the Phipps

Houses, these new apartment buildings epitomized a generation of new thinking on the housing problem.

What these sites have in common is that each was possible only because the land was obtainable "at prices low enough to warrant the construction of these buildings."[27] If land prices had been comparable to Manhattan, none of these admirable affordable housing experiments could have been realized. Henry Wright was blunt: "There is, in fact, no magic formula by which low-cost housing can be produced in a way to absorb high land costs." He decried "futile attempts at cheap housing on expensive land; land crowding and room crowding have been the natural result, and low standards have also been taken almost for granted."[28] That Sunnyside Gardens and the Phipps Garden Apartments combined affordability and quality in both design and materials proved his point.

A Partnership Ends

The last project Stein and Wright worked on together was Chatham Village, a community built outside of Pittsburgh in the early 1930s. Henry Buhl, Jr., owner of the Boggs and Buhl department store, bequeathed $13 million to create a foundation to benefit the people of Pittsburgh. In 1929, the directors determined to build model housing for low-income residents. Stein and Wright were brought in as site planners and design consultants; the architects of record were Ingham & Boyd, a local firm.[29]

Wright was largely responsible for the plan for the hilly site. "He had a feeling for the shape of the ground and what could be done to mold it to the practical needs of home and community that seemed superhuman," wrote Stein. "He appeared to sense the site possibilities long before the

Rendering of homes at Chatham Village. (Published in Henry Wright, *Rehousing Urban America*, Columbia University Press, 1935.)

Interior pathway through a greenway, Chatham Village, 1964. (Urban Explorer, the John Reps Travel Photographs, John Reps Papers, Division of Rare and Manuscript Collections, Cornell University Library.)

surveys were made." Furthermore, he "went to the roots of the basic problems of development costs."[30] As at Sunnyside and at Radburn, the row houses faced a common greenspace.

The first section was well under construction in 1932, and with the economy at a low ebb, labor and construction costs were much lower than projected. After visiting the site, Stein wrote, "The group of brick houses are simple in design but charming, partially because of the careful way in which they have been related to the site and to each other and partially because of the infinite care with which every simple detail has been studied. The construction is very good." He thought it "the best moderately priced housing development," but not quite as successful "as Radburn in meeting the problems of the motor age."[31]

Sadly, as Chatham Village was under construction, the partnership between Stein and Wright came to an end. Henceforward, Wright would be a consultant to Stein rather than a partner. In August 1933, Wright wrote to Stein informing him that he had, "after a long struggle, come to the conclusion that it would be wiser for me to withdraw from the association of the past 10 years." Stein saw that his collaborator of the past decade was "becoming more and more of a teacher and a theorist, with fewer and fewer moments to spare in criticism of my work." The break had been coming for some time, as Stein took on more of the work. In a letter to his wife, he reflected, "I owe much to Henry, so much I can never repay him. That flame of his has helped light me on my way. It would have been somewhat different without it." But he had clearly moved on in his own mind, explaining, "I have come to enjoy being on my own, completely, even in those problems of town planning that I formerly left mainly to his guidance."[32]

Within a year, Wright joined the faculty at Columbia University in the new program in town planning and housing studies, and in 1935 published his book, *Rehousing Urban America*, laying out the ideas and solutions he developed with Stein and the other members of the RPAA. He died the next year. Stein never completed his own book on housing, though he worked on it intermittently over the years. In 1950 he did finally publish a book about his work with Wright and his own projects, *Toward New Towns for America*. Fittingly, he wrote much of the manuscript in Wyldes, the former home of Sir Raymond Unwin.

6

⁞⁞⁞

Foreclosure

The Great Depression and the End of a Dream

FOR AMERICA'S CITIES, the Great Depression brought an unprecedented level of unemployment and the nearly total collapse of a cornerstone of urban prosperity: the real estate market. While not exclusively an urban problem, unemployment was certainly more visible in the cities, and by their numbers and the nature of their demands the jobless soon overwhelmed all sources of private charity. Families had to make bitter choices between food, shelter, and other necessities, and with so many out of work, unable to pay their rent or keep up with mortgage payments, evictions and foreclosures, often enforced by city marshals, became tragically common. In 1932 alone, financial institutions across the nation foreclosed on a quarter of a million properties; by the time Franklin Delano Roosevelt took office in March 1933, the foreclosure rate was up to a thousand a day.[1]

The sight of a family forced out on the street, surrounded by their possessions, multiplied by the thousands, translated into that most unusual of urban problems: a housing glut. Existing apartments remained vacant as would-be tenants, if they were fortunate, doubled up with friends or relatives in already crowded homes, or lived in "Hoovervilles." Unable to afford a place of their own, young couples moved in with parents or put off marriage altogether. Housing values fell precipitously, leaving many homeowners owing more than their property was worth. The construction of new housing virtually ceased, leading to a crisis in the building trades and deepening the cycle of stagnation and unemployment.

The economic boom of the 1920s was nowhere more evident than in Queens, and like everywhere else during the Roaring Twenties, the real estate explosion in Queens had been built on credit. By mid-decade, however, the downturn in Queens real estate had already begun. The high point in the value of building permits came in 1925, and by 1928 the total had slumped by nearly a quarter, from close to $200 million to less than $150 million. After racing upward in the early 1920s, mortgage investment, too, leveled off after 1926.[2]

Still, in the autumn of 1929 expressions of business confidence were abundant. President Herbert Hoover assured the country that the business of the nation, "the production and distribution of goods and services, is on a sound and prosperous basis." In September, just weeks before the stock market crash, V. H. Vreeland, the president of the Long Island Real Estate Board, stated proudly, "Yes, the future is bright."[3]

New York City was perhaps unique in both the magnitude of its problems and in the scope of its solutions. Queens prospered mightily during the boom years of the 1920s, but after the Wall Street collapse, the already slowing rate of real estate investment plunged dramatically (see Table 2). Banks which had eagerly granted mortgages during the 1920s foreclosed on those same properties in the early 1930s, and as a result they had little capital to invest in new housing even if there had been a demand. Employment in Queens dropped rapidly in the first year after the crash, and it continued to fall in each succeeding year.[4] Almost overnight the mood

Table 2. Permits for New Housing in Queens, 1921–1935

Year	Permits	Estimated $ in millions
1921	6,851	39.1
1922	21,321	133.1
1923	25,021	157.8
1924	24,610	160.3
1925	31,527	172.9
1926	24,151	186.6
1927	22,641	179.6
1928	18,710	146.5
1929	11,843	87.5
1930	11,213	70.0
1931	12,554	68.5
1932	4,015	12.8
1933	2,142	11.7
1934	3,314	10.1
1935	6,126	24.1

Source: "Queens Building Totals $1,46 0,000,000 in 15 Years," *Queensborough*, May 1936.

of optimistic boosterism yielded to cries for governmental action to ease the crisis.

Queens was then, and remains today, a borough of homes built and financed by the private sector. As the Great Depression deepened, an increasing number of homeowners faced the dreaded prospect of foreclosure. From January 1929 to February 1933, a total of 15,728 homes were foreclosed in the borough. This was, in truth, a national problem, as the average homeowner by 1933 was two years behind in mortgage payments and local taxes. Economist A. Anton Friedrich of New York University, a homeowner in Sunnyside Gardens, stated that "the critical situation which faces the urban homeowner will probably continue for a long enough period to bring about wholesale foreclosures and dispossession of homes unless constructive remedial action is undertaken by the Federal Government."[5] Never had the federal government intervened in the housing market, let alone extended aid to individual property owners.

The City Housing Corporation in Crisis

Sunnyside Gardens may have sprung from the minds of housing reformers, but clear-eyed capitalists provided the funding. Founded as a limited dividend enterprise, the City Housing Corporation nonetheless operated on sound business principles, sound in the context of the housing boom of the 1920s, at any rate. The common mortgage arrangement during the 1920s had insurance companies or savings and loan institutions issue the first mortgages, which typically covered barely half of the appraised value. Buyers usually had to take out costly second and third mortgages to make up the difference.[6]

On that basis individuals without sufficient income or assets were able to purchase properties. Looking back decades later, Clarence Stein wrote, "As the 'home-owner' has only a minority holding on his house, when inevitable depression comes, he discovers that 'home-ownership' for those with low incomes is a myth."[7] Stein, of course, had readily endorsed the provision of mortgages on those terms to buyers in Sunnyside.

At Sunnyside, the City Housing Corporation guaranteed the first mortgages provided by the Equitable Life Assurance Society of the United States and the Irving Trust Company, and the CHC itself issued the second, using capital obtained through the sale of bonds to philanthropists like the Rockefellers and the Russell Sage Foundation. Because dividends were capped at 6 percent, borrowers received a better rate than they would have received on the open market, where interest rates ranged between 10

HOW the MORTGAGE DISAPPEARS.

Down payment of 10% pays for the house up to the dotted line. Figures below show how the mortgage, represented by solid green, gradually disappears

After 5 years 11½% of the mortgage paid.   *After 10 years 27% of the mortgage paid.*   *After 15 years 47½% of the mortgage paid.*

After 20 years 76% of the mortgage paid.   *After 23 years entire mortgage cleared away.*

Compare these carrying charges with your present rent

In order to make the Sunnyside Finance Plan still more clear, below is given a list of house prices and payments in the group now ready for sale:

Type	Price	Down Payment	Total Monthly Charges		Payment on a/c of Principal
One Family	$8,830	$883	$66.78	including	$13 24
Two Family	11,800	1180	89.87	including	17.70
Three Family	19,250	1925	149.60	including	28.87

"How the Mortgage Disappears," City Housing Corporation brochure, 1926. (Clarence Stein papers, Division of Rare and Manuscript Collections, Cornell University Library.)

and 15 percent. To further reduce costs to the purchaser, the CHC serviced the loans itself, collecting a single payment covering interest, amortization, taxes, water bills, and court maintenance fees. Payments were scheduled to decrease by 30 percent in 1932. In 1921, New York State enacted a ten-year exemption from real estate taxes for new construction; when the taxes kicked in, the CHC would modify payments so owners could cover the increase while the overall carrying charges remained about the same. If all went as anticipated, borrowers would own their homes outright in twenty-three years.[8] This arrangement guaranteed a flow of capital to the CHC while permitting the company to advance its agenda. At the same time, buyers interacted with the CHC, not the financial institutions that had actually lent the money, masking the economic realities that underlay the company's financing.

The CHC's business model depended on continuous construction and expansion. They sold stocks and bonds backed by the mortgages issued to buyers in Sunnyside and Radburn. As long as timely mortgage payments continued, the company could further its grand design of building garden suburbs. But if families defaulted on their obligations, and if economic conditions worsened more and more, the City Housing Corporation would be unable to build its way out of financial difficulties, let alone pay investors.

When ground was broken for Radburn in early 1929, the company seemed well positioned to grow and profit. All the homes in Sunnyside had been sold; homeowners were faithfully making their monthly payments, and the apartment buildings were fully rented. The CHC had $4 million in assets and looked forward to an additional $3 million in new capitalization. John D. Rockefeller had recently lent the company $5 million. Behind that ledger, the picture was less rosy. After 1929, the CHC no longer paid out dividends from earnings, only from cash on hand, and by 1931 the company was running a deficit. With a growing number of Sunnysiders falling behind in their mortgage payments, the CHC was hard pressed to meet its own obligations.[9]

Financial failure was not unique to the City Housing Corporation, of course, but as both a reform enterprise and a capitalist investment it was caught in a peculiar bind. The company had built an almost personal relationship with homeowners in Sunnyside, which led to exaggerated expectations about what the company should do in response to the expanding mortgage crisis. CHC had set out to build not houses, but a community, and in the 1930s it was clear that they had succeeded more than they ever expected.

Quite literally, the Great Depression hit home in Sunnyside Gardens. In August 1932, residents formed the Consolidated Home Owners' Mortgage Committee and began to organize to resist threatened foreclosures. More than 300 of the 563 homeowners joined the protest. Six months later, 411 Sunnysiders signed a petition addressed to the CHC protesting that mortgage payments had become an "uneconomic burden." Property values had fallen, and Sunnysiders owed more than their homes were worth. The petitioners wrote: "To meet this situation, a promise of relief to 'cases in extreme need' and a promise of an indefinite reduction of interest rates is not enough. To put Sunnyside Gardens on a solvent basis and to make it financially safe for those of us who have invested our savings and our energies to make this an attractive home community, the full program as (a) interest reduction, (b) three-year waiver of amortization, and (c) writing-down of the mortgage principal, is absolutely necessary." At this early stage of the crisis, the company assured the petitioners that they would endeavor to reduce the interest rate, but they could not promise any reduction in the outstanding principal.[10]

In February 1933, two Sunnyside homeowners, A. Anton Friedrich, an economics professor at New York University who also did work for the National Recovery Administration, and Gaylord Herendeen, a statistician with the American Telegraph and Telephone Company, conducted a survey "to establish the actual current economic status of the home owners in Sunnyside." They sent out 503 questionnaires and collected 302 responses. The findings were grim. Of those responding, income had been halved, disposable income was down by two-thirds, and three-quarters of all bank accounts had been completely drained since 1928; many respondents had unpaid medical bills and debts to lending institutions. The primary breadwinner in four in ten families had been unemployed for fourteen months or longer, and overall net worth had fallen 78 percent. An astonishing three-quarters of the homeowners were down to five cents on the dollar of their 1928 net worth. To underscore their plight, the Consolidated Home Owners' Mortgage Committee sent the report directly to President Roosevelt and members of Congress.[11]

Ironically, the crisis intensified after Franklin Delano Roosevelt entered the White House promising "a new deal for the American people."[12] Two developments in 1933 doomed the homeowners. First, New York governor Herbert Lehman refused to use state power to declare a mortgage moratorium. This was not a demand of Sunnysiders alone, but a statewide issue. Republican Fiorello La Guardia, in the midst of his campaign for mayor (he had lost his seat in Congress in the Roosevelt landslide the year before), supported the homeowners and railed against shady bankers and corrupt financiers. La Guardia urged the governor to call a special session of the legislature "to save the homes of thousands and thousands of families." On August 1, homeowners from across the metropolitan region rode special trains to Albany to plead for a moratorium on foreclosures. But when Governor Lehman did offer mortgage relief, his modest proposal would apply to borrowers behind in principal only, not interest, taxes, and other arrears.[13]

The second ominous development was the worsening financial condition of the City Housing Corporation itself. The company had been far from unresponsive to residents. In 1932, they had made financial adjustments to the extent they could, reducing rents, waiving mortgage payments in a few cases, and advancing interest payments on mortgages it had co-signed. In all, they expended $45,000 to assist two hundred homeowners in Sunnyside. Company president Alexander Bing asked bondholders to waive interest payments temporarily, until the general financial situation improved; remarkably, three-quarters of them did so. The report by Friedrich and Herendeen did influence the actions of the CHC, at least to the extent the company could modify its actions within steadily tightening financial constraints. In their tenth annual report in May 1934, the CHC explained that they had "worked in close cooperation with the Committee representing Sunnyside owners," and noted with appreciation the committee's efforts to work out solutions in difficult cases. But between these outlays and reduced income from the mortgages, the company was in a death spiral. The CHC had repossessed thirty-nine houses, seventeen in 1933 alone. Furthermore, the company was $500,000 in the red.[14]

The Mortgage Strike

How successful the CHC had been in creating a community was evident in the way Sunnysiders responded to the crisis. They organized; they lobbied and protested; and neighbor helped neighbor. J. Charles Laue, secretary of the mortgage committee, said, "Economic pressure is forcing people who have always met their obligations to stop paying. We also find those who are in the 25 per cent [sic] class unwilling to sink further money into those houses until an adjustment in the mortgage structure is made." The committee demanded "blanket relief," with a temporary suspension of mortgage payments and a permanent reduction in mortgage rates. Furthermore, they wanted the 6 percent interest rate to be halved, a moratorium on foreclosures declared, forgiveness of all outstanding fees, and a 95 percent cut in the value of the second mortgages to reflect the decline in property values. "Sink or Swim, we will stick together," resolved the residents at a mass meeting. They avowed they would withhold payments until the mortgage terms were adjusted.[15]

The early years of the Great Depression brought out significant tenant resistance to evictions and rising rents. Often, these rent strikes occurred in tenement districts where communists had a visible presence.[16]

At Sunnyside, it was a strike by property owners, not renters, but many Sunnysiders had come from the tenement districts, and there had always been a number of Communist Party members or sympathizers in the community. That certainly accounts in no small measure for the rhetoric and passion of the mortgage strikers, but it was also the temper of the times. Communists tapped into genuine fears and resentments, and that resonated beyond the dedicated party members. As party leader Earl Browder declared, "Communism is twentieth-century Americanism."[17]

In his autobiography, David Horowitz, sixties radical turned conservative, wrote that his parents, both members of the Communist Party, moved to Sunnyside in 1940. They could have bought a house for $4,000 but disdained property ownership on principle. "To my parents and their friends property was theft; the right of owners did not exist in any reality they recognized." The Horowitzes did finally buy in 1949, paying $18,000. Sunnyside was attractive to them because "the name was like an emblem of the radical fantasy they would impart to me the way other families transmitted a religious faith." They saw this "model housing development for working families" as "a reproof to capitalist chaos." According to Horowitz, it was not simply the idea of Sunnyside that attracted communists; the party identified the Gardens as a target of opportunity and moved its activists in.[18] But while the Communist Party may have labored to exploit the situation, residents of all political perspectives joined together.

Obviously, the company could not accede to the demands of the homeowners' committee, no matter how much they may have wanted to. In the first place, the company had secured the first mortgages and thus had to gain approval from the lending institutions before reducing principle or interest. In the second place, the company had taken out second mortgages that went to secure a bond issue. The mortgage holders themselves were squeezed, philanthropic purpose or no.[19] In other neighborhoods, each homeowner arranged his own mortgage, which meant that several banks were involved and that the foreclosures would not hit everyone at once. In Sunnyside, however, one institution held all the mortgages, so many homeowners faced foreclosure at the same time. Despite the fact that several financial institutions were involved, it was the City Housing Corporation alone residents interacted with.

As more and more residents in Sunnyside and Radburn fell behind in their mortgage payments and the number of foreclosures mounted, the CHC could not meet its obligations to bondholders, and with no capital on hand the company could not build its way out of trouble, even if there had been a market. Finally, inevitably, the company filed for bankruptcy in 1934.

Dissatisfied with the CHC's response—it was in bankruptcy and thus its freedom of action was drastically circumscribed—and frustrated by the lack of governmental intervention, the Home Owners' Committee began their mortgage strike on March 24, 1935. In a remarkable show of solidarity, half the residents stopped making payments on principal, interest, and taxes, vowing to continue to withhold payments until the company acceded to their main demand, that the interest rate on their mortgages be reduced from 6 percent to 3 percent. One observer wrote, "By a turn of fate, under stress of hard times, the community spirit thus fostered became the seed for the owners' organization once the strike was on. The common greens and meeting places were put to collective and then to rebellious use."[20]

At the end of March, Laue and Meyer Parodneck, the group's attorney, traveled to Washington and met with John Fahey, chairman of the Home Owners' Loan Corporation (HOLC), to press their case that the 6 percent interest rate on their mortgages was unrealistic under the current circumstances. Not surprisingly, they received no immediate assistance, only a referral to the HOLC's manager for New York. Launched in 1933, the HOLC refinanced one in ten mortgages across the county, but did not act to aid the Sunnyside homeowners. One possible answer is that the properties were deemed high risk as they were located adjacent to the railroad yard and the industries of Long Island City. What had been a virtue when the CHC acquired the property was now classified a liability by federal housing bureaucrats looking at land use maps, where undesirable neighborhoods were outlined in red (the literal origin of the term "redlining").[21]

Lewis Mumford had a steady income writing for the *New Yorker*, so he could meet his obligations, but his neighbors could not. Decades later, Sophia Mumford recalled that "eventually we just felt we had to stand by our neighbors." They joined the mortgage strike "sadly and reluctantly. We withheld payments for a year, then we left."[22] The Mumfords moved upstate to Amenia, about two hours north of Manhattan.

While many mortgage strikers undoubtedly hoped to reach an acceptable agreement with the lenders, more militant voices were emphatic that no compromise was possible. The strike would continue, they insisted, until all demands were met and all residents retained their homes. One bulletin from the committee called the threat of foreclosure "a gigantic bluff" intended to scare them. "THEY CANNOT AFFORD TO GO THROUGH WITH THE FORECLOSURES. All we need to do to beat them is not to pay City Housing a nickel. Let us keep our lines fast."[23] What the committee missed, of course, was that the bankrupt company had no leverage at all.

When the mortgage strikers refused to make scheduled payments, the CHC had no choice but to begin eviction proceedings, serving papers on fifteen members of the Consolidated Home Owners' Mortgage Committee. Bing stated plainly that "the residents have refused to make their mortgage payments and there is nothing left for us to do but foreclose." To reinforce solidarity, the committee staged a meeting in the park house and presented to homeowners who had been served with papers "service flags," a blue border around a white field with an evergreen positioned in the center.[24]

Incensed, the fifteen men sent telegrams to President Roosevelt and Governor Herbert Lehman demanding help. "We ask for your intervention," the telegram to the president read, "since the HOLC and other alphabetical organizations so far have failed to act. With billions at your disposal, surely something can be done for the home owners." To Governor Lehman, whom they had lobbied without success for a mortgage moratorium in 1933, they wrote: "One of the powerful institutions which pledged to you on Feb. 25, 1933, that no foreclosures would be started against homeowners without negotiation, has now taken lead in instituting foreclosure action in Sunnyside Gardens and is steadfastly refusing to discuss mortgage question. Foreclosure summonses have been served on leaders in drive to intimidate model community of 600 houses built by City Housing Corporation in which your family made investment. Pledge of Equitable and other financial institutions was used with your consent to forestall enactment of protective legislation. You alone can now step in to demand Equitable not foreclose without living up to pledge."[25]

The mortgage strikers kept up the public pressure. Unable to move the CHC or obtain help in Washington, the Home Owners' Committee attempted to insert themselves into the reorganization proceedings in federal bankruptcy court. Their main contention was that the company had misled them when they signed the mortgages. The committee argued that the company presented itself as a philanthropic venture, but in reality it was a creature of the banks. George W. Alger, representing the second mortgage holders, in return described the strike as the action of a "semi-communistic organization." Federal Judge John C. Knox offered the Sunnysiders little encouragement, remarking that he had little sympathy with those trying to "put the squeeze" on others in order to get out of their own obligations. A few weeks later he urged the striking homeowners and the mortgage holders to compromise, but neither side could.[26]

In October, Charles Weis, president of the Home Owners' Committee, and Meyer Parodneck met with attorneys from the Equitable Life Assurance Society, the holder of about 130 first mortgages on Sunnyside homes,

to request reduced interest charges. Equitable replied that such a prop-
osition could be considered only if all arrearages were fully discharged.
This would have included payment of interest and other charges accrued
on the second mortgages held by the City Housing Corporation, but since
the Committee had filed suit against the company, they had to reject Equitable's tentative offer.[27]

The strikers became adept at the theater of protest, understanding well
that if they kept their issue before the public they had at least a chance.
They picketed the 45 John Street offices of the Merchants Fire Insurance
Company, of which John D. Rockefeller was a director, carrying signs
proclaiming "Rockefeller puts families out of homes." In November 1935,
they sued again, this time naming Bing, Stein, Wright, and other CHC
board members, including Eleanor Roosevelt, even though she had left
the board in 1928. The First Lady was served with a summons as she entered the grand ballroom of the Hotel Commodore to address a luncheon
of the National Public Housing Conference on the subject of abolishing
the slum. The suit sought damages of $850,000 on behalf of 217 property
owners. Bing dismissed the suit as "a repetition of the false and misleading
charges which the home owners have been misled into making," adding
that the same charges had been used as a defense in the first foreclosure
proceedings and in that case all fraud charges were withdrawn.[28]

In December, J. Charles Laue saw his home and two others sold at auction on the steps of the Queens County Court House in Long Island City.
His neighbors danced and carried brooms, and to the tune of "The Battle
Hymn of the Republic" sang their strike song: "Sunnyside is on a mortgage holiday./Sweeping 6 per cent philanthropy away./Second mortgages
can't make these houses pay/Although their sales go on." And the chorus:
"Glory to the 6-per-centers,/Who are out to make us renters,/What a pity
we're dissenters,/We'll stay in Sunnyside." When the auction began, one
Sunnysider bid a homeowner's Harvard diploma and American Legion
membership; it was not accepted.[29]

Laue was finally evicted the following August. On the eve of the eviction, two hundred neighbors gathered outside his home for a wake. When
the sheriff arrived the next day he met a crowd of one thousand attending
the "funeral." The doorway had been draped with somber black crepe and
the mourners offered eulogies around a coffin bearing the legend "Here
lies the deed to our home. We mourn our loss!" An American flag flew at
half-staff in the yard.[30]

Gussie Plimack, a woman who lived through the evictions, recalled
that the marshals did not have an easy time of it. "Whenever the marshals

would carry the furniture out the front door," she said, "we'd carry it around to the back door and put it back in the house." At one meeting of the mortgage strikers, the committee presented James Gilleeny a medal "for activity in the interest of better housing" because he "came off best in a dispute with four process-servers serving a summons on a neighbor."[31] Soon after, Gilleeny himself was served with an eviction notice for his home at 45-18 Middleburgh Avenue (Thirty-Ninth Avenue). In an unusual twist, the Equitable Life Assurance Society attempted to serve a writ on Sheriff William F. Brunner to show why he should not be held in contempt of court for delaying the eviction. Sheriff Brunner had actually met twice with Governor Lehman, imploring him to intervene on behalf of those facing eviction. "It is with sincere regret that I was obliged to evict the Gilleenys," explained the sheriff, "and I wish it were a discretionary power on the part of the Sheriff rather than a mandatory power. The court ordered the eviction and there was nothing else I could do."[32] The Gilleenys were evicted on March 10 and moved to a rented house in Flushing. Still, Gilleeny remained the lead plaintiff in the case against the City Housing Corporation, a case not finally dismissed until 1939.[33]

In a dramatic move, the committee installed a siren above the front door of Corrine Thal's home on Forty-Fourth Street. When the authorities arrived, the siren sounded and dozens of neighbors filled the house, making it impossible for the eviction to proceed. But such defiant acts of solidarity only delayed the inevitable. The Thals were evicted a month later, after their home had been sold to the Merchants Indemnity Corporation of Manhattan, the holder of the mortgage. A crowd of more than two hundred filled the courtyard and blocked the sheriff and his men, but after breaking a window, they gained entry. The Thal's furniture had been weighted down with concrete blocks to prevent its removal, but carried out it finally was. Inside there was a scuffle, and six individuals were arrested and charged with disorderly conduct, including one man who had run for office on the Communist Party line. To prevent the mortgage strikers from moving the Thal's furniture back into the house, three special policemen were stationed inside. Putting a brave face on the situation, Charles Weis declared, "This shows that the expense of taking over the homes will be such that the owners will not be able to sell or rent them and make any money."[34]

The Communists may have been determined, but communistic fervor was no match for a capitalist legal system. In January 1936, federal judge John C. Knox denied the application of the Home Owners' Committee to sue the CHC and its directors for damages, effectively closing out their

legal options. A final appeal to Governor Lehman to intervene on their behalf was rebuffed. "While I have much sympathy with all those in financial
straits," responded Lehman, "I do not consider it to be the proper function
of the Governor to conduct negotiations for the modification of private
contracts between private individuals."[35]

As the contentious situation worsened, residents redefined the history
of the CHC entirely. While its dividends were capped at 6 percent, there
was no such limit to the company's profits, they reasoned. Profits above the
6 percent cap would be reinvested, as indeed was the case. The CHC put
the profits earned at Sunnyside toward the construction of Radburn; that
was, in fact, their business model. Sunnysiders, however, now saw the company as just another example of the wealthy taking advantage of the little
guy. By the middle of 1936, fifty-two residents had lost their homes to
foreclosure, and an additional 175 foreclosure actions were in progress.
In their suits against the CHC, the homeowners contended that they had
purchased their house on the basis of "cost plus" and that the company
had exaggerated those costs.[36]

Foreclosure judgments and evictions continued into the spring of 1936,
but after all the bad publicity and protracted legal proceedings, the bondholders finally offered a compromise. They had been prodded to the table
by Mayor La Guardia, who had First Assistant Corporation Counsel William C. Chanler participate in the discussions. In a letter to residents, Lawson Purdy, chairman of the Sunnyside Bondholders Protective Committee
and a member of the board of trustees of the Russell Sage Foundation,
offered a reduction of interest rates to 4 percent, and a blanket 25 percent
reduction on second mortgages, so that the total owed on the first and second mortgages did not exceed the true value of the house. The letter said,
"It has become increasingly apparent to our committee that a considerable
part of the home owners now represented by the Sunnyside Home Owners' Committee have neither the intention nor the ability to preserve their
homes by making any payments on their obligations, and are simply hoping
to protract the period in which they can live rent free in their houses."
Purdy went on to state that "this substantial group has, we feel, become an
increasing peril to all other home owners." But, with foreclosures certain
to continue, the bondholders finally recognized that they had to adjust the
terms. Dozens of Sunnysiders accepted the deal. Equitable also modified
the terms of mortgages they held.[37]

Even then the protests did not end. Three months after the compromise offer, thirty people protested outside the Equitable headquarters
at Thirty-Second Street and Seventh Avenue, holding placards reading,

"Policy Holders: Equitable Life Is Using Your Money to Evict Us" and "Is 6 Per Cent More Sacred Than Our Homes?" Mrs. Toni Maxwell, who was evicted the previous year, attempted to present to the company president a mound of hamburger meat, representing "a pound of flesh."[38] Clearly, more than a resolution of the mortgage issue, some of the mortgage strikers were more interested in making a larger political point.

While Sunnysiders publicized their plight and barricaded themselves in their homes, there was little such drama at Radburn. Also faced with foreclosure, residents there neither actively resisted nor initiated legal action. Perhaps this was because in Radburn the homeowners were more upper middle class and included a good many professionals. Perhaps it reflects the absence of the Communist Party there. CHC counsel Charles Ascher recalled how wrenching it was to act as an "untrained social worker." The unemployed homeowners, young engineers, and junior executives could not pay the mortgage interest, and each expressed confidence that he would get another position soon. "Well," thought Ascher, "who was I to tell them they weren't going to get a job soon?" He did his best for them, but all he could offer was, "If you can't pay the full interest, what could you do?" According to one historian, "Radburn residents quietly accepted foreclosures, and either continued to live in the repossessed houses as tenants or moved elsewhere." At the end of 1931, with the CHC out of capital and headed for bankruptcy, Ascher resigned. As far as he was concerned, the "truncated experiment" was at an end.[39]

In the end, more than half of all Sunnysiders lost their property to foreclosure, and the dream of building a new urban community through architecture and planning evaporated, even as the houses and the garden suburb plan endured. When the CHC could not meet their demands for mortgage relief, residents blamed the company and turned against it. Writing twenty years after the events, Clarence Stein commented that the residents "were wrong, no matter how just might be their resentment."[40] The City Housing Corporation went bankrupt, and with that went the grand dream of demonstrating a profitable alternative to urban congestion and suburban sprawl.

7

###

Envisioning the Future City

WITH SUNNYSIDE GARDENS, the Phipps Garden Apartments, and the first section of Radburn complete, Clarence Stein and his colleagues had reason to be optimistic. The City Housing Corporation was in every way a success. They had built attractive, quality homes and provided an opportunity for home ownership to families otherwise shut out of the market. The ultimate measure of success, of course, was a return on investment, and the company had exceeded expectations there too. They had demonstrated that it was indeed possible to solve the housing problem, but it required the commitment of public spirited citizens willing to accept a lower return on their investment. For those who embraced that vision, it was a small price to pay for a public good.

Perhaps the City Housing Corporation could have continued its upward trajectory, building out Radburn and embarking upon a third garden suburb. Perhaps other builders, seeing the economic benefits of the Radburn idea and the lesson in civics that was Sunnyside Gardens, would have followed the company's lead. Others might have been inspired to adopt the limited dividend model; Alexander Bing certainly thought that the great philanthropic organizations, such as the Carnegie and Rockefeller foundations, should do so.[1] But the experiment ended abruptly. The stock market crash in October 1929 shook the nation's confidence, and conditions only worsened over the next three years. By 1933, the company was but a legal shell, and Stein walked away just before it went into bankruptcy.

Stein may have left the City Housing Corporation behind, but he was as confident as ever in the correctness of his vision of an urban future. Writing in the *New York Times*, he outlined his vision of how cities could be remade. "Our present cities are physically obsolete," he wrote. "They are unable to either satisfy the demands made by modern living or to make efficient use of opportunities offered by modern technics." The "cancerous growth of slums and blighted areas" made for a dismal prospect, socially no less than economically. "The basic flaw in our present city pattern is its lack of any functional form, or at least the fact that its form no longer functions. Laid out almost entirely from the point of view of ease of speculation in real estate, the plan has no relation to the human needs of living and working and so no sense of the possibility of permanence."[2] The only solution, thought Stein, was to build anew. "There is no reason why even large cities should not remake themselves by the development of new and complete planned communities, instead of mechanically adding streets and blocks without any organized scheme," he argued. As new towns arise, each built according to a rational plan, the older, decaying slums of the central city could be wiped away and a rational and verdant plan imposed.[3]

The reality of mass building across the country in the 1920s was "endless rows of jerry-built, unrelated houses badly fitted to badly shaped lots and unpleasant surroundings. This is quite as wasteful and unsatisfactory as though each individual had really built his own house." By contrast, Stein envisioned construction on the neighborhood level, "the natural basic planning unit which permits the greatest degree of economy and freedom in the layout of blocks, streets, business centres, schools, recreation spaces and houses." Fostering vibrant community life was to be a primary motivation of building these new towns.[4]

The election of Franklin Delano Roosevelt in 1932 brought the promise of relief, recovery, and reform. Indeed, many of the men and women who flocked to Washington to join the New Deal had gained their earliest experience during the Progressive Era. Furthermore, many of them were New Yorkers, and several members of the Regional Planning Association of America (RPAA) found opportunities there. Benton MacKaye and Tracy Auger worked with the Tennessee Valley Authority; Frederick Bigger was chief of the planning staff of the greenbelt program; Robert Kohn was appointed head of the Public Works Administration Housing Division; and Catherine Bauer had a position in the Federal Housing Administration (FHA).

For the first time, the federal government would be motivated to address conditions in America's cities. U.S. Secretary of the Interior Harold Ickes was responsible for crafting and implementing the programs that would remake the cities. While economic recovery was the most immediate goal, Ickes also believed that "the reform of our housing on a tremendous scale must take a first place."[5] This was the opening for the large-scale application of the ideas long espoused by the RPAA.

Secretary Ickes embodied the ideas of urban progressivism. He recognized the maleficent influence of the slum and how those conditions were an impediment to the fostering of strong family life. He went even further, advocating the use of federal funds to address those concerns. In *Back to Work: The Story of the PWA*, he wrote, "I believe that every American family is entitled to decent living conditions. . .to light, to air, to sunshine, to clean streets, to healthful surroundings, to an absence of preventable fire hazards, to parks and playgrounds in order to give the children now playing among noxious garbage cans in filthy alleys a chance to grow into normal and healthful American citizens. If such a home cannot be provided without a subsidy from the government, then I, for one, am for a subsidy."[6] Such thinking animated the New Deal.

At the same time, he was careful to stipulate that this was not a program to compete with private industry. "By confining the work of the Emergency Housing Corporation . . . to the clearance of slums and the production of a like number of low cost units, limited as to rentals and restricted as to occupancy to the low income groups," he wrote, "the Administration can stimulate one of the basic industries without encroaching upon its field of future opportunity." Until the private sector recovered and consumer demand returned, and in cases where local agencies were unable or unwilling to act, his Public Works Administration (PWA) would take the initiative "in the interest of unemployment relief and recovery." Convinced that the only solution to the crisis was for the federal government to build housing directly, Ickes hoped to outwit greedy land speculators and corporate investors, and thereby prevent, or at least minimize, the siphoning off of federal dollars for private profit.[7] "It quickly became obvious," he wrote, "that our much vaunted private initiative, as so often happens when the goal is a social good instead of a private profit, was unable or unwilling to undertake the job."[8]

To lead this effort, Ickes selected Robert D. Kohn. During the First World War, Kohn had headed the housing division of the U.S. Shipping Board, where he became acquainted with Wright and Ackerman. He was well acquainted with Stein also, having been a founding member of the Regional Planning Association of America, and a collaborator with him on the designs for Temple Emanu-El and the Fieldston School. As director of the Housing Division of the PWA, Kohn found a parallel with his experience during the war. He maintained that although this was an emergency organization, there was nothing temporary about its program, its aim being not just recovery but the "prevention of such conditions in the future." The PWA, according to Kohn, was not in competition with the private sector because, in the first place, they worked with local contractors, suppliers, and architects, and, second, because "nobody is doing the job of providing adequate housing at rents the majority of the population can pay." At the same time, he did not hold unrealistic expectations about what he could accomplish. It would not be possible to supply housing for the poor without substantial subsidies. His objective was to produce urban housing that could serve as a model for the future, and obviously, he was sympathetic to designs in line with the garden city ideals.[9]

Flush with praise for his work at Sunnyside and at Radburn, Stein's exuberance at seeing the ideas of the men and women behind the RPAA embraced at the federal level was certainly understandable. He could see all future suburbs patterning themselves after Radburn, whereas in cities Sunnyside Gardens and the Phipps Garden Apartments would serve as models. With the federal government welcoming proposals to remake blighted cities, he could reasonably expect that the pioneering work of the City Housing Corporation would be honored as a beacon illuminating the way to our urban future.

Hillside Homes

In the first round of federal financing of local housing construction, the Housing Division offered up to 85 percent of the necessary funds to either limited dividend corporations—private entities that capped profits at 6 percent—or municipal housing authorities. Like other states, New York lacked the legal apparatus to accept funds for public construction of low-income housing; consequently, the first proposals submitted to Washington came from limited dividend corporations. Of the hundreds of such applications submitted to the Housing Division from across the country, Harold Ickes approved only seven, committing about $11 million for the construction of 3,065 units. Two were in New York: Hillside Homes in the Bronx, and Boulevard Gardens in Queens; the others were in Altavista, Virginia; Euclid, Ohio; Philadelphia, Pennsylvania; Raleigh, North Carolina; and St. Louis, Missouri. By April 1935, three of the projects were occupied, three were under construction, and one was just starting construction. Following this tentative beginning, Secretary Ickes suspended the program. For the next three years, the Housing Division operated as the client, working directly with architects, contractors, and suppliers. In New York, the two projects completed in this way were the Williamsburg Houses and the Harlem River Houses.[10]

With his friend and former colleague Robert Kohn writing the checks, Stein saw his opportunity. He was "anxious to see whether the Radburn idea of a community developed around common interests, large open spaces, and safety of number, could be built into a community consisting entirely of apartment houses." He identified a large site in the Bronx, owned by philanthropist and housing advocate Nathan Straus, suitable for "a community of some six or eight thousand people with all the safety features of Radburn." Writing to Mumford, Stein enthused, "It is wonderful what one can do if the plot is large enough and it is possible to change the location of streets, or altogether, eliminate a good many of them."[11]

Despite his earlier experience, Stein was hopeful that he could convince the city to accept a design predicated upon the closing of streets. "What I want to do is to get them to take a space equal to the streets closed and put it altogether [sic] in a single park, which will be placed across the road from the existing school." He was not entirely optimistic, however. "It is astounding, as soon as one gets into really good, large-scale planning, how many laws or regulations one has to break or have changed. So, even if we are able to get money to finance any of these large operations, which is still very questionable, we are going to have our hands full inducing the city to permit us to do something good."[12] Predictably, the city denied his request, and again Stein had to adapt plans to the urban grid.

In September 1933, the PWA approved a $5.06 million loan at 4 percent interest to the Hillside Housing Corporation. Nathan Straus had volunteered to serve as president of the company, and he sold the property to the company for 70 cents per square foot, significantly below market rate. Only the low cost made it possible to build affordable housing. Stein's design was based on Phipps Garden Apartments, but on a greatly expanded scale: 108 four-story walk-up buildings and 4 six-story elevator buildings, 4,948 rooms in 1,416 units, including 188 garden apartments. The buildings covered 38 percent of the site, enclosing landscaped courtyards with sitting areas, gardens, and playgrounds. Here, he incorporated a central walkway running through and connecting each of the five blocks. In a sense, that unifying element created a virtual superblock. Just as he had at each of his previous projects, Stein built into the design space for children's activities, clubs, and community meetings.[13]

As construction was underway at Hillside Homes, the other PWA-funded apartment complex was going up in Queens. Boulevard Gardens,

Rendering of Hillside Homes, Clarence Stein, April 1934. (Marjorie Sewell Cautley Collection, Architectural Archives, University of Pennsylvania.)

located only a short walk from Phipps, was built by the Cord Meyer Company. The Housing Division signed a $3.21 million loan agreement with the company on November 11, 1933, and work was completed within two years. With private capital scarce and the housing market uncertain, federal funding was a lifeline for Cord Meyer, and the company was well positioned to take advantage of this unprecedented opportunity. Cord Meyer had been a major force in the growth of Queens since the 1890s, building subdivisions in Elmhurst and Forest Hills, including Forest and Arbor Close (1927–1928), blocks of two- and three-story Tudor row houses surrounding private courtyards—designs clearly echoing Sunnyside.

Cord Meyer had the design and the architect in hand, contractors and suppliers at the ready, and the management experience to carry a large project through to completion. It would have been impossible for state or local government to design and build on the scale of Boulevard Gardens in 1933, as evidenced by the New York City Housing Authority's initial effort, First Houses on the Lower East Side. Designed by architect Theodore H. Engelhardt and landscape architect Charles N. Lowrie, the eleven-acre complex had 10 six-story elevator buildings—a total of 968 apartments. The buildings covered only 23 percent of the site, the remainder given over to generous landscaping and a children's playground. Boulevard Gardens follows the garden apartment precedent of Jackson Heights, Sunnyside

Gardens, and Phipps, with the buildings around the perimeter enclosing a landscaped green.

In form, the H-shaped buildings resemble Engelhardt's six-story Kelvin Apartments, a complex built by Cord Meyer in Forest Hills in 1928.[14] In contrast with Stein's experience with Hillside Homes, the builder at Boulevard Gardens was able to create a superblock on the irregular site, rather than fitting the buildings into the street grid. The reason, perhaps, is that the site backed onto a railroad embankment. To accentuate the visual separation from the surrounding low-rise blocks, the buildings sit on a landscaped berm. The handsome brick buildings feature ornate neo-Georgian entries, with an arched opening leading through to the courtyard within, not unlike Phipps. The brick facades feature minimal ornament, the scale broken by shutters on the second- and fifth-floor windows. Entries are situated on the short sides or the corners, leaving the longer facade to face the landscaping uninterrupted.[15]

In "The Sky Line," Lewis Mumford generally praised Boulevard Gardens for its scale and the "extremely generous" interior courts, but thought the architecture lacked "positive conviction and gives no positive pleasure." He was especially critical of Engelhardt's choice of ornament, "the few half-hearted Georgian touches" and "the row of shutters—yes, shutters." Still, he thought it "miles ahead of the ordinary commercial development," and far, far better than the first municipal housing project completed that same year. Mumford called First Houses "downright terrible . . . precisely how not to house lower-paid workers, and above all how not to rebuild the blighted areas of New York."[16]

The residents of Boulevard Gardens certainly appreciated their opportunity. The inaugural issue of their newsletter exulted, "Boulevard Gardens was never planned to be just another mass of walled-in cubicles: it wasn't erected for private profits . . . nor was it built or intended as a charity offering from the government to its poor. Boulevard Gardens was intended to be . . . a gigantic community of happy people, all interested in making a success of a new type of living. Government money and private enterprise has made possible perhaps the most unique development ever conceived in the history of this greatest of cities." They were certainly aware that there was more to living there than just paying rent. "We are all pioneers in a new kind of life," wrote the editor, "and on our shoulders rests the fate of a tremendous new social scheme."[17]

Within two years of the start of construction, the first residents arrived at Hillside Homes, and almost all of the 1,400 units were occupied by the spring of 1936. A crowd of five thousand gathered in the playground in the middle of the project for the dedication ceremony on June 29, 1935. The occasion provided elected officials an opportunity to express their commitment to housing reform. "The splendid project exceeds my expectations," exclaimed Governor Herbert Lehman. "I have always considered good homes as being the soil in which good citizenship is rooted," he said, reiterating a central tenet of urban progressives. "Light and fresh air bring happiness and contentment and this project, with its maximum of open space is ideal." Nathan Straus stated that "the right of every citizen to a decent home is at least as important as the right of citizens to an education."[18]

Beyond the quality of the new buildings, the alternative presented by Hillside also offered additional impetus for slum clearance. The governor expressed his confidence that "in the near future we will see a rapid disappearance of slum areas." What was required was land and capital, and the PWA offered the latter. Lending funds to a limited dividend entity afforded "little or no burden to the taxpayers, because they are largely self-liquidating and self-supporting." Darwin Jones, head of the State Housing Board, added that this success was "an excellent illustration that private business can march hand in hand with State and Federal Government."[19]

Clarence Stein also spoke at the opening, although the *New York Times* story did not so much as mention his name. In his remarks, he highlighted

Courtyard, Hillside Homes, circa 1936. (Marjorie Sewell Cautley Collection, Architectural Archives, University of Pennsylvania.)

the design, which brought a bit of nature into the city. "Blight has destroyed the social as well as the economic value of a large part of New York," declared Stein. But Hillside will be "different from the rest of New York. . . . a quiet, peaceful park surrounded by homes. . . . a place of safety and repose, a place of sunlight. From every room one will look out on broad vistas of gardens and restful lawns or gay play places."[20] These were the values animating the design of Sunnyside, Radburn, and Phipps.

The enlightened design of Hillside would inoculate the complex from blight, suggested Stein, for it "was planned, was built, and will operate as a complete integrated neighborhood. It will control its own environment. It will be managed by a company that knows that its success depends on the preservation of its unique features." Here was another principle underlying all of the work by Stein and his circle. The quality of the housing affects, and could even determine, the character of the residents. A blighted environment generates blighted people, and he had confidence that Hillside Homes would endure. "Above all," he said, "the people who live here will preserve and develop the gardens and recreation spaces that offer an opportunity for a finer and more abundant community life."[21]

Such faith in the enduring qualities of his design was rewarded. Hillside remained a stable, working-class enclave for decades. But the decline and decay of the Bronx in the 1970s finally infected this grand complex. Even a plan respectful of human scale and incorporating humanistic values could not immunize the place against the social ills surrounding it. By 1990, half of the units were vacant, 132 illegally occupied by gangs and drug dealers. The walls were covered with graffiti, and there were four thousand broken windows; public spaces were dominated by drug dealing and other antisocial and criminal behavior. New owners brought the place back, however, beginning with the renovation of the playgrounds, landscaping, and community rooms. In this they recognized, above all other factors, a safe and pleasant public realm that was necessary for a community to thrive. That principle had been the foundation of Stein's design. But revitalization also required a break with the past. Hillside Homes was renamed Eastchester Heights.[22]

"The City"

Stein hoped that he would play a major role in developing housing policy in Washington and that the garden city would become the official goal. In that, he would be disappointed, even though Frederick Bigger, a founding member of the RPAA, was in charge of the greenbelt program. Stein and

Wright were brought in as consultants for the new towns program of the Resettlement Administration, but Stein did not gain the commission he had hoped for (his reluctance to relocate his practice to Washington was perhaps a factor). After meeting the architects for Greenbelt, Maryland, Stein wrote with exasperation, "The plans were unpardonably wasteful. They had nothing to do with low-cost housing. They were the result of the architect's desire to have every American live like a king or better, a suburban bank president. . . . We finally had to rip into the plans." Even though he had only a peripheral role, Stein could not accept such misguided designs. "The possibility of building Garden Cities means too much to me [to] let the whole thing be set back because the first ones are so extravagant that they become the laughing stock of all practical builders." He owed it to "the memory of old Ebenezer Howard." When he revisited the site a year later, he exulted, "They have the beginnings of a Garden City! If old Ebenezer were only here to see it."[23]

The 1939 New York World's Fair offered Stein and Mumford an opportunity to bring their ideas before a wider public. The means was a film illuminating the ills of contemporary cities, strangled by congestion and beset by pollution, and the golden future of the garden city. He organized Civic Films under the wing of the American Institute of Planners and named to the board old friends from the RPAA—Frederick L. Ackerman, Tracy Auger, and Robert Kohn, who was also a member of the fair's Board of Design, and chairman of the Committee on Theme. With a $50,000

Greenbelt, Maryland, 2017. The Resettlement Administration built this community based on the Radburn Idea between 1935 and 1941. (Author's photograph.)

grant from the Carnegie Foundation, he approached Pare Lorentz, the documentary filmmaker who produced "The Plow That Broke the Plains" in 1936 for the Resettlement Administration and "The River" in 1938, a documentary about the Tennessee Valley Authority. Lorentz prepared the shooting script, and Mumford wrote the narration. Documentary filmmakers Willard Van Dyke and Ralph Steiner were brought in to shoot the film, and Aaron Copeland composed the score.[24]

In structure, "The City" offers a progression from innocence through experience to higher innocence. It begins in the pastoral village of Shirley, Massachusetts, the home of Benton MacKaye, the originator of the Appalachian Trail, a founding member of the Regional Planning Association of America, and a life-long friend of Stein and Mumford. For his script, Mumford reached back to his 1931 book, *Brown Decades*, which outlined the virtues of the ideal New England village and decried its loss: "planned as a definite communal unit: the pattern of common, school, church, town hall, inn, and houses had been worked out in relation to the need to exercise the direct political and economic functions of the community. . . . But the precedent was ignored. The greed to own land and profit by its increased increment outweighed the desire to build permanent and useful habitations."[25]

That idyllic past is lost as industry and pollution obliterate any possible connection to nature. Intending to demonstrate the impossibility of a good life in a noisy, crowded, and congested metropolis, the film shifts to scenes of New York City. Stein's description of life in obsolete "dinosaur cities" is brought to life on the screen: "the turbid mass of traffic-blocking streets and avenues, the slow-moving crowd of people clambering into street-cars, elevateds, subways, their arms pinioned to their sides, pushed and packed like cattle in ill-smelling cars. . . ."[26] Interestingly, that sequence was incorporated into the 1948 film "Mr. Blandings Builds His Dream House," to suggest why Cary Grant and Myrna Loy were decamping for the suburbs. As the scenes of the chaotic city build to a climax, a rational, human-scaled alternative emerges; images of life in a garden city present the possibility of a serene future and a pleasant environment.

Stein and Mumford obviously intended to advance their idea of the garden city by showing the wholesome family life in Radburn and Greenbelt, but more than that, the film expressed the values behind the creation of those places. Mumford's didactic script incorporated all of the ideas he and Stein and the other members of the RPAA had been advocating for decades, and the narration tells viewers how they should interpret what they are seeing: "This is no suburb where the lucky people play at living in the country. This kind of city spells cooperation. . . . Each house is grouped with other houses close to schools, the public meeting hall, the movies and the markets. Around these green communities a belt of public land preserves their shape together." And then: "New cities are not allowed to grow and overcrowd beyond the size fit for living in. The new city is organized to make cooperation between machines and men. . . . The motor parkways weave together city and countryside. . . ."[27] This was not Sunnyside Gardens, Radburn, and Greenbelt. This was the urban utopia of their dreams.

Constant in their thinking was the certainty that the congestion in cities, the unrelenting pace of urban life, and the limited and unfulfilling opportunities for leisure overwhelmed the individual and diminished the possibility of a genuine community of spirit. The built form of "dinosaur cities" was itself the problem. The film exhorted viewers to support the idea that we deserve better and that we can do better. Not all viewers were convinced, however. Planner Mel Scott thought that "somehow the closing shots of children riding their bicycles along tree-shaded paths and of parents smiling at gurgling babies were anticlimactic after the brilliant sequence of urban horrors. The planned community was as dull as it was healthful and peaceful."[28]

The optimism of the World's Fair quickly gave way to the grim realities of war. Stein and Mumford continued writing and advocating for their ideal, but their window of opportunity had closed. After the Second World War, Stein again advanced the idea of the regional city, now as a civil defense measure. Dispersing population and production would enhance survivability in the event of nuclear war, he reasoned.[29] But his ideas were largely irrelevant. Postwar America would indeed be suburban, but the result was more sprawl than thoughtful planning. Postwar public housing ignored the precedents of Phipps Garden Apartments and Hillside Homes, and Levittown did not even nod in the direction of Radburn.

PART II

PRESERVATION

8

🁢

Preserving the Historic Garden Suburb in London and New York

ONCE THE GARDEN SUBURB was the future of urban living. Lewis Mumford called them "harbingers of a new age."[1] That first generation of planned communities is now a century old, but while they are surely of the past, they are certainly neither obsolete nor irrelevant in the present and, one assumes, the future. Even the best built homes can deteriorate over time, however, and we must ask how best to restore them, or whether it would be better to replace the entire structure and build something reflecting contemporary needs and taste. The question, then, is whether the "Garden Cities of To-Morrow" are sustainable today.

That the garden suburbs around London and New York endure in their original form is remarkable in itself. They remain highly desirable among home buyers despite, or more likely because of, the controls and regulations imposed upon residents. "How lucky we are to live here," exclaims the cover of a Hampstead Garden Suburb Residents Association brochure. Inside the text continues: "It's not just luck. The Suburb has been kept the way it is as a result of the concern and involvement of the people who have lived here since the beginning."[2]

In all the discussions of sustainability, historic preservation rarely makes an appearance. Energy efficiency, recycled materials, green roofs, LEED certification, solar power and windmills, even bike racks—all are popularized as essential elements of sustainable architecture. Economic justice, social justice, and environmentalism are the primary concerns of sustainability advocates. Environmentalists address the preservation of open space and greenbelts, but rarely the preservation of the built environment. Restoring or maintaining historic buildings is generally not counted as green by environmental advocates. But really, the greenest building is the one that is already built. Whether considering the natural materials utilized—stone, terra cotta, brick, wood, plaster; embodied energy—the labor and resources that went into producing the structure; or simply not contributing to the waste stream—construction debris is perhaps the largest single contributor to landfills—historic buildings are inherently sustainable.

Considering the entire life cycle of a structure, "older buildings compare quite favorably to new construction."[3] But they do age, and the needs, tastes, and values of the society which must maintain them are surely different from those of the society that built them.

Managing the English Garden Suburb

The survival of Letchworth, Welwyn, and Hampstead is not accidental. Each has been highly regulated from its inception, with limitations on new construction and controls over alterations to existing homes extending even to plantings and paint trim. Historians have long studied these planned communities, but their focus is on the original design and construction, the historical context for their creation, and the social, economic, and cultural ideas of the planners. Rarely is the story carried forward through the tedium of maintenance, regulation, lawsuits, and demographic change to discuss the mechanisms put in place to enforce aesthetic standards and to sustain these places over the decades.[4]

Raymond Unwin understood that regulation was essential if the beauty and harmony of the architecture and overall plan were to be preserved. This was particularly difficult in a residential context at a time before architectural regulation was accepted as a valid regulatory practice. In 1909, a few years after he began working at Hampstead, he wrote, "The external appearance of a building is so much more important to the public at large than it is to the individual occupant or owner, that there would seem to be clear justification for the exercise of some public supervision of the designs of buildings; and unless improvement can be brought about by an educated public opinion, there is little doubt that sooner or later definite public control will be demanded." The question, of course, is whether such public control would have a deadening influence on architectural innovation and creativity, and unduly constrain property owners. Unwin was confident that it was "possible by means of suggestion and supervision to obtain a certain minimum standard of design, to secure a certain degree of harmony, and at any rate to avoid the perpetuation of such monstrous examples of ugliness as too often disfigure the country to-day."[5]

One innovation applied from the onset in both Letchworth and Welwyn was "use zoning," a practice "secured by covenants under leases." Commercial activities were limited to specific sections and generally excluded from residential blocks, with signage limited to a single name sign "of a type to be approved in detail" for each business. Leases stipulated that "the plans and external appearance and materials of all buildings, including extensions, are subject . . . to the approval of the companies' architects." At times drastic action had to be taken against leaseholders who disregarded the guidelines. Frederic Osborn, estate manager at Welwyn, learned that "control had always to be sympathetically exercised, but became easier as time went on, and the character of the town became established and recognized. Public taste improved, and protests against lax consents were useful as a counterweight to the far more frequent and intense resistances to control." Oddly enough, he learned that "in practice there is more danger of laxity than of aesthetic tyranny."[6] Absent rigorous and consistent enforcement of design standards, the aesthetic integrity of the place would be compromised and ultimately lost.

At Letchworth, First Garden City Ltd. retained control over all buildings and landscaping until 1962, when an act of Parliament transferred all assets, rights, and responsibilities to a new public entity, the Letchworth Garden City Corporation.[7] In 1995, a subsequent act of Parliament transferred the entire estate, then valued at £56 million, to the Letchworth Garden City Heritage Foundation.[8] Today, the foundation "proactively" manages its commercial assets; the income generated supports its charitable activities and funds maintenance. The guiding principle is that "value is predominantly created from our property portfolio and therefore the successful management of this portfolio is critical to our success." The end, of course, was "the maintenance and enhancement of the physical, economic and social environment of Letchworth Garden City." With that goal ever in mind, the foundation draws a direct connection between preservation and sustainability: "This objective is driven by our commitment to sustainability. This is about helping to maintain and enhance the town to ensure that its success continues for the long term. This can be achieved through the positive and environmentally sensitive management of the Garden City Estate, combined with investment in our charitable commitments to support the town's social and economic infrastructure."[9]

Far from a tangential concern, assuring the continuity of the design was one of the paramount concerns of the Heritage Foundation from the outset. Recognizing the historic significance of the first garden city, their

2011 strategic plan noted that the strict and consistent standards were "created to help safeguard the town's existing physical character for the benefit of all local communities and future generations—locally, nationally, and internationally." They strove to have Letchworth stand as "a living model of an environmentally sustainable town." To achieve that goal, the foundation understood that they had to meet the needs of the business community, because a "strong economic environment" was necessary to assure the town's future prosperity and desirability.[10] At the same time, the foundation grasped that only through strict regulation could they maintain economic value, the underpinning of environmental and social sustainability.

Like Letchworth, Welwyn Garden City thrives under a management scheme intended "to ensure that homes and street scenes are kept in harmony with the original design and concept of the time." But concern for aesthetics and history alone would not justify strict regulations covering extensions, alterations to or replacement of windows and doors, garden structures, walls and fences, hard surfaces, and trees and hedgerows. The management scheme is important because "inappropriate development, poor quality alterations to buildings and erosion of the special character of the environment will lead in turn to the lowering of neighborhood values both in visual and economic terms." The challenge is to "manage change whilst at the same time ensuring that the fundamental aesthetic, amenities and values of the garden city remain intact." By such means, Welwyn would exemplify a "sustainable" community.[11]

Of course, preservation does not mean freezing a place in time. In 1980, the Housing Committee of the Welwyn Hatfield Council voted to demolish five hundred homes in the garden city. Designed in the 1920s by Louis de Soissons, the original Welwyn architect, the homes were among the earliest examples of load-bearing concrete walls. After half a century, however, many houses were unsound. With window frames rusting and heating systems failing, the Council determined that demolition of the still attractive houses and the construction of replacement homes was the most economical and sustainable solution. Although the new homes maintained the traditional scale and adhered to the historic plan, they exuded far less charm than the originals. Such a bold decision was certainly at odds with the preservation ethos, but to the managers of the estate, the economic sustainability of the garden city demanded nothing less. Still, an individual commenting on the Our Welwyn Garden City web page lamented, "Why, when they knocked down these beautiful looking and designed houses, did they rebuild them with soulless and lifeless boxes?"[12] In this instance,

Welwyn's guardians failed by emphasizing economic viability to the exclusion of aesthetic and historical imperatives.

From the start, Hampstead Garden Suburb, too, was governed by a trust empowered to control all new construction and alterations to existing structures. Aesthetic considerations in particular were singled out among the founding principles. "The houses will not be put in uniform lines nor in close relationship built regardless of each other or without consideration for picturesque appearance," the rules stated. "Great care will be taken that the houses shall not spoil each other's outlook, while the avoidance of uniformity or of an institutional aspect will be obtained by the variety of the dwellings, always provided that the fundamental principle is complied with so that the part should not spoil the whole, nor that individual rights be assumed to carry the power of working communal wrong." The founders understood that the long-term integrity of the Hampstead Garden Suburb depended upon that fundamental principle, that all residents accept a common set of design standards. As early as 1909, Unwin recognized that "the difficulties of such public control are undoubtedly great, but the evils which result from absolute lack of control are even greater."[13]

This paternalistic system of regulation worked well until passage of the 1967 Leasehold Reform Act, which fundamentally changed the relationship between estate owners and their tenants across the United Kingdom and presented a serious challenge to the character of the garden suburbs.[14] Prior to 1967, the Trust owned all homes in Hampstead, and the old leases contained covenants providing the ground landlord with the control necessary to protect his investment. The new legislation removed those provisions, and for the first time, residents could purchase the freehold of their houses. The cohesive character of residential areas previously ensured through oversight by a single landlord now could be compromised by the interests of newly enfranchised homeowners wishing to maximize the economic potential of their new asset or to assert their own individual taste over established community standards. But the Leasehold Reform Act 1967 also enabled the ground landlords of "well run" estates to apply to the high court to set up a scheme of management to control alterations to houses and grounds.[15] Accordingly, residents of Hampstead reestablished the Hampstead Garden Suburb Trust and set up such a scheme of management "for the purpose of ensuring the maintenance and preservation of the character and amenities" of the suburb.[16]

Letchworth Garden City Corporation initially applied for an exemption to the Leasehold Reform Act, but when that was denied they submitted their scheme of management for the court's approval in short order. In a deliberate attempt to provide "continuity with the previous leasehold covenants," the new covenants explicitly required that the exteriors of buildings, hedges, and fences meet standards set by the Letchworth Garden City Corporation. Owners could not "alter, extend or rebuild without written Corporation consent." Without these new controls, it is unlikely that the character of the garden city could have been preserved. Even so, "visually unsympathetic alterations" utilizing inferior materials have proliferated.[17]

In the mid-1960s, not unlike changing attitudes toward urban renewal in American cities, public sentiment in the United Kingdom was turning away from the wholesale demolition and rebuilding that had characterized England's postwar reconstruction. Many questioned why historic buildings and even entire blocks had to be sacrificed for highways or uninspiring housing. Even the profoundly beautiful city of Bath saw block after block of Georgian town houses demolished to make way for modern homes. A small book chronicling this outrage was provocatively titled *The Sack of Bath*.[18] Liverpool experienced a similar awakening. The city's population fell 15 percent between 1950 and 1975, and the once great port was falling into disuse. As economic and demographic decline threatened the city's historic buildings, civic leaders sought to alert the public as to what was at risk.[19] It is intriguing to note that historic preservation gained traction in New York and in England at about the same time.

In response to such critiques, the United Kingdom adopted more proactive preservation measures. Beginning as early as the 1880s, the government acted to protect sites of historic and archaeological interest. Today, Historic England oversees a list of over four hundred thousand places. Grade I sites "are of exceptional interest;" Grade II* includes "particularly important buildings of more than special interest;" and Grade II buildings "are of special interest." The churches designed by Edwin Luytens at Hampstead are Grade I; the Spirella Factory at Letchworth is Grade II*, and the Shredded Wheat Factory at Welwyn is Grade II. District councils handle applications for alterations and extensions, but they must consult Historic England "about wholesale demolition of all grades and about all work to grade I and II* buildings."[20]

The idea of defining a "conservation area" to protect entire communities was introduced in 1967. Under that designation, "the local authority had a duty to identify, designate, and to administer policies for their preservation and enhancement." Hampstead (1968), Welwyn (1968), and Letchworth (1974) each received that additional layer of protection. The Town and Country Planning Act of 1968 mandated that owners of listed buildings now had to obtain prior consent if they wished to demolish, alter, or expand their properties. Adhering to those higher standards often comes with higher costs. The Letchworth Garden City Heritage Foundation "offers modest grants to householders . . . to assist bridging the cost gap between plastic-framed windows and concrete roof tiles (both widely used in housing modernization) and the more authentic timber windows and clay plain tiles."[21]

Facing newly empowered residents whose status had changed from leaseholders to freeholders, the Hampstead Garden Suburb Trust was once again armed with the authority to enforce strict controls. In 1971 the Barnet London Borough Council granted the Trust powers overriding "permitted development," work "that has had a cumulative corrosive impact on the visual integrity of the overall character elsewhere." As one resident put it, after five hundred buildings were listed, "It is odd. You pay more to live here, and you can do less. You can't change your windows, create a driveway or do anything really to alter your house. But people like it here. We must be mad."[22]

Even with the protections of the conservation area designation, threats loom from two opposite yet interrelated directions. First, the "spectacular rise in housing prices has fueled pressure for changes to (and redevelopment of) the existing housing stock," and second, the government is demanding that all local planning authorities advance proposals to build affordable housing, notwithstanding status as a conservation area. The question now is whether Hampstead, Letchworth, and Welwyn can embrace change while protecting the qualities that make these places special.[23]

With homes in Hampstead Garden Suburb selling for between £800,000 and £3 million (2012),[24] homeowners understandably want what they want, even if their plans are contrary to Trust regulations. Therein lies a fundamental contradiction. Strict regulation keeps the Suburb a highly desirable place to buy, but at the same time rising property values attract individuals who chafe under controls enforced by an external authority. Mervyn Miller describes this as "rising affluence begetting unrealistic expectations," with "growing pressure for demolition and replacement by 'super-houses,' unsuccessfully attempting to incorporate characteristics of suburb architecture."[25]

In recent years, the courts and the Lands Tribunal have both affirmed and rejected the Trust's power to regulate. In one case, the Trust had denied an application for a new residential unit above a garage, arguing that it "was out of keeping with the design of the principle part of the house and of others in the area, would reduce views of greenery and would set

⹂HAMPSTEAD ⹂ GARDEN ⹂ SVBVRB ⹂ TRVST⹂

862 Finchley Road Hampstead Garden Suburb London NW11 6AB
Telephone: 020-8455 1066 and 020-8458 8085 ~ Facsimile: 020-8455 3453 ~ email: mail@hgstrust.org

Notice to Freeholders

Please remember that, under the Scheme of Management operated by the Hampstead Garden Suburb Trust, you are required to obtain the prior approval of the Trust before altering the external appearance of your property including the garden.

A non definitive list of alterations which require the consent of the Trust is detailed below:

- Changing windows (including double glazing) and external doors
- Extensions, porches & other alterations
- Work to patios, driveways & paved areas in gardens
- Erecting garden sheds
- Re-pointing
- Removing hedges and any work to trees
- Re-roofing
- Chimney alterations
- Replacement of guttering or down pipes
- Erecting satellite dishes
- Installing air conditioning units and extract flues

and

- Converting a garage to another use.

Applications for consent must be made in writing and approved before work commences. Application forms are available from the Trust office or from www.hgstrust.org. To arrange an appointment with the Trust's architectural advisers or tree consultant please telephone the office.

If you are in any doubt about whether Trust consent is required under the terms of the Scheme of Management, or have any other queries, please do not hesitate to contact the Trust Office on 0208 455 1066 during office hours Mon-Fri, 9.00-5.00pm.

Thank you for your co-operation.

February 2011

Notice to Freeholders, 2011. Even after decades of tight regulation, the Trust reminds residents that they must obtain prior consent for all work listed here. (Hampstead Garden Suburb Trust.)

an undesirable precedent across the Suburb." After the Trust prevailed, Chairman Angus Walker commented, "As the Lands Tribunal noted, a guiding principle of the Suburb's founders was that the interests of the wider community should prevail over the interest of any individual."[26] The Trust was also sustained in demanding that another homeowner remove six-foot high security gates installed without permission.[27] In another case, however, the same tribunal allowed demolition of a well-maintained and handsome house by J.C.S. Soutar—who had been appointed Trust architect in 1915—and the construction of two houses in its place. Future battles are to be expected. "The very high value of Suburb property," wrote Trust Manager Jane Blackburn, "means that some owners and developers feel it is worth their while to challenge Trust decisions preventing inappropriate demolition or development through the courts."[28]

Because Hampstead, Letchworth, and Welwyn have remained such desirable places to live in, especially given their proximity to London, home prices have risen beyond the means of most middle-class families. In actuality, the entire region has an affordability crisis, but the growing demand for new construction challenges the ability of these places to maintain their historic character. In March 2012, the government created the National Planning Policy Framework, which "introduced a presumption for approved sustainable development," with affordable housing listed as a "statutory planning requirement."[29]

This conflict between the historic garden city and a requirement for new affordable housing arose almost immediately at Letchworth. In 2015 the foundation offered a plan to erect more than fifteen hundred new homes in the greenbelt, including 111 acres of farmland. Residents were outraged and organized a protest. "I really do think they are committing a crime," said one woman. "I see it as destruction of the concept of the garden city." Others expressed concerns about crowded schools and increased traffic, but above all residents were shocked that the greenbelt, the defining feature of their garden city, would be violated.[30]

A supporter of the proposal could offer only economic justification for building. "It is increasingly difficult, if not impossible, for middle-income households to buy in Letchworth," said the head of North Hertfordshire Homes, a development company. "Our concern is that if the houses aren't built, then that affordability situation will get worse and worse and worse. . . . And where do future generations live? Where do young people who aspire to live in the town they were born in go if there is no building?" The alternative to "sacrificing a relatively small level of green belt . . . is that Letchworth becomes pickled in aspic."[31]

The rub, of course, is that only about 40 percent of the new homes would be affordable, the majority being offered at market rate. With such a minimal contribution to easing the housing crisis, the sacrifice of the greenbelt seems a high price to pay. What is clear is that two social goods are in conflict, and the solution will be imposed by political forces. In that arena, it is unlikely that local interests will prevail over national policy.

Preservation in New York

Aesthetic regulation was entirely alien to the city of New York prior to the enactment of the landmarks law. That was not because of an absence of public sentiment in favor of such. Far from it. The fact is that it took many decades of effort before the state legislature passed the enabling legislation authorizing the city to preserve its historic buildings and neighborhoods. After several lamentable and well-publicized losses, including Pennsylvania Station in 1963 and the Brokaw Mansion on Fifth Avenue in February 1965, Mayor Robert F. Wagner finally signed the New York City Landmarks Law on April 19, 1965.[32] Even with the authority granted under the new law, the Landmarks Preservation Commission moved with caution in the early years, and the number of designations grew slowly. Prior to the law, and for most of the city for decades after, any efforts to protect places of historical or architectural significance had to be either voluntary or contractual, that is, through legal encumbrances attached to a deed.

In many ways, Forest Hills Gardens, described by Robert A. M. Stern as "the most English of American planned suburbs," consciously followed the goals and standards of the English precedents.[33] From the very beginning, the place was subject to uncompromising aesthetic standards. The Covenants and Restrictions imposed in 1913 "run with the land and are binding upon every property owner." The mandate was quite explicit: "No building, fence, wall or other structure shall be erected or maintained nor any change or alteration made therein, unless the plans and specifications therefor show the nature, kind, shape, height, material, color-scheme and location of such structure," without approval by, at the time, the Homes Company. When the Russell Sage Foundation sold its holdings in 1922, it created the Forest Hills Gardens Corporation and "transferred to that entity title to the common spaces and granted it authority to enforce the restrictions." The Corporation issued "Procedures and Guidelines" to help homeowners by providing "uniform and consistent standards." The ultimate purpose, of course, was more than aesthetic. "The value of our homes and the existence of Forest Hills Gardens, as we have known it," states the document, "depend upon our cooperation in the maintenance of architectural standards."[34]

As at Hampstead Garden Suburb, an independent organization has the legal authority to regulate all aspects of the place. The Forest Hills Gardens Corporation is an organization of property owners, answerable only to its members. It regulates the buildings and actually owns the streets, a situation unique in the city of New York. "To preserve the original aesthetics and design of our community," the corporation enforces controls over all new construction and alterations. A realtor in Station Square noted, "People understand that their property value has remained strong because of the ironclad covenants and restrictions."[35] As at Hampstead, aesthetic regulation is deemed crucial to long-term sustainability and to maintaining strong property values.

All proposed work, from additions and new construction down to ordinary maintenance, required the approval of the corporation's architecture committee. Their decisions take into consideration "consistency and/or compatibility with adjoining or nearby structures" and "visual conformity to the high standards of architectural and site design." Those standards mandated "red clay tiles" for roofing, copper gutters, and a specific concrete mix. Replacement windows were to conform to the original configuration, and new storm windows were prohibited. Should a homeowner proceed in violation of the rules, the corporation would "exercise such options" as "withholding of parking decals" (not a trivial matter when the corporation owned the streets and booted cars lacking permits) and place a "Notice of violation in the resident's file or property's title, legal suit, and the right of abatement."[36]

Forest Hills Gardens is self-regulating; through the corporation the community sets and enforces its own standards. The only option available to other places is designation as a historic district under the landmarks law. As of 2020, there were 150 historic districts and district extensions in the five boroughs.[37] After designation, property owners must obtain permits from the commission for any changes to the facades and hardscape, including doors and windows, fences, skylights, paint trim, even repointing, not to mention additions and new construction. On the whole, this has worked remarkably well, fostering restoration of historic features on designated properties while gradually remediating inappropriate changes that had accrued over the decades. Had they not been designated, it is unlikely that the character of the city's historic neighborhoods could ever have been sustained.

Immediately adjacent to Forest Hills Gardens is Kew Gardens, a similar suburban development of one-family houses and apartment buildings developed at the same time. In the 1920s, Kew Gardens attracted a colony of Broadway entertainers and film stars, including Charlie Chaplin, Will Rogers, and George Gershwin; by 1940 it was entirely built out. Unlike Forest Hills Gardens, however, Kew Gardens never had a governing authority to enforce aesthetic regulations. For generations, the quality of the architecture, combined with a common value system among the residents, seemed sufficient to sustain the character of the place. In recent years, however, new residents embracing a different aesthetic and expressing different wants and needs, and often possessing higher levels of disposable income, have significantly altered or even replaced the original homes.

Alarmed by this growing cancer, the Kew Gardens Improvement Association sought protection under the New York City landmarks law. Sylvia Hack, president of the association, asserted, "For over eighty years, the people of Kew Gardens have valued what they had and have. Now it is all too apparent that unless we achieve historic designation and recognition, the next generation may inherit only a shell of what exists." Unfortunately, their years-long campaign gained no traction at the Landmarks Preservation Commission, and Kew Gardens remained vulnerable to market forces and the vagaries of individual taste. From the perspective of the longtime residents seeking protection, the city "sacrificed neighborhoods by short-term thinking when the longer view would have been wiser."[38] It is the embrace of the longer view that distinguishes the management of Forest Hills Gardens and the English garden suburbs from the marketplace of individual desires and tastes in unprotected places like Kew Gardens.

This suggests another aspect of a regime of strict regulation. While design standards inhibit what one can do with one's property, the same controls also limit what one's neighbors can do. The certainty that comes with landmark designation or a private scheme of management protects the homeowner's investment and increases the value of the property as a home. Conversely, the absence of such controls can in some instances inhibit sales to would-be home buyers, particularly in highly desirable areas attracting interest from developers or investors.

Brooklyn realtor Donald Brennan contends that there is an enormous downside to owning property outside a historic district. By his calculation, "the cost of having to use a certain type of window is worthwhile insurance to make sure that my neighbor doesn't let his property devolve, or turn around and sell his building to somebody else and it disappears, and then I have a problem as to what will go on next to me." During periods of intense development pressures, there are tremendous risks. "The pro-landmarking argument that values will only rise," says Brennan, "is not as compelling as the argument that values will likely diminish in the absence of designation."[39]

To be clear, the decline in value is not strictly financial; all too often, in fact, the value is primarily the lot, the quality of the structure built upon it being irrelevant. As more and more original homes in a neighborhood disappear, the value of the remaining houses as residences per se decreases.

A perfect example of this is Old Astoria along the East River in Queens. As late as the 1990s, almost all of the stately antebellum houses remained, and several had been lovingly restored. But some property owners balked at the idea of becoming a historic district and the Landmarks Preservation Commission showed no interest in the area. Now, many of the historic houses have been demolished, and it would be difficult to create a historic district out of what survives.

The second garden suburb in Queens was Jackson Heights. The Queensboro Corporation began building in 1911, and the community was largely built out by 1930. Robert A. M. Stern calls Jackson Heights a "model urban suburbia" demonstrating "what high-density housing in the city could be." From the beginning, the Queensboro Corporation imposed design standards on land they sold to developers, assuring a harmonious ensemble of high-quality buildings. After World War II, such restrictions were abandoned, and the remaining lots sprouted buildings of lesser architectural character.[40]

The innovative feature of the new garden apartments was the landscaping. Each building is set back from the street to provide a small garden in front, and the landscaped courtyard in the center of each block provides an unprecedented expanse of green visible from every apartment. In terms of scale and architectural quality, there was nothing like it anywhere in the city. With his buildings in Jackson Heights, architect Andrew J. Thomas "established humane and practical standards for housing in the city."[41]

A renewed building boom in the 1980s targeted underbuilt sites, primarily the free-standing one-family houses and low-rise commercial blocks, and "a number of buildings were bulldozed or 'improved' to the point where [they] were unrecognizable." What saved Jackson Heights from the fate of other Queens neighborhoods was its density and the quality of the housing—brick as opposed to wood-frame, and attached and semi-attached houses as opposed to free-standing dwellings. The buildings were already as large as the zoning permitted, so there was little danger that the larger garden apartment blocks would be demolished, but it was quite possible that architectural elements could be stripped from the facades in the name of safety or economics. In 1980, after a pedestrian was struck and killed by a piece of a cornice falling from a Manhattan building, the City Council enacted Local Law 10, which mandated the inspection of "exterior walls and appurtenances."[42] Not surprisingly, many building owners wasted no time in stripping all architectural ornament from facades.

In 1988, fearing that incremental changes would undermine the harmony of the architecture and ultimately threaten property values, residents formed the Jackson Heights Beautification Group. Their goal was to maintain the character of the historic blocks and push for protection under the landmarks law.[43] After five years of advocacy and outreach to residents, elected officials, and citywide preservation organizations, the Beautification Group succeeded. The Landmarks Preservation Commission designated Jackson Heights a historic district in 1993, protecting thirty-eight blocks of garden apartments and one- and two-family houses.[44] Since then, the Landmarks Preservation Commission has regulated all buildings and open spaces in the district. The Beautification Group has continued to lobby for an expansion of the protected zone, as several important apartment buildings had been left out of the original district.

A garden suburb is sustainable only as long as it remains economically viable and is perceived as a desirable place to live. Strict guidelines also contribute to a distinctive sense of place and thus enhance the attractiveness to potential residents by assuring that their investment will be protected. In the case of these landmarks of planning, aesthetic regulation has been a major factor in maintaining property values, and it is indeed likely that without such controls, these places would have been lost, absorbed by the sprawling city.

At the same time, the early-twentieth-century garden cities are worthy of preservation in their own right. They represent an optimistic moment in the history of urban housing and design. Having only plans and photographs would scarcely substitute for wandering the streets. It is not enough to know that Ebenezer Howard lived in the garden city he built; we have to be able to see his house. Urban historians and planners continue to admire and study these historic garden cities, but these places are home to individuals with diverse taste, needs, and wants. If the goal of long-term sustainability is to be realized, the suburbs have to adapt to contemporary living, but not at the cost of lower standards of regulation. Only through strict and consistent regulation can homeowners be assured that property values will remain solid, because that is the best guarantee that the community will endure. Indeed, only tight controls will ensure that Letchworth, Hampstead, and Welwyn, and Forest Hills Gardens and Jackson Heights remain intact to celebrate their bicentennials.

9

⁙

Preserving Sunnyside Gardens

SUNNYSIDE GARDENS IS SURELY an icon in the history of urban planning, but its persistence was not an act of God. Nor can we attribute the preservation of its most significant design elements to the innate qualities of the plan, qualities that discouraged individualistic expression and encouraged adherence to a common aesthetic. Sunnyside Gardens has been under a strict regime of regulation for almost its entire existence. Without those controls, it is unlikely it could have remained as intact as it has.

When the City Housing Corporation built the community in the 1920s, they inserted into every deed covenants "running with the land" to remain in effect for forty years. In drawing up the documents, Lewis Isaacs specifically referenced the creation of Gramercy Park by Samuel Ruggles in 1831 and the legal status of that private park. The covenants were limited to forty years because that was the "economic life" of the buildings, based on a depreciation rate of 2½ percent per annum. "We did not want to put the dead hand of the past on the future," said CHC counsel Charles Ascher. Still, the documents did outline the aspects of the plan and the architectural features meriting protection, and each successive purchaser "assumed this contractual obligation," agreeing to "never build anything that would limit the freedom of the interior space." Together, the physical plan and the legal protections "operated to minimize ill-considered selfish action."[1]

For Sunnyside's first four decades, these restrictions effectively protected the open spaces, walkways, and architectural details. The covenants were quite explicit, specifying paint colors for wood trim, fenestration

and doors, the size and type of fencing, even plantings. Homeowners understood and accepted these controls, and the court associations actively
enforced those rules, confronting neighbors over violations no matter how
trivial. A five-member committee consisting of two representatives of the
City Housing Corporation, two property owners, and one independent
individual was charged with ruling on all proposed building modifications,
maintaining the courts, and assessing the monthly charges. After the CHC
went bankrupt, residents formed the United Trustees to perform those
same functions, with members selected by property owners.[2]

In 1956, the United Trustees, fearing that their "small oasis of grass,
trees, and flowers in the center of a city of cement and stone" would
become a "jungle of fenced plots, indifferent gardening, and all sorts of
sheds" when the controls expired, approached Ascher, who had admin-
istered the covenants in the 1920s. He advised that "the only thing they
could do to extend these restrictions was to get every property owner to
sign a fresh document." He volunteered his students at Brooklyn College
to ring doorbells. "Most of the owners, 35 or 37 years later, knew nothing
of the legal basis of any of this," he said. "When they bought their house
no lawyer explained to them that they were inheriting these obligations."[3]
All that most residents experienced were the limitations placed on their
property, not the social benefits such limitations were intended to foster.
The effort did not make great headway, although 54 of the 60 homeowners
in Hamilton Court signed on.

The fears were realized when the easements on Colonial Court lapsed
in 1964. Over the next five years each court saw the restrictions lifted in
turn, depending upon when the blocks were completed, until in 1968 all
had expired. With the expiration of the covenants, the United Trustees lost
all authority and ceased to function. There was no longer any mechanism
to collect and administer funds for common purposes.[4]

When the covenants lapsed, some homeowners responded like it was
the Oklahoma Land Rush. To their shock and dismay, neighbors awoke
to discover that a fence was being erected along property lines across the
walkway and into the middle of the heretofore sacrosanct court. What had
been "the common" was being privatized. By the time the city imposed
new regulations in 1974, only six of the fifteen center courts remained
inviolate. A number of homeowners paved over front yards to create driveways, enclosed porches, or built dormers and rooftop additions. Those
actions had been strictly prohibited, but now there was no regulatory
authority to maintain common design standards. While remarkably few
homeowners transgressed those norms, it took only one to compromise

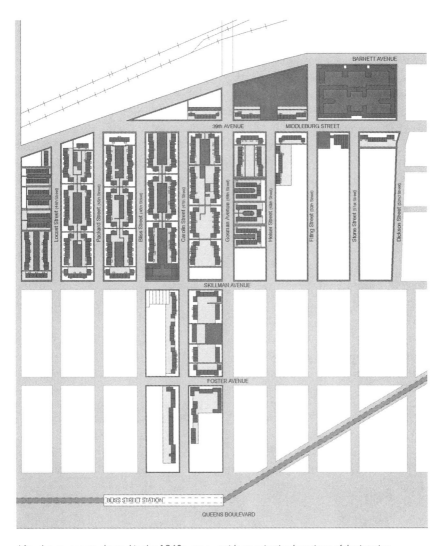

After the covenants elapsed in the 1960s, many residents privatized portions of the interior courtyards, compromising the integrity of Stein and Wright's plan. Darker sections in the common areas denote intact common spaces, lighter areas show where fences went up. (Laura Heim Architect.)

the integrity of an entire court. Each material change was an affront to the social ideals and planning principles advanced by Clarence Stein, Henry Wright, and Lewis Mumford.

In truth, after the easements expired, homeowners were reclaiming their own property. They had always paid taxes on their full lot, even if the covenants denied to them the active and exclusive enjoyment of their portion of the central court. "Bitter arguments broke out between neighbors, pitting preservationists, many of them older residents, against those seeking privacy or merely asserting their new property rights," wrote one resident. "Spite fences were erected, followed by retaliatory hedges to cover the fences. Friends stopped speaking to one another, and some families even moved away."[5]

As the first section completed, Colonial Court was also the first to lose protection. Chain link fences now divide one building from the next, both on the street side and within the courtyard itself. This makes it impossible to experience the plan as originally intended, and certainly impedes the possibility for casual interaction among neighbors. When the covenants expired the next year in Roosevelt Court, the yards quickly became so badly mauled with fences, sheds, and other intrusions that the interior court is all but inaccessible except through the houses; the collective aspect has been lost, the common not even a memory. Today, only Hamilton Court remains intact. There, an active court association continues to assess dues, maintain the interior gardens, and actively monitor new work.

Jefferson Court and Madison Court North, with their mews configurations, present a distinct case, for here the front door of each house faced the common area. The alleyways behind, however, became a jumble of

Fences in the common space at the north end of Lincoln Court. (Author's photograph.)

additions, dormers, opaque fencing, obtrusive decks, and not a few illegal parking pads. The apartment buildings of Carolin Gardens, Monroe Court, and Wilson Court remained virtually intact, but only Carolin Gardens has managed to maintain a semblance of the landscaped common, with a well-maintained garden running behind the five buildings. Its immediate neighbor, Monroe Court, has seen the rear yard completely paved over, and fencing went up on the property lines. At Wilson Court, the private landscaped rear garden envisioned as an essential amenity for residents is today devoid of plantings and entices no one.

The erosion troubled those Sunnysiders who recognized the clear connection between the standards established to maintain the uniformity of the architecture and the social goals of the designers. There is no question but that the earliest residents accepted the regulations imposed by the City Housing Corporation. The modest houses spoke of egalitarianism, and the rules expressed a common purpose that demanded the willing participation of all residents. With the loss of the protections provided by the covenants came the loss of the "community spirit . . . grounded on certain legal obligations to maintain the common land . . . and a common set of social values."[6] Were those social values essential to the preservation of Sunnyside Gardens as the place its builders intended?

The Special Planned Community Preservation District

After almost a decade of ugly and destructive incursions—and it is remarkable that there were as few as there were—it was clear that without a new form of regulation the planned community would be lost. In 1974 the Department of City Planning created a new zoning category to address threats to Sunnyside and other planned communities. The Special Planned Community Preservation District was an innovative designation specifically drafted to protect four places: Parkchester in the Bronx, the Harlem River Houses in Manhattan, and Fresh Meadows and Sunnyside Gardens in Queens.

The purpose of the new zoning resolution was "to preserve communities which are superior examples of town-planning or large-scale development; to preserve and protect the character and integrity of these communities, which by their existing site plan, pedestrian and vehicular circulation systems, balance between buildings and open space arrangement and landscaping as to the quality of urban life; to preserve and protect the variety of neighborhoods and communities that presently exist which contribute greatly to the uniqueness and livability of the city; to maintain and protect the environmental quality that these communities offer to their residents and the city-at-large, and to guide the future development within these areas consistent with the existing character, quality and amenity of the Special District." The regulations stated clearly that "no new development, enlargement which may include demolition of buildings, or substantial alteration of the landscaping or topography is permitted within the area designated as a Special Planned Community Preservation District except by Special Permit of the City Planning Commission after public notice and hearing and subject to Board of Estimate action."[7] (The Board of Estimate had authority over budgetary and land use issues; the mayor, city council president, and controller each had two votes, and each borough president one. The U.S. Supreme Court ruled it unconstitutional in 1989.) The new zoning protected the plan, the footprint of the buildings, and the open space, but not the architecture. That would fall under the prevue of the Landmarks Preservation Commission, that is, if that agency chose to designate.

John Zuccotti, chairman of the City Planning Commission, explained, "These sites represent superior examples of large-scale developments and of town planning. These sites also have large open spaces that could be developed and we think these open spaces should be preserved." The intention was not to deny the owner the right to use his property, but "to subject his plans to closer scrutiny. We are aiming to preserve the special character, the integrity and the fine human scale of the projects."[8] This was a proactive initiative that came out of the Department of City Planning, not an administrative response to grassroots activism.

The impetus for this welcome regulatory designation can be traced to the actions of real estate mogul Harry Helmsley, whose Helmsley-Spear Corporation seemed to be specifically honing in on planned communities. The company had recently lost a battle to build on open space in Tudor City in Manhattan. In 1968, Helmsley-Spear acquired Parkchester, the stylish middle-income complex built in the Bronx by the Metropolitan Life Insurance Company between 1938 and 1942. The lead architect was Richard Shreve, architect of the Empire State Building, and Gilmore Clarke was the landscape architect. Four years later, the company purchased Fresh Meadows, the distinctly modernist complex of garden apartments and apartment towers built by New York Life Insurance Company in 1949 (Voorhees, Walker, Foley & Smith, architects). Given the Tudor City episode, residents of Fresh Meadows worried that the generous open space there—barely a fifth of the 150 acres was built upon—might be lost to new construction. There was a precedent. In 1960, New York Life

Fresh Meadows, circa 1950. Like Sunnyside Gardens, Fresh Meadows was designated a Special Planned Community Preservation District in 1974. (Courtesy of the Queens Borough Public Library, Archives, Illustrations Collection.)

received a zoning change to erect a ten-story, 209-unit affordable housing tower. So the tenants association took their concerns to the City Planning Commission.[9]

In retrospect, it is extraordinary that the City Planning Commission recognized the unique character of these places and acted as quickly as it did. The idea for the special district grew out of a committee at the Landmarks Preservation Commission that studied several planned communities, but the commission concluded that those places were not old enough to merit designation as historic districts. The landmarks law required that designated places be at least thirty years old, so in fact only Fresh Meadows, completed in 1949, was too recent to qualify for designation. What the commission implied was that these were architecturally different from row house neighborhoods like Brooklyn Heights and Park Slope. The Landmarks Preservation Commission, it seemed, was not yet ready to appreciate that a modernist planned community was as worthy of designation as brownstones in Brooklyn. Nonetheless, the commissioners recognized that something should be done to preserve such unique places.[10]

When the proposal came to a hearing, the Municipal Art Society and the American Institute of Architects testified in favor. Surprisingly, there were no voices in opposition at the hearing held at Queens Borough Hall, but residents of Parkway Village, a garden apartment complex built in 1947 between Union Turnpike and Grand Central Parkway for employees of the United Nations, took that occasion to lobby for the inclusion of their homes under the new special zoning. Their elected officials testified in support, as did Parkway Village resident Roy Wilkins, president of the NAACP, who said that inclusion was necessary to "preserve the integrity and character of the community."[11] City Planning did not accede to their request, however, and in fact never granted to any other places the protections afforded the original four. In the 1990s, despite overwhelming support among residents and their elected officials, the Landmarks Preservation Commission declined to consider Parkway Village for designation as a historic district.

Reaction to the Planning Commission's action was overwhelmingly positive. One Fresh Meadows resident exclaimed that the proposal "shows the city's awareness, however belated, that unless certain unique neighborhoods are guaranteed protection, developers will scar their faces beyond recognition." The president of the Fresh Meadows tenants group said, "It is a beautiful, open place. We are not prepared to surrender our lovely neighborhood to the forces of urban decay that so inevitably accompany mammoth new construction." Sunnysiders expressed similar feelings. "We don't want any residential construction that is out of character with the community," said one woman. Only Harry Helmsley offered a negative word. "It's unconstitutional," he declared, "but that doesn't seem to mean much anymore."[12]

A *New York Times* editorial praised the new layer of protection: "Increasingly, the city has been recognizing environmental and social values in its zoning legislation; it has, in fact, treated these regulations as a tool to improve New York or safeguard what is good about it. In this case, it has been understood that not only historic districts require the protection available through designation by the Landmarks Preservation Commission; districts with less architectural significance but with exceptional features through planned design are acknowledged to be equally deserving of recognition and conservation. By establishing the desirability of this special community character, the Planning Commission has taken an important step forward. New York's planners are continuing a trend toward the progressive and creative interpretation of zoning in the interests of a more livable city."[13] While embracing the significance of these places in terms of urban planning, the *Times* seemed to accept the inferiority of the architecture as a given. That was clearly not the case. Rather, the city was not yet prepared to accept a modernist aesthetic as historic.

At Sunnyside Gardens, the new rules limited the ability of homeowners to build additions or enclose porches, banned fences in or across the common areas, prohibited the removal of mature trees, and banned new driveways and curb cuts. "We're concerned about fences," said one woman. "One of the treasures of our community are our free and open spaces but some of our neighbors are threatening this with fences." To explain the new rules, City Planning prepared a brochure with clear illustrations showing exactly what was prohibited under the special zoning without a special permit. The most glaring defect in the new zoning was that it was not retroactive and tacitly legalized the fences, driveways, and additions built since the easements lapsed. Further, enforcement proved difficult, as the city had to distinguish between existing fences and new ones.[14]

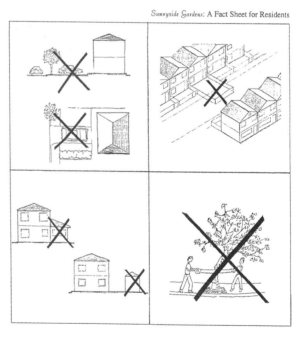

-3-

Alterations Not Permitted Without Special Permit Approval

No demolition, new development, enlargement or alteration of landscaping and topography is permitted within the Sunnyside Gardens district except by special permit of the City Planning Commission. The following are just some of the actions that require a special permit approved by the City Planning Commission.

- The cutting of curbs or paving any portion of existing yards
- The erection of fences or barriers of any kind which serve to partition the central garden areas
- Alterations to houses and yards, such as the construction of rear yard decks and the removal or addition of porches
- The alteration of landscape, such as the removal of trees or the creation of new paths

If you do one of the above without a special permit, you risk a fine from a City agency and will be destroying the character of Sunnyside Gardens.

Sunnyside Gardens: A Fact Sheet for Residents

Sunnyside Gardens: A Fact Sheet for Residents, 1975. The pamphlet explained to residents what was prohibited under the new Special Planned Community Preservation District zoning. To the dismay of many Sunnysiders, the City Planning Commission removed these protections from Sunnyside Gardens when the zoning was changed after designation as a historic district, leaving the Landmarks Preservation Commission the sole arbiter of what is permissible in the district. (Department of City Planning.)

The city had no problem enforcing the rule against driveways and curb cuts. In 1988, the Department of Buildings mistakenly allowed a driveway, but quickly revoked the permit when they realized that the address was within the special district. The owner went ahead anyway. He was fined $250, and then he proceeded to spend thousands of dollars in legal fees fighting for his driveway. Five years after the issuance of the faulty permit, Judge Bernard Greenbaum ordered the owner to remove the offending curb cut. "Every one of us is governed by the zoning law," said the judge, "and we can't change it. It's a criminal offense." In 1993, a man bought a home on Forty-Third Street and proceeded to pave over his front yard to park his two cars there. Again the city ordered the parking pad removed. Penny Lee of the Queens office of the Department of City Planning said, "The whole notion of a special district designation is that all the houses were developed under one comprehensive plan. Sunnyside Gardens was intended not to have driveways."[15] In the first instance, the driveway was indeed removed; the second illegal parking pad inexplicably remains.

The Sunnyside Gardens Conservancy

By the time the easements lapsed in the mid-1960s, that early cooperative moment when neighbors would together enforce design standards was barely a memory. Was it even possible to regenerate the original intent of the designers and the social goals expressed in their designs? And if so, how? Writing in *City Limits*, a journal offering a left-liberal perspective on urban affairs, especially housing issues, editor Tom Robbins recognized that "handing down social ideals from generation to generation is hard enough within families, let alone communities. They need to be reborn outside the formality of deeds and restrictive covenants."[16]

Under the leadership of attorney Franklin Havelick, an advisor to Mayor Ed Koch, and local realtor Dorothy Morehead, a small core of residents formed the Sunnyside Gardens Conservancy in 1981 in an effort to re-ignite that original spirit. They recognized that their neighborhood was distinguished by both its history and its design, and they believed that those attributes were worth preserving. This was a challenge, said Havelick, because "the structures in the Gardens which had people talking to each other had disappeared." In particular, the court associations had largely ceased to function.[17] When the covenants expired, there was neither legal nor moral authority to protect the courts, only a tradition upheld by older residents.

To reinforce the distinctive character of Sunnyside Gardens, the Conservancy embarked on a few high-visibility projects. They successfully lobbied the city to restore the original street names, such as Bliss Street, Packard Street, and Middleburgh Avenue, and soon new signs included both the old name and the number. Street trees, especially the majestic London planes arching over the streets, received overdue attention. Homeowners were offered matching grants to repoint the brick facades.[18]

In 1986, the organization, now ambitiously renamed the Sunnyside Foundation for Community Planning and Preservation to reflect a broader mission, moved into its own storefront on Skillman Avenue and grew to four paid staff. They lobbied the Parks Department to plant new trees along Skillman Avenue and convinced the Public Development Corporation to finance the rehabilitation of that short commercial strip. Landscape architect Signe Nielsen redesigned the streetscape, with new brick paving, benches, historic lampposts, and even playful round kiosks for public notices.[19] What made these successes all the more significant was that the city was only slowly recovering from its near bankruptcy in the mid-1970s, and there was precious little funding for such public realm enhancing frills as the Sunnyside Foundation was advocating.

In an effort to further preservation goals, the Sunnyside Foundation, with the assistance of the Trust for Public Land, initiated a campaign to obtain preservation easements from residents. A publication by the Trust for Public Land defined such easements as "a legal agreement a property owner makes to restrict the type and amount of development that may take place on his or her property. Each easement's restrictions are tailored to the particular property and to the interests of the individual owner."[20] For granting the Sunnyside Foundation the preservation easement, the owner would receive a tax benefit in return. The foundation explained that the purpose of a conservation easement "is to support the original concept of our historic and socially significant neighborhood, and to protect it from future risk." In effect, they were attempting to recreate the regulatory regime that existed under the original covenants "to meet the needs of the community in protecting common gardens, community walkways, trees and landscape; to create realistic standards for these protected areas which are both flexible and enforceable; to provide an incentive for individual homeowners to adopt the easement and to contribute to the upkeep of the protected areas voluntarily." These were to be perpetual easements, attached to property records so that it would appear in the title insurance report. Homeowners who accepted these new easements were also obligated to make an annual contribution toward the maintenance of the common areas; in return, they received a tax deduction.[21] Only a handful of homeowners signed up, however, and the easements seem to have been forgotten with the disintegration of the Sunnyside Foundation in the late 1990s. New homeowners often have no idea that their property is covered by such restrictions.

The organization achieved a major success in listing Sunnyside Gardens on the National Register of Historic Places. In the application submitted in 1983, executive director Nina Rappaport wrote that the place "is significant to American History and architectural history because of its pioneering garden city–type community housing plan, its low-cost handsome brick houses, and unique social history. Recognition of its merit as one of the finest, most livable garden communities—not only in New York but in the entire world—is long overdue." The National Register listing was bestowed on September 4, 1984.[22] Radburn had secured that honor almost a decade before. In practice, however, this federal designation is only honorific. It provides no real protection to the architecture, the plan, or the landscaping.

The logical next step should have been designation as a historic district by the Landmarks Preservation Commission. But the pro-preservation Sunnyside Foundation faced significant opposition within the community from residents who felt that designation by the city would interfere with their property rights. According to Havelick, "The community became bitterly divided on the merits of conservation." Also, given the political climate in Queens, such an effort would not have been a sure thing. Every designation had to be affirmed by the Board of Estimate, and Queens Borough President Donald Manes was notoriously unsympathetic to preservation. Following his lead, the Board of Estimate had overturned six designations in Queens since 1974, and the Landmarks Preservation Commission was understandably reluctant to designate sites in the borough.[23]

The Sunnyside Foundation's success brought out new critics, but, oddly enough, the most vocal were not property rights advocates, as might have been expected, but residents who identified with Sunnyside's radical tradition. One unnamed community activist exclaimed flatly, "They're out to gentrify the neighborhood." That critique saw preservation as a way to boost property values (at the time, one-family houses were selling for about $140,000, and two-family houses for $190,000). In defense, Havelick said that the foundation was "mindful of the problem of gentrification. This is a community that wants and needs its older residents." At the same time, he reiterated the goal of neighborhood restoration: restoration of the original plan and restoration of the sense of community. "There are a lot of competing visions of what this community could become. But we're not highbrow preservationists. I don't care if it takes ten years or twenty years for the fences to come down. What's more important is that we establish a sense of community."[24]

Here was a conflict between two competing progressive values. One expressed the fear that gentrification would drive up rents and the price of homes, a situation already evident in parts of Manhattan and Brooklyn as the city's real estate market recovered after the fiscal crisis of the mid-1970s. The other built a grassroots organization of residents fighting to protect their quality of life. Normally, *City Limits* would have been openly sympathetic to the anti-gentrification voices, but in this case, editor Tom Robbins clearly sympathized with the foundation, in part, no doubt, because of Sunnyside's heritage as an embodiment of communitarian values. The "semi-utopian community," he explained, was "trying to rebuild the system of open space, buildings and people" which made up the "egalitarian plan" conceived to "forge a true democratic community."[25]

Preserving Radburn

Compared with Sunnyside's contentious path to preservation, Radburn had a much smoother history. Design controls were in place at the City Housing Corporation's second project from the beginning. Even before the first residents arrived, the company established the Radburn Association as a private, nonprofit corporation "to assure the permanence of the open spaces, to assure controls of the community by the residents." As at Sunnyside, Radburn had privately owned house lots. But where in Sunnyside ownership extended to the common areas, with each property owner owning a portion of the courts and walkways, the Radburn Association held the common parkland in trust for the community in order to protect it from "private speculation and development."[26]

On the whole, the self-governing Radburn Association has proven an adequate vehicle for the maintenance of Radburn's historic features. Its ownership of the parks and interior walkways continues, and the association still enforces the protective covenants. The architectural and open space restrictions in place since its founding have prevented such egregious changes as high fences and inappropriate additions, even though some design elements have been inevitably lost.[27]

In addition to preserving the common areas and parkland, the association was also charged with implementing and enforcing the regulations outlined in the Declaration of Restrictions, a document that was prepared even before construction began and, by and large, is still in force. Its purpose was to maintain Radburn's architectural integrity and "protect atmosphere and appearance." To enforce that goal, "architectural, property line, open space, and landscaping controls were conveyed as part of the property deeds."[28] That, the founders believed, would impede "thoughtless or inconsiderate purchasers" who would destroy "the harmony or spoil the plan by building structures inappropriate in design or location." At the time of purchase, every homeowner had to acknowledge receipt of "the Green Book," which contained the Declaration of Restrictions and a copy of the association's bylaws. An additional fee based on the assessed value of the property funded the association. The original purpose was the protection of the City Housing Corporation's investment, but the structure remained in place even after the CHC went bankrupt during the Great Depression.[29]

The Declaration of Restrictions was intended "for the more efficient protection of the community and control thereof by the inhabitants." CHC Counsel Charles Ascher crafted the document after consulting with several experts, including Luther Gulick of the National Municipal League and Charles A. Perry of the Russell Sage Foundation, and examining the restrictions governing Forest Hills Gardens and Roland Park in Baltimore. He believed that the emphasis ought not be on "which restrictions can be put in print, but which restrictions *work*, which are accepted by the community without friction, are sustained by public opinion and are enforceable without resort to the courts." Radburn was thus the "most complex civic unit to which government-by-contract has been applied; and its scheme of administration seems as notable an experiment as its town plan."[30]

The Radburn Association had complete authority over all work. The rules were clear: "No building, fence, hedge, wall, sign, billboard, awning, pole, radio antennae or other structure of any kind, whether similar to the foregoing or not, shall be commenced, erected, or maintained upon The Property or any part thereof, nor shall any addition thereto, or change or alteration therein be made, unless the design thereof in such form as The Radburn Association may demand, shall have been submitted to The Radburn Association, and the nature, kind, shape, height, materials, floor plans, elevations, color scheme, location of such structure upon the building site, grading plans of the building site, and plans for the disposal of sewage and wastes, if any, shall have been approved in writing by The Radburn Association." Most crucially for the garden suburb's future integrity, the association was empowered to withhold approval for alterations on strictly aesthetic grounds.[31]

At Sunnyside Gardens the covenants expired after forty years, leading to unfortunate encroachments upon the common areas to the detriment of the original plan. At Radburn, the restrictions were to remain in effect until 1960. But the CHC had the foresight to have the covenants automatically renewed for another twenty years, and for every twenty years thereafter, with the proviso that they could be altered or overturned entirely only after the filing of a written agreement no less than five years prior to the expiration.[32] Under that arrangement, the sustainability of the Radburn plan was virtually assured in perpetuity.

Based on the earlier experience at Sunnyside, with its several court associations enforcing the rules, each according to its own judgment, the CHC determined that a single central organization was preferable.[33] Charles Ascher believed that "the kind of issues arising among people living together in a community were not resolved by adversary processes. An administrative framework was needed." Enforcement required a certain degree of flexibility. The CHC did not want tall fences obstructing views of the common areas, but recognized that a homeowner might want to protect his lawn and garden. They accordingly ruled that two and a half feet would be the maximum height, and they convinced a local hardware store to carry that stock size. Ascher recalled that the Radburn Association had "control of exteriors of houses, including the color of paint. So we persuaded the local hardware store to stock our approved colors at a reduced price to meet the Spring Saturday afternoon impulse to repaint the porch with what the association deemed discordant colors."[34]

In the first twenty years, only six unauthorized changes came before the trustees. The Radburn Association had the right to pursue legal action against violators of the restrictions, but only once in the community's first two decades was that necessary. In 1938, a homeowner applied to enclose and enlarge his porch. Although the Borough of Fair Lawn found the proposed work to be in compliance with its zoning code, the Radburn Association's Architectural Committee denied the application. The man proceeded with the work regardless. Lengthy legal action ensued, but in the end the transgressing individual was permitted to keep his illegal addition, while acknowledging the association's right to control such matters. Historian Daniel Schaffer concludes that "personal interaction—in this case more than legal precedent—was the source of the community's success."[35]

For Ascher, this episode confirmed that "the sanctions of private covenants are slow, expensive, and uncertain." Nevertheless, "the constant vigilance of the association in support of the desires of most of the residents has served to check the thoughtless or selfish, more by explanation, mediation, and adjustment of differences than by police action." He drew a clear lesson on the attempts at aesthetic regulation in Sunnyside Gardens and Radburn. "The art of administration," Ascher believed, "is the free rendering of the black and white of legal documents in the pastel shades of human conduct and desire." To maintain its authority, the homeowners association had to carefully pick its battles. Ascher learned this from James C. Nichols, developer of Country Club District in Kansas City, who told him, "We've trained ourselves to look up the other side of the street when we pass buildings which clearly violate the controls. But there's just nothing we can pick a fight about."[36] This measured approach stands in sharp contrast to the aggressive stance of the Hampstead Garden Suburb Trust and the Forest Hills Gardens Corporation, both of which operate on the principle that compromise with transgressors will only encourage others to follow suit, and that legal precedent is precisely what maintains their authority.

In 1975, Radburn was listed on the National Register of Historic Places, and in 2005 the U.S. Department of the Interior designated Radburn a National Historic Landmark. The district's "boundary is defined by the roads designed and laid out by the City Housing Corporation," even though that encompassed many non-contributing buildings constructed after the period of significance.[37] Both designations are largely honorific and lack any enforcement powers. Even so, residents believed this would bolster their efforts to maintain its historic character. On the occasion of the public celebration of the National Register listing, seventy-six-year-old Fred McMullen, a Radburn resident since 1930 and the community historian, said that the new designation would give them every right to enforce the long-standing restrictions. "We've had some 'free-thinkers' in the past few years who thought they could change the outside of their homes," he said. "We hesitated before bringing them to court. This gives us more wallop."[38]

The contrasting histories of Sunnyside Gardens and Radburn highlight the need to enforce strong and clearly defined design controls in a garden suburb from the very beginning. Sunnyside demonstrates just how fragile a planned community is, while Radburn provides an example of the benefits of consistent regulation. There, design standards have remained essentially unchanged since 1929 and have been enforced by the residents themselves through the Radburn Association.

When the original covenants expired after forty years, Sunnysiders lost almost all control over the regulation of their community. Under the Special Planned Community Preservation District designation approved in 1974, it was the city which would determine what was allowed and what was prohibited. The Sunnyside Foundation attempted to restore the original community spirit, but their success depended upon the voluntary cooperation of residents. The next step was to achieve designation as a historic district, with a more intense regulatory regime enforced by the Landmarks Preservation Commission, not by the residents themselves.

10

###

The Fight for the Historic District

WHAT NEITHER THE SPECIAL DISTRICT designation nor the National Register listing protected, of course, was the architecture, leaving facades vulnerable to the gradual erosion of features like multipaned wood windows, doors, and slate roofing. In 2003, a woman who had lived in Sunnyside for fifty-four years expressed her frustration with the situation and her hope. "Some people buy homes and have no idea it's an historical area," she said. "If it were landmarked, it will be noted on the deed when you buy the home. If they're not interested, maybe they wouldn't purchase their home and if they are interested, then they will follow the rules."[1]

The Preservation Alliance

By 2000, the Sunnyside Foundation was no longer viable. The organization had purchased an original Sunnyside house on Forty-Seventh Street in 1989 for $225,000, intending to use it as offices and an exhibit space. But they could not maintain that momentum. Staff were let go, advocacy efforts ceased, and eventually the house became just another rental property. Into that void stepped a new group. Concerned that their neighborhood's defining features might be compromised or lost, Herb and Liz Reynolds brought residents together in 2003 and formed the Sunnyside Gardens Preservation Alliance. Their avowed purpose was to gain designation as a historic district. One of their first steps was to contact the Historic Districts

Council, a citywide advocacy organization that had successfully guided several communities through the designation process.[2]

Almost immediately a clique arose in opposition, with media-savvy academics taking the lead: Susan Turner-Meiklejohn, a Sunnyside homeowner and a professor of urban planning at Hunter College; Warren Lehrer, an art professor at Purchase College; and his wife, author/performer Judith Sloan. They argued that only the plan of the community was significant and that the architecture was not distinguished in any way. Brick houses were common throughout Queens, after all. They often referenced the *AIA Guide to New York City*, which called Sunnyside "an urban delight, where the architecture is unimportant—even insipid."[3] They argued that the primary motivation of the founders of Sunnyside Gardens was not architectural, but social, seeking to create a community that would promote a mixing of classes, and thus designation "really flies in the face of what they were trying to do." Furthermore, they suggested that landmarking would only intensify the process of gentrification, driving up property values and making it more expensive to make repairs or renovate. Representing opponents, attorney and Sunnyside homeowner Ira Greenberg said, "landmarking would be inappropriate for us because it focuses so much on buildings and architecture, but what makes Sunnyside Gardens so great is the walkways and outdoor spaces, not the architecture." Furthermore, he claimed that designation would drive up the cost of repairing the slate roof of his house. Most damning of all, and clearly intended to foment ethnic animosities, opponents proclaimed that the drive for creating the historic district was motivated by anti-immigrant bias.[4]

According to Turner-Meiklejohn, "The zoning district has worked to protect the most significant element of the neighborhood, the open space." She was correct. The Special Planned Community Preservation District designation imposed in 1974 worked very well as far as it went. The rules were strictly applied and the process for obtaining an exemption—for a curb cut, an addition, or fencing—was onerous. But perhaps that was the point, to protect the significant aspects of the place rather than make the path easy for those who would compromise the neighborhood's coherence for their own advantage. During the more than thirty years the rules were in effect, only one applicant went through the process to enclose his porch in brick (a few residents had made such changes illegally, without obtaining the necessary permits, but then they did not obtain permits from the Department of Buildings either).

The limitations of the special zoning can readily be seen in Fresh Meadows. Built by the New York Life Insurance Company between 1946 and 1949 on a former golf course (site of the PGA tournament in 1930 and the U.S. Open in 1932), the complex consisted of garden apartments and 2 thirteen-story apartment buildings. The plan remains intact because of the special district regulations. In the 1990s, the management most unhappily mangled the clean modernist architecture by affixing vinyl fluted columns supporting vinyl pediments. The changes were jarringly inappropriate. Still, the remodeling was entirely acceptable under the rules of the special zoning, which protected the plan and open space, but not the architecture.

Tom Angotti, Turner-Meiklejohn's colleague in the Urban Planning Department at Hunter College, lent support to the anti-landmarking side in the online publication *Gotham Gazette*.[5] Angotti opposed preservation in general, viewing it as an issue thrust upon poor neighborhoods whose residents have *real* concerns. He asserted that historic preservation leads to gentrification (never mind that the process is usually the reverse), decreases affordability, and assaults established working-class or minority communities. "Historic preservation has mostly been a tool for the preservation of property values in elite neighborhoods," he contends quite erroneously. "Elite conceptions of historic value are entirely bound up with property values and elite interpretations of history." He does acknowledge that a handful of the city's historic districts protect working-class neighborhoods, but those are exceptions and "not a common concern of preservationists."[6]

That statement is an irresponsible misreading of the history of preservation in New York City, not the least by labeling preservationists as elitists. No community is immune to feeling a deep sense of loss when a historic structure is lost. Far more than a narrow economic interest, preservationists are motivated by a love of their historic city. What else explains the fact that preservationists support designations in places where they do not own property? Furthermore, it is profoundly condescending to lower-income and minority residents to dismiss their desire to demonstrate pride in their historic architecture and to protect their neighborhoods from out-of-scale development.

Concerning Sunnyside, Angotti maintained that historic district designation, while preserving the architecture, "would make the housing there unaffordable to the moderate-income working class population that is at the core of the garden city concept." In the same vein, Turner-Meiklejohn argued that "the key goals of the Garden City were not architectural but social."[7] How the social goals were to be sustained eighty years after first articulated and the architectural context jettisoned she left unexplained.

Fresh Meadows, circa 1950, with the original modernist entries and fenestration. Garden apartments in 2020 with redesigned front entries permitted under the Special Planned Community Preservation District zoning; also, the original casement windows have been replaced. (Top: Courtesy of the Queens Borough Public Library, Archives, Illustrations Collection; Bottom: author's photograph.)

The City Housing Corporation had set out to build for families of moderate means, but that dream came to an end during the Great Depression. Neighbors banded together to resist foreclosures and evictions, but they ultimately succumbed to economic realities. That is a history worth commemorating, and the best way to commemorate it would be to protect the historic character of the buildings, not by encouraging the gradual decline in the planned community's coherent and uniform design. If nothing else, designation would honor that first generation of residents by preserving the homes they fought to keep.

Usually, opponents of landmarking can be categorized either as real estate interests seeking to maximize development potential without what they consider unnecessary and intrusive regulation by the city, or staunch advocates of private property rights who see preservation as tantamount to a taking. No one can tell me what I can or can't do to my property, they cry. As one Sunnyside resident put it, "Enough rules already. This is my home. Why does somebody have to tell me what kind of window or what color?"[8]

The most odious aspect of the campaign by opponents was the attempt to tar proponents as anti-immigrant, if not racist. Turner-Meiklejohn contended that what was really driving preservationists was their discomfort with recent demographic changes. Half the residents were foreign-born, she claimed, and non-Hispanic whites made up only about 40 percent of the residents. She concluded from those numbers that "the social base for new restrictions is in that minority of 'old timers'"[9] implying that those "old timers" ought not to have a say in the future of their neighborhood. During a discussion on the *Brian Lehrer Show* on WNYC, Turner-Meiklejohn repeatedly harped on the anti-immigrant theme, suggesting that the presence of new immigrants led to the "tremendous unease . . . that gave rise to this effort to make this community more expensive and more exclusive."[10] Such assertions may be perfectly apt in an academic text where the prevailing wisdom is that gentrification is a plot to preserve racial and cultural hegemony, but evidence backing such an assertion was lacking in this case.[11]

The Sunnyside Gardens Preservation Alliance gained the support of at least three-quarters of the residents, a sentiment that was especially pronounced among longtime residents and senior citizens. They had lived in their homes for decades and understood and appreciated the value of clear regulations applied to all and accepted by all. In more than one public meeting indignant individuals stood up and stated that they were immigrants and supported the historic district.

Angotti saw a much larger problem. "The argument in Sunnyside," he wrote, "reflects a debate taking place throughout Queens, where some residents blame immigrants for changes in the urban landscape. Justified concerns about out-of-context building conversions often get mixed with disdain for new foreign-born residents. Crackdowns on building violations and demands for downzoning sometimes target the new populations instead of trying to accommodate them and go after the violators."[12] From this perspective, property owners are to be condemned as anti-immigrant bigots for attempting to protect their investment—in quality of life no less than economic—by seeking enforcement of building codes and zoning rules. Complaints, it would seem, should be addressed by considering who is making the complaint, and who is being complained about. Following his logic, an illegal cellar apartment or a front yard paved over for parking would be acceptable in some cases but not in others.

Proponents and opponents staged their own public meetings. At one anti-landmarking event, organizers used their platform to condemn neighbors for turning in neighbors for building code violations (there had been a recent spate of violations issued for illegal decks, and they blamed landmarking proponents, though violations hit homeowners on both sides of the issue). An opposition fact sheet stated that despite assurances by the Landmarks Preservation Commission (LPC), not all preexisting alterations would be retroactively legalized, or "grandfathered in." Of course, no illegal work, work done without first obtaining the proper permits from the Department of Buildings, could ever be grandfathered. Playing up this fear, they wrote, "Once the floodgate of neighbors reporting on neighbors really becomes unleashed in this neighborhood, everything done in the present, past, and future can and will be subject to violations."[13] "Stop snitching," is how Warren Lehrer summed it up (that loaded phrase came out of inner city neighborhoods, a warning not to call the police on drug dealers or street thugs, usually uttered by those same elements; a rap video out of Baltimore in 2004 popularized the phrase and the concept behind it). That existing laws and codes should be enforced is a legal matter; whether they are best for the city is a political question.

Another aspect of the controversy concerned the question of diversity. Rather than preserve the best from the past, why not champion the changes brought by generations of newcomers? "While it is a good idea to have strict but sensible regulations that promote good design and aesthetically pleasing neighborhoods," wrote Angotti, "there is a fascination and a value in the immense variety of ways that people alter and decorate

During the campaign to gain historic district designation, landmarking proponents prepared these Photoshopped images to show what was allowable under the Special Zoning and why protection under New York City's Landmarks Preservation Commission was necessary. (Laura Heim Architect.)

their homes. Some of these efforts are beautiful, others are mediocre, and still others are incredibly ugly. The shape, colors, and textures go from glorious to garish. But that is what makes a walk down a New York street exciting."[14] Neighborhoods across the city have sought the protection of the Landmarks Preservation Commission precisely because they do not wish to be subjected to such chaotic excitement. The goal of preservation-minded residents in Sunnyside Gardens was not social conformity, but the protection of the historic plan and the historic architecture.

In response to suggestions that the architecture was insignificant, architect Laura Heim prepared a set of photo montages showing just what could happen under existing regulation. They depicted Sunnyside's brick row houses faced in stucco and vinyl siding, splashed with garish paint colors, and featuring oversized Palladian windows. Unveiled at a public meeting attended by representatives of the Landmarks Preservation Commission, the images elicited gasps. That a single homeowner could disrupt the harmony of the whole for an expression of individual taste was an uncomfortable prospect. Some who had been undecided up to that point came over to the preservationist camp.

More than any other recent preservation battle, the struggle to designate Sunnyside Gardens attracted a surprising amount of press. Indeed, there was an almost gleeful tone to the coverage of a question pitting neighbor against neighbor in a seemingly privileged enclave. As one reporter put it, "Friendliness has melted into anger." Elisabeth de Bourbon of the LPC remarked, "I don't know what accounts for the level of disagreement, and the intensity of the disagreement." The *New York Times* described the tone as "sour." Susan Turner-Meiklejohn, seemingly oblivious to her own contribution to the atmosphere, remarked, "There's noticeable anger. It's particularly inappropriate when the historic intent of the community was to dispel hostility between neighbors. I mean, what would Lewis Mumford think?" A pro-preservation stalwart, Irma Rodriguez, said, "It's become personally offensive. Because I'm a supporter of landmarking, I've been characterized as being anti-immigrant or elitist," adding, "opponents have become vocal and nasty."[15]

Designation

Preservationists may hope that designations are decided on the merits, but the decision rests ultimately in the political arena, where not a few have been mauled by lions. No matter the architectural, cultural, or historical attributes of a site, the Landmarks Preservation Commission is unlikely to designate without the approval of the local city council member. In Sunnyside, opponents lobbied elected officials vigorously, and they gained support from a state senator—who had never before made any comments on any preservation issue—and the two local Democratic committee members. Advocates counted two members of the New York State Assembly and the borough president, the Queens Civic Congress, and the Queens and New York chapters of the American Institute of Architects.

On the fence sat term-limited councilman Eric Gioia. His unwillingness to take a public position only encouraged opponents and contributed greatly to the sour discourse. Shortly after the commission calendared Sunnyside Gardens for a public hearing, he told a reporter, "It is imperative that we protect the character of the neighborhood. Opponents have raised valid concerns which I take seriously and am now raising with the commission. I have spent the past few months listening to friends and neighbors. I am intent on ensuring all voices are answered and a consensus built."[16] The low point came at the Landmarks Preservation Commission hearing. The councilman did not attend personally, but before dozens of his constituents, his representative read a statement in which he encouraged all to participate in the process and assured everyone that he was considering all sides of the question. A profile in courage it wasn't. The public hearing is the moment of truth, but Gioia ducked. That a lone council member lacking courage and commitment could thwart such a popular movement is dreadful to contemplate, but that was the situation. Gioia, who presented himself as a reformer, never did explain why he finally came around to support designation.

The Landmarks Preservation Commission does not impose a historic district designation on an unwilling community. The commission responds to requests from the public, and the process leading up to the public hearing generally takes years. In the case of Sunnyside, the commission staff held five information sessions at the local community board between September 2002 and February 2007. The commission also sent out notices to property owners three times in the four months before they voted to calendar the proposed district for a public hearing. During that entire time, commission staff surveyed the condition of the buildings and compiled historical research for the designation report.[17]

In the end, of course, after all the wrangling at public meetings, all the fire-fueling press, and all the testimony, the Landmarks Preservation Commission designated Sunnyside Gardens. Explaining his vote to designate, Commissioner Stephen Byrnes stated, "There may be certain naysayers who desire no limitations on altering their property, but this goes way beyond that. The ideals of light and air for all at a reasonable profit, matched with quality design and landscaping are a national treasure and represent what is great about America."[18]

Still, the opponents warned that the cost to homeowners would rise. Ira Greenberg, attorney for the Sunnyside Gardens Preservation group, said, "We don't know what landmarking will do, but to follow the rules you have to keep submitting every little thing about your house and that is more than a burden." Countering that line, Catherine O'Flaherty exclaimed, "The only thing that's going to change is that people won't be able to break the rules."[19]

After much "soul-searching," Eric Gioia supported the designation when it came up for a vote in the city council. Even then, he declined to acknowledge his constituents who had worked so hard for that day and watched from the gallery. The last word belongs to LPC Chair Robert Tierney. After the LPC had voted to calendar Sunnyside Gardens and the Phipps Garden Apartments in March 2007, he remarked to a reporter, "It's a great area. Fifty years off, if that's allowed to go away, we should be very embarrassed."[20]

Restoration and Transformation

The boundaries of the Sunnyside Gardens Historic District included all the original buildings constructed by the City Housing Corporation, with the exception of a commercial building at Forty-Seventh Street and Queens Boulevard and the parking garage designed by Clarence Stein at the edge of the district on Forty-Eighth Street. There were two other anomalies. Although the LPC declined to include the commercial buildings facing the district across Skillman Avenue, they did include a row of mid-1930s stores with apartments above, across from Phipps. In 1931, unable to raise additional capital to build, and with a growing number of Sunnysiders falling behind in their mortgage payments, the City Housing Corporation had sold those lots to a commercial developer.[21] The LPC also included the vacant lot adjacent to those stores that for fifty years had been a children's playground for families living in Phipps; it had been fenced off since the 1980s. By including that lot, the LPC was signaling that it would guide any new construction on the site to assure that it would be appropriate, that is, in conformity with the defining characteristics of the historic district.

Have the fears of the opponents of the historic district proven justified? Property values have indeed risen, but to what extent the rise was because of the new protections under the landmarks law as opposed to the general rise in housing costs citywide is an open question. In 2006, the year prior to designation, a one-family house sold for $460,000; in 2013, six years after designation, a similar 952-square-foot home sold for $810,000. By 2017, the price broke the million-dollar barrier, and within a year rose by another quarter-million dollars.[22]

Ironically, designation also introduced new uncertainties. The Special Planned Community District designation had served Sunnyside well for over thirty years, and landmarking advocates had blithely assumed that when Sunnyside Gardens was made a historic district those regulations would remain in place, or at least that the Landmarks Preservation Commission would incorporate those rules into their own guidelines. In that, they were mistaken.

The Department of City Planning, which enforced the special district rules, had no interest in maintaining them after landmarking, and the Landmarks Preservation Commission was committed to defining and applying its own standards. The two agencies explained that eliminating the special zoning would streamline the permit process for residents, because they would only have to go to one agency rather than two. Incorporating those rules into new LPC guidelines was never considered, apparently.

Two years after designation, City Planning rescinded the special district status and also changed the zoning in such a way as to leave each house in the district with excess volume in the building envelope. John Young, director of the Queens Office of City Planning, explained that they did not want to "shrink-wrap" the buildings. Such an approach displayed a profound misunderstanding of Sunnyside Gardens, for throughout its history regulations had been in place to do just that. At the city council hearing about the proposed zoning changes, the Historic Districts Council testified in opposition: "By removing the protections of the PC District, the door is now wide open for applications for driveways, fences, sheds, carports, parking pads while mature trees will have no protections whatsoever. Equally important, almost all the buildings in the district are grievously under-built with regard to their lots. . . . Yes, the Landmarks Preservation Commission will still regulate these buildings on the basis of appropriateness—but through this zoning change, the bar for what could be appropriate is fatally lowered. In a perfect world, the LPC would somehow enforce all the rules of the PC District, thereby making enforcement more efficient, while not sacrificing any of the protections the neighborhood has previously enjoyed."[23] The zoning change was easily approved; the community's concerns were dismissed.

With the revocation of the Special Planned Community Preservation District protections, the designation report prepared by the Landmarks Preservation Commission became the guiding regulatory document. These reports explain why a district merited protection and documented in great detail the features to be protected and the condition of each property at the time of designation.[24] One way to assure that a clear and common set of standards would be applied is through the creation of a master plan. The Jackson Heights Historic District has a master plan for storefronts. The master plan for Douglaston covers additions and alterations, the form and footprint of new construction, materials, window replacements, fencing, and HVAC units.[25] Apartment buildings along Park Avenue have master plans for window replacement and the insertion of air conditioners. Such a master plan was not prepared for Sunnyside, but two years after designation, the LPC issued "Doing Work in Sunnyside Gardens: A Homeowners Guide to the Landmarks Preservation Commission Rules." The intent was to explain the "existing rules" and how they were "intended to allow changes to buildings while preserving the special architectural character for which the district was designated."[26]

The document did note several features unique to the district and explained how regulation here would differ from other row house historic districts. There the commission would allow "more extensive work" on rear facades, including rear-yard additions and rooftop additions. "This presumption will not apply in Sunnyside Gardens," the guide states. "Because the layout of the rear yards, with common gardens and walkways is so integral to the design . . . , and because the massing and character of the rear of the buildings affects the design and experience of site plan, the existing rules . . . *shall not apply*." Even so, homeowners wishing such additions were welcome to bring their application before a public hearing of the commission.[27]

Windows on primary facades were to have a six-over-six configuration, but on facades in the rear the commission would permit the installation of other styles. The commission simply inserted its own rule, one that was completely at odds with the original design. The guidelines permit the use of materials at variance with historic precedent for rear porches so long as they are "*not visible from a public thoroughfare*."[28] This rule, while perhaps motivated by a desire to ease the process for homeowners, contradicts the design intention of Stein and Wright. At Madison Court, all of the wood porches facing the court are identical. Permitting the use of other than traditional materials and form would compromise the court's integrity.

Since designation, Sunnyside Gardens has indeed seen improvement, but overall the record has been mixed. Under their regulatory guidance of the Landmarks Preservation Commission, many homeowners have indeed restored historic features that had been lost or altered over the decades. But other homeowners have done work without any LPC permits, resulting in inappropriate and discordant changes. In several instances, the commission has approved such work after the fact. As at Hampstead Garden Suburb, eternal vigilance is the price of protection.

In 1940, and again in 1980, the city of New York photographed every building in the five boroughs for purposes of taxation. Available through the Municipal Archives,[29] those images offer, literally, a snapshot in time, and are a godsend for homeowners and their architects engaged in a restoration project. That is especially the case in Sunnyside Gardens, because the 1940 photographs show how the community appeared while the covenants were still in place and thus what modifications had been allowed. It is a relatively straightforward matter to use the photograph as a guide in restoration of a facade, matching as closely as possible the windows, doors, lighting, and hardware. The 1980 photographs reveal changes that had been made in the period between the expiration of the covenants and the imposition of the special district zoning.

Even with such documentation available, the LPC not infrequently disappoints preservation-minded residents by approving applications for work that denies the precedent of decades of controls. Sunnyside Gardens was the first planned community protected by the LPC, and the agency has wrestled with exactly how to regulate it, particularly the rear facades facing the courtyards. Historic districts in New York commonly contain buildings constructed at different times and in varied styles. This is not the case in Sunnyside Gardens, which was built to a uniform plan within a five-year span. The district has a simple palate of materials and colors, but the prevailing mantra at the commission is that "anyone can apply for anything." In a sense that is true, but this planned community has a degree of uniformity that had to be underscored, not negotiated. As the commission considers applications on a case-by-case basis, some applicants have been permitted changes that would have been prohibited under the original covenants or the special district zoning.

The counsel at the Landmarks Preservation Commission has described their function as "we regulate work." If a homeowner undertakes no changes, there will be no interaction with the agency. But for almost all work, an owner must obtain a permit. Most applications are handled at staff level, but if a major alteration is proposed, or if an owner has been issued a violation and seeks redress, the matter goes to a public hearing.

A two-family house in Colonial Court at the time of designation and after conversion into a single-family residence after designation, 2010. (Laura Heim Architect.)

The first project brought before the commission after designation presented a situation where the tax photo was irrelevant. The owner of a one-family house in Hamilton Court needed to replace an unsightly and deteriorating dormer facing the interior courtyard. This addition would have been allowed under neither the original covenants nor under the special district zoning, so the first issue was to determine when it was built and whether it had been done legally. Once its legality was confirmed, the question was how to configure its replacement. Architect Laura Heim convinced the owner to shrink the volume and pull it back from the roofline. The result utilized traditional materials to create a clearly contemporary feature. The fenestration in the new volume clearly expresses that the dormer was not original but of more recent vintage.[30]

In the earliest courts, the homes had open porches, but the residents almost immediately began to enclose them. Today very few retain that original open condition. Stein and Wright clearly intended that the porches, whether facing the street or the interior courtyard, present a uniform appearance. The enclosed porch provides a charming, light filled connection to the street, a dramatic spatial sequence from the public realm to the private home. Originally open above and below, rear porches on the two-family homes provided both homeowners and upstairs tenants a connection to the landscaped court. After the expiration of the covenants in the 1960s, many were remodeled using discordant materials and awkward fenestration. Lower porches were enclosed to create an additional room, and in some cases even the upper space has been enclosed, thus compromising the intent of the planners. Since designation several front porches have been restored closer to the original design.[31]

Originally, many of the three-family houses featured an open wrought iron porch, with a terrace above for the tenant. Today, more of these are enclosed than open, often in a disharmonious or careless style. Enclosing an open porch involves zoning issues, as the interior volume is being increased. During the designation process, the Landmarks Preservation Commission agreed that any proposals for additions would receive special scrutiny, meaning the application could not be approved at staff level but would have to come before a public hearing.

What was deemed adequate for a family in 1925 is woefully inadequate by twenty-first-century standards. The original kitchens were small and inefficient, separated from the dining room by a non-bearing wall. There were only one or two electric outlets in each room, and the capacity is certainly not adequate for the many devices requiring power. The original designs did not consider the recreational aspects of the private rear

A 1926 City Housing Corporation promotional brochure showing a kitchen in a one-family house, and a remodeled one-family house. In recent decades many homeowners removed the wall between the kitchen and the dining room to create an open floor layout. (Top: Clarence Stein papers, Division of Rare and Manuscript Collections, Cornell University Library; Bottom: Laura Heim Architect.)

yards; the plans labeled the space "drying yard." Some mews houses, including the row where Lewis Mumford lived, could access the yard only from the cellar. Over the decades, homeowners modified the interiors to accommodate contemporary living, often removing the wall between the kitchen and dining room. Homeowners frequently include changes to the rear facade for a more efficient interior layout and more natural light. Not infrequently, the dining room window would be replaced by sliding doors.

As part of their commitment to keeping Sunnyside affordable, the planners included two- and three-family houses, reasoning that the rental income would make it possible for someone otherwise unable to buy a home to pay their mortgage. At the same time, rental units opened the community to individuals unable to buy a home. Today, those larger houses are being converted into single-family residences, invariably by new buyers. In these conversions, the first floor becomes the open public area, with living and dining rooms, kitchen, and a new powder room; upstairs, what had been the tenant's apartment becomes the family's private space, typically with three bedrooms and two bathrooms.[32]

Even after designation, some residents have simply defied the authority of the Landmarks Preservation Commission. Most egregiously, one woman suddenly installed a locked gate across the path from the street into the courtyard. The walkway had been open since 1927. Her neighbors were not pleased, to say the least, and several reported the transgression to the LPC. Had this happened while the Special Planned Community Preservation District designation was in effect, the Department of City Planning could have applied legal muscle to order the removal of the gate. The LPC immediately issued a notice of violation, but the agency has no power to enforce its decision. Only if the woman seeks another permit from the LPC or the Department of Buildings can the city compel compliance.

In another instance, a homeowner installed a metal spiral staircase off the back of his house (a feature without precedent in the district), paved over the rear yard, and replaced his slate roof with synthetic materials. He received violations, but appealed his case. At the public hearing, rather than confront the illegality of the work, the commissioners simply discussed various aesthetic considerations and then granted a legalization. What is especially disturbing is the message this decision sends out to others— namely, that it is better to seek forgiveness than to ask for permission.

Such violations set a terrible precedent, for there is less incentive for others to follow the rules. The rules are complicated, involving zoning constraints and the buildings code, as well as the regulations of the Landmarks Preservation Commission. But if the Landmarks Preservation Commission does not set and enforce high standards, there is little chance a historic district can remedy its defects. One can only hope that the example set by homeowners who abided by the rules and received preapproval for work will prove a stronger influence in the long run.

Notwithstanding the loss of the Special Planned Preservation District controls, and even with the sometimes uncertain regulation under the Landmarks Preservation Commission, there is no question that the creation of the historic district was essential for the long-term security of Sunnyside Gardens and Phipps Garden Apartments. New work in the district has been far more respectful of historic precedent than had been the case before designation, at least with those who received permits before commencing work. One disappointment, however, is that none of the fences intruding into the courtyards has been removed.

When proposals come before the Landmarks Preservation Commission, residents are free to offer their input, but the agency is not bound to follow their opinions. The commission is free to render decisions according to its own standard of appropriateness, regardless of whether or not a proposal follows precedent or conforms to the original intent of the planners. With designation, Sunnyside's future was secure, but at the same time, for good or for ill, Sunnysiders had lost their capacity for self-regulation, and once lost, it would not be regained.

11

⁞⁞⁞

A Question of Appropriateness

The Aluminaire House Controversy

THE SUNNYSIDE GARDENS HISTORIC DISTRICT faced its first public controversy in the fall of 2013. Architects Michael Schwarting and Frances Campani, professors at New York Institute of Technology (NYIT), proposed siting the Aluminaire House, a 1931 housing prototype, on the only vacant site in the district, an abandoned and fenced off children's playground across from Phipps Garden Apartments. The reaction from the community—largely negative and surprisingly angry—and the way the issue was presented and discussed in preservation circles offer a lively narrative of the meaning of architectural significance, preservation, and appropriateness.

The Aluminaire House presented a preservation conundrum. Preserving an architectural treasure was set in opposition to protecting the integrity of a historic district. Preservationists on either side could offer compelling arguments, but in the end it came down to the elusive question of appropriateness, the term in the landmarks law covering alterations to designated structures and new construction in historic districts. The Landmarks Preservation Commission has never clearly and definitively defined appropriateness, yet that is precisely the quality on which they must hang their decisions. An exhibit at the Museum of the City of New York celebrating the fiftieth anniversary of the landmarks law noted, "This open-ended concept has left it up to different generations of commissioners to interpret the word when reviewing proposals." In the volume accompanying that exhibit, architect Francoise Bollack wrote, "in considering interventions to landmarked buildings or in landmark districts all approaches are valid: the only meaningful questions are 'What is the right thing to do for this building, for this neighborhood?' and 'What is a positive contribution from the perspective of design and preservation?'"[1] Over the decades, the commission has certainly embraced contemporary design solutions inserted into historic districts, but this was something different—the insertion of an architectural icon into a historic context.

A. Lawrence Kocher and Albert Frey designed the Aluminaire House in 1931 for the Architectural League's Architectural and Allied Arts Exposition held at the Grand Central Palace, an exposition hall that covered the block between Forty-Sixty and Forty-Seventh Streets, Lexington to Park Avenues. Kocher had been an editor of *Architectural Record*; Frey had worked in the office of Le Corbusier in France before coming to New York. The experimental structure was the sole example of the emerging International Style included in the show, during which gold medals were awarded to the firm of Shreve, Lamb & Harmon for the Empire State Building and Eliel Saarinen for the Cranbrook Academy of Art in Michigan.[2]

Constructed in ten days, the Aluminaire House was recognized as significant from the moment it went on display. Architecture critic Paul Goldberger has suggested that Kocher and Frey sought to demonstrate "the applicability of modernist theory to middle-class housing, to hold out the promise of a light, airy, open new world. Here, in this house of prefabricated panels of polished corrugated aluminum and glass, the dream that modernism would show a new way of life to the masses actually had a flicker of reality to it." In contrast with his own time, with its ubiquitous suspicion of technology, Goldberger saw this house as "a kind of a challenge, a clarion call to a new age in which technology would liberate building, and building, in turn, would liberate society."[3] In that sense it was not so different from the impulse behind the garden city, the deliverance of urban dwellers from the dreadful conditions of the late nineteenth century cities and the unleashing of human potential stifled by those conditions. While the garden suburbs of the early twentieth century utilized traditional materials and applied traditional design principles, Frey and Kocher employed modernist style and materials for their own version of societal transformation and liberation.

Writing in *Architectural Record* in early 1930, Lewis Mumford seems to have anticipated the Aluminaire House. Mass production must surely come to housing, he wrote, because there is no other way to provide quality homes for industrial workers cheaply; traditional methods of construction and the craftsmanship of the building trades result in either higher

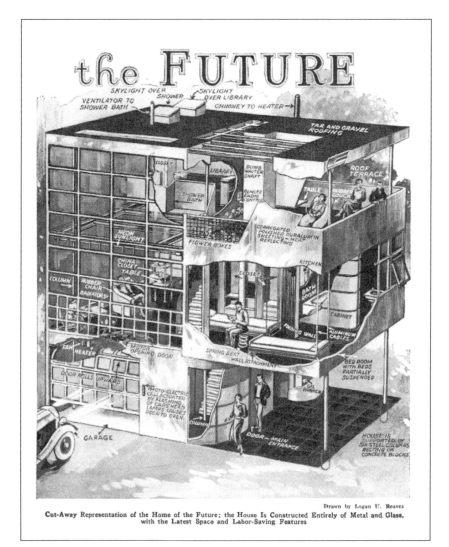

Isometric section of the Aluminaire House. (Illustration by Logan U. Reeves, published in *Popular Mechanics*, August 1931.)

costs or lower standards. Imagining the mass-produced house, he thought that it would "probably be placed on a platform, if not on a pedestal, in order to provide garage space and avoid the expensive cellar; the plans would be standardized; the pipes and fittings and fixtures would be integral with the walls and ceilings, joined together by the turn of the wrench; the use of light insulating materials would both facilitate transportation and permit the design of large windows which would otherwise, in cold weather, make a great drain on the heating system." Mumford saw that the mass-produced house would also provide an avenue for general social improvement, bringing together a "corps of experts, sanitary engineers, heating engineers, hygienists, to say nothing of professors of domestic science," who would "hasten the rationalization of the modern house."[4] Such confidence in the knowledge, experience, and ethics of experts applied toward advancing a societal good was surely an artifact of his time.

Mumford identified a problem that was at once philosophical—how ought urban dwellers live so as to foster their most positive qualities—and practical—what form should those dwellings take, and how can they be made affordable to all classes. If houses were designed for workers the way they were for the upper middle class, "the costs were so high that only the middle class could afford to live in them." And if strict price limitations were imposed, then all variation or innovation in design had to be eliminated. The only option, he concluded, was a factory-produced home with integrated fixtures. The downside, of course, was that "the charm of good building, the charm due to the carpenter's or the mason's feeling for his material and site, would disappear." To compensate, "there would be the austere charity of good machinery; and since this charm is already a sentimental memory in most of our building, it is an illusion rather than a reality that it would be destroyed." With all that, the final cost would not be significantly lowered, because land, materials, and financing were more or less fixed costs. In the end, Mumford came back to the superiority of "the finer rows and quadrangles of Sunnyside" over any manufactured home.[5]

In their prospectus for the exhibition, Frey and Kocher explained that their house "was designed to meet the needs of present day life—the life of the near city," and offered "better light and air with mechanical conveniences and efficiency of arrangement" than was to be found in typical suburban architecture. With its light metal framework and "a manner of construction that is suited to standardization with its many economic advantages," the house utilized metals and synthetic products in a new way: "The outside walls are faced with aluminum, a material that is weather-resistant. It is in the form of sheets slightly ribbed to break glare, and to care for expansion and contraction in varying temperatures. It also has more stiffness than flat sheets and lends itself to ease of joining. This aluminum is backed with insulation that makes its three-inch wall more effective in excluding heat and cold than customary heavy masonry. Windows of ultra-violet glass extend the entire width of rooms to make them as well lighted as the sun porch."[6]

Architect Francis Keally noted approvingly, "In the hands of an artist aluminum, like any other metal, may be made to achieve a beauty equal to its economy and practicability. The light, rectilinear effect of this house suggests the simple elegance of line of Japanese houses, a similarity very apparent in our modern design. The use of metals in building is only in its infancy, and now that modern engineers and modern industry have given us metal on a vast scale for entire building construction it remains for the architect to take over this new medium and furnish such design as will suit the material."[7]

Frey and Kocher's work offered a striking contrast to the more traditional architecture that dominated the Architectural League's show. To accentuate that point, Philip Johnson brought together young architects to show their rejected works in a vacant storefront at 171 West Fifty-Seventh Street. The models exhibited there represented the insurgent International Style without apology.[8] A year later, Johnson and Henry-Russel Hitchcock curated the historic show on the International Style at the Museum of Modern Art (MoMA). They included only six examples from the United States, and one was the Aluminaire House. The curators of the housing portion of the MoMA show were Clarence Stein and Henry Wright, with assistance from Catherine Bauer, and Lewis Mumford wrote the introduction to the catalogue.[9] The Aluminaire House may not have resembled the brick homes in Sunnyside Gardens, but it was certainly a member the same family of reform-inspired housing.

Two years after its exhibition, the house was one of the few individual works featured in *The Arts in American Life*, a report commissioned by President Herbert Hoover as part of a series investigating various aspects of American society. The book highlighted what authors Frederick P. Keppel and R. L. Duffus considered new and innovative, and they were certainly aware of the MoMA show. In particular, they pointed to the skyscraper and the garden suburb as the dual manifestations of the spirit of innovation in the contemporary city. At the same time, they noted the appearance of "stripped architecture." While "not uniquely American," they wrote, "its boldest and most massive exemplifications are to be found in the United States." Even so, they contended that "the test of a nation's architecture will not be in its public buildings, its railway stations, its skyscrapers, its churches or its factories but its homes."[10]

In the early twentieth century, the dominant theme in domestic architecture, especially suburban architecture, was nothing if not historicist. Even the simple brick houses in Sunnyside had a few colonial touches. Keppel and Duffus noted that a "small group of American architects have treated the dwelling house as a fresh problem, to be solved wholly in terms of modern conditions and materials, with no regard whatever for historic styles." The "functionalist" house, or "dwelling machine," would be approached as if it were a "new invention," and it was from that vantage point that they appraised the Aluminaire House, which they called a "house for contemporary life." They tempered their enthusiasm, however, by recognizing that in the domestic field, "functionalist" design was "a conception rather than an actuality."[11]

The house did not at all resemble a suburban cottage, though its proportions were similar. Recognizing its futuristic orientation, Keppel and Duffus observed that "modern civilization has two aspects, as yet imperfectly reconciled—the workaday, which is dominated by machinery, and the traditional, which has its roots deep in the handicraft psychology of the past. Handicraft conceptions have obviously lingered in the home longer than anywhere else. The shiny and efficient factory-like home, with its metallic surfaces, its severe economy of space and its banishment of much that was implied in the original use of the word homey, will possibly be slow in making its way." Although the Aluminaire House represented such a breakthrough, the authors rightly concluded that "the architectural millennium does not seem to have arrived."[12]

Frey and Kocher had designed and constructed the house specifically for the Grand Central Palace exhibition. Had it been ridiculed, or worse, ignored, it might have been immediately discarded, preserved only in drawings and photographs in Albert Frey's files. But it was hailed from the start, and it could not be so easily trashed. Wallace Harrison, just entering the prime of his career, purchased the house for one thousand dollars and had it reassembled on his eleven-acre estate in Huntington, on Long Island, where he had already constructed his own modernist home. Over the years Harrison introduced additions and modifications, and he twice relocated it on the grounds. Eventually, the Aluminaire House fell into disrepair.[13]

Harrison sold his estate in 1974 (he died in 1981). In 1986, the new owner announced plans to build suburban homes on the property and received a permit to demolish the Aluminaire House. By then it was not particularly attractive; still, it was just as Harrison had left it. Even though it had been out of the public eye for many years, the prospect of losing this "icon of modernism" sparked renewed interest. The house, wrote Paul Goldberger in the New York Times, "deserves to remain, not only as an object in itself, but as a relic of an age when modernism represented not only sleekness, but earnestness as well."[14]

With demolition looming, Michael Schwarting negotiated the donation of the house to New York Institute of Technology, on the condition that it be dismantled and removed as soon as possible. Schwarting and Frances Campani, his colleague, partner, and wife, directed students as they documented and dismantled the house, and then supervised the reassembly and restoration on the NYIT campus.[15]

That ought to have been the happy ending, but soon the house was again in peril. NYIT decided to close the Central Islip campus in 2004. Students and faculty would move to the Old Westbury campus, but the Aluminaire House would not, even though the ample grounds of the former estate offered several possible sites for relocation. In 2010, the school transferred ownership of the house to Schwarting and Campani's Aluminaire Foundation, and a search began to identify a new location for what they hoped would be Aluminaire's permanent home.[16]

With a single exception, the Sunnyside Gardens Historic District was completely built out, meaning that every lot had housing on it and that what was built was as much as the zoning allowed. Unlike most other historic districts, there were no vacant lots or underbuilt soft sites for new construction. The one exception was the 100-by-100-foot lot at the corner of Thirty-Ninth Avenue and Fiftieth Street. Originally an outdoor nursery and children's playground for the use of Phipps residents, the corner had been fenced off for three decades.

The Landmarks Preservation Commission specifically included the site within the district because the playground had historically been part of Phipps, but also to assure that what was ultimately built would complement the district's architecture and character. The Real Estate Board of New York has criticized the LPC for including vacant lots within historic district boundaries,[17] but time and time again such actions have proven to be prudent. The buildings ultimately approved by the Landmarks Commission fit well into their context and, indeed, are architecturally superior to what otherwise would likely have been built.

Clearly, designation of the historic district was not intended to foreclose development of the former playground. In 2008, the Queens office of the Department of City Planning, in consultation with the Landmarks Commission, approved new zoning for Sunnyside to supplant the 1974 Special Planned Community Preservation District. Under the old special district designation, driveways and curb cuts were banned. Homeowners could apply for a special permit, but no such permit was ever approved. The new zoning imposed after designation specifically barred new curb cuts

The reassembled Aluminaire House on the campus of New York Institute of Technology. (Courtesy of the Aluminaire Foundation.)

anywhere in the district, with the exception of a single curb cut permitted for the former playground.

The architects learned of the vacant site across from Phipps Garden Apartments, and found the owner amenable to placing Aluminaire there. In return for a ninety-nine-year no-cost lease for the land under the house, Schwarting and Campani agreed to design, for no fee, the eight units of housing the owner intended to build there. It seemed like a workable solution, especially since the owner, Harry Otterman, was intent on building on the lot in any event. For his part, Otterman "thought it was a little gem that would shine up the neighborhood." It was, he thought, "just a nice thing to do."[18]

But eighty years after Aluminaire had its debut, the architectural millennium had still not arrived, certainly not in Sunnyside Gardens. While the experimental house boasted a compelling history of its own, the question ultimately came down to what was best for the historic district, not the house.

The matter of new construction was not a small issue. This was a once-in-a-lifetime opportunity to build in the spirit of Sunnyside Gardens and the Phipps Garden Apartments on the only vacant site in the district. Kenneth K. Fisher, attorney for the owner, said he was "pleasantly surprised" when Sarah Carroll, then director of preservation at the Landmarks Commission, told him that she was not only familiar with the Aluminaire House but wanted to see it preserved. The staff thought this was an inspired idea and encouraged the application. Had Carroll "thrown cold water on it in my first conversation with her," recalled Fisher, "I would have told the client, let's not waste our time."[19]

Fisher, who had served in the city council in the 1990s and had been chair of the Landmarks subcommittee, believed this application could succeed for two reasons. First, while the house was "not of the style of the district, it was of the era of the district and it was of the theory of the district," namely, providing "high quality, low cost housing for working people, something better than the product that was available to them." Second, in terms of scale and plan, with the town houses framing the house, he thought it looked right. That Aluminaire, contrasted with its context, was an asset, he thought, not a problem. "You want the clean delineation between new and old," he said. "You don't want fake old."[20]

The housing Schwarting and Campani designed, however, fell short. The scale was right, but the materials and detailing were not. Indeed, they went out of their way to reject brick, the district's defining material, in favor of oversized ceramic panels in a terra cotta tone (they used similar

Rendering of the Aluminaire House and the proposed new housing on the site of the former Phipps Playground. (Courtesy of Michael Schwarting and Francis Campani.)

materials on a rebuilt tenement on the Lower East Side in 2010).[21] In essence, they took their clues from the Aluminaire House and dismissed the core elements of the historic district. The fatal flaw, in Fischer's analysis, was that the architects "did not pay as much attention to the location of the house as they did to the house itself. It was just a location to them." Their message was that "it didn't really matter where the house went."[22]

The proposal was publicly announced in the spring of 2013, and the community's immediate response was outrage. That June, over a hundred residents jammed the monthly meeting of the community board to make their objections known. Here, in their first public presentation to the community, Frances Campani stated that Sunnyside Gardens was an appropriate location because the house and community are contemporaneous. "It was an early example of modern architecture in America using American materials of aluminum and steel," she said. But it was clear that whatever aesthetic or historic arguments she offered would not be well-received. Community board chairman Joe Conley called the house "totally out of character with the neighborhood," and noted that "the number of people who have complained about this proposal is overwhelming." The Sunnyside Gardens Preservation Alliance called the proposal "horrendous" and rejected the design as "jarring and inappropriate." It was apparent, however, that the Preservation Alliance would not merely oppose the Aluminaire House, but they would attempt to block construction of anything on the former playground.[23]

In 2015, Phipps Houses announced plans to construct a ten-story, 210-unit building of affordable housing on a parking lot between the existing apartment buildings and the railroad embankment. The Preservation Alliance and residents of Phipps opposed that plan also. Councilman Jimmy Van Bramer, citing the passionate opposition expressed at the town hall meeting where Phipps presented their proposal and the petition in opposition with two thousand names on it, blocked the project. "Just because you are progressive and believe in affordable housing doesn't mean that every single affordable housing project is right for every single proposed location," he explained.[24]

The Aluminaire House was in fact different in style and appearance from the housing in the district. It was free-standing, while the houses in Sunnyside were all attached; it was metal, not brick; and finally, it featured a garage, where only a handful of homes in Sunnyside Gardens were built with garages. As Van Bramer put it, "How can a house that in some ways resembles a spaceship be plopped down in the middle of this neighborhood?"[25] (When first presented with the proposal in a private meeting, Van Bramer thought the idea intriguing, but did not like the proposed housing; once he realized the plan was not popular among residents, he came out in opposition.) Many opponents rejected the house on that basis, but some also offered arguments on behalf of the old playground.

Marjorie Cautley designed the playground in conjunction with her design of the Phipps grounds. Landscape architect Michael Gotkin argued for the preservation of the playground. "Cautley's landscape . . . became a defining feature of the community," he contended, and was in fact "one of the last intact Progressive Era playgrounds in New York City." To bolster his case, he referred to the U.S. Department of the Interior's 1996 *Guidelines for the Treatment of Cultural Landscapes*, which stated: "A property will be used as it was historically, or be given a new use that maximizes the retention of distinctive materials, features, spaces, and spatial relationships." Notwithstanding the fact that the corner had been fenced off for decades, Gotkin argued that while "the site appears diminished, all of the playground's visual and spatial qualities along with its architectural and landscape features are remarkably intact." But how does this qualify as a "cultural landscape" meriting preservation? Gotkin concluded that "the extant structures reflect both the period of design and use and can continue to serve the community in new ways. The playground links the Sunnyside Gardens and Phipps communities together and is the sole surviving landscape that can testify to that significant aspect of the Sunnyside Gardens vision."[26]

In September, shortly before the proposal would come before the community board and then for a public hearing at the Landmarks Preservation Commission, the Historic Districts Council (HDC) sponsored an information session at Phipps, where Schwarting and Campani could give the community a full presentation of the proposal in a calm setting. While polite, the audience was far from receptive.[27] Again, the tone was not, "What an interesting idea, but it's not for us"; it was, "How dare you." The proposal next received a cold reception at the community board; Chairman Joe Conley said, "The Aluminaire House and the design of the units seem inconsistent with the whole purpose of landmarking Sunnyside Gardens."[28]

The campaign to block the proposal enlisted local elected officials. Councilman Van Bramer stated that more than 350 constituents had contacted his office to voice their opposition, while only 5 endorsed the plan. State Senator Mike Gianaris stated he had "never seen such opposition as with this project."[29] Even Congressman Joseph Crowley was prodded to voice his opposition.

The Landmarks Preservation Commission hearing on October 15, 2013, was packed. Forty persons testified in opposition and 14 in favor. Counted against stood Councilman Van Bramer, the Historic Districts Council, and dozens of residents, many bussed in by the Preservation Alliance. Speaking in favor were the Municipal Art Society, Docomomo, and a handful of architects and architectural historians.[30]

The first question before the commission was whether it was appropriate to place the Aluminaire House at this location. Second, if placing the house here was deemed appropriate, was the proposed housing scheme correct? Third, if they voted against siting the Aluminaire House there, would it still be appropriate to construct new housing, and if so, should the proposed design solution be accepted? This was a complex issue, but almost without exception, advocates and opponents discussed only the house itself.

Residents testified passionately that the Aluminaire House was wrong for the district and that the abandoned playground meant a great deal to them, speaking as if it were still a vibrant amenity rather than a fenced off lot. But questions regarding the use of the site were beyond the LPC's compass. The Historic Districts Council, which had been testifying before the LPC on Certificate of Appropriateness items for decades, offered the most cogent arguments in opposition. "If the appropriateness of rebuilding the Aluminaire House was judged by the standards of new construction in an historic district, which is essentially what is happening—especially considering the likely amount of new materials the building would require—it would fail," they said. "The building does not relate to the district through its materials, massing, or design, all factors the Landmarks Preservation Commission regularly considers and discusses at great length." Furthermore, "appropriate new construction also has a chance to grow historically with its district—it is a clean slate with no prior history." By contrast, this house "brings its own history, an interesting one that reflects some of the issues Sunnyside Gardens dealt with, but a different one." Finally, HDC reminded the commissioners that this was not an academic exercise, but "a building that does not fit in the unified, cohesive architectural milieu of the historic district."[31]

Few on either side even mentioned the eight new homes that would go up around the Aluminaire House, but that was an integral part of the proposal. Income from the sale of the units would fund the Aluminaire House Foundation. HDC contended that the new construction related more to the house than to the district, suggesting that "the use of terra cotta rain screens, rather than bridging between the aluminum house and the landmarked brick buildings as the applicant has suggested, only introduces yet another new material to the district." Other aspects of the design—rooftop terraces and pergola, inset balconies, an entry atop a high stoop—likewise had no reference points in the historic district.[32]

The Municipal Art Society supported the proposal, but they did not comment on the proposed housing. Architect Kenneth Frampton of Columbia University voiced his support, as did architectural historians Andrew Dolkart of Columbia and Marta Gutman of City College. Dolkart thought relocating the house to Sunnyside was "a fantastic idea," suggesting that it "will only add to the neighborhood's importance as a center of forward-looking housing and planning." Gutman testified that this project would help Sunnysiders and all New Yorkers "grasp the history of affordable housing in their city—and the various means activists used to make high quality examples available." She noted that, considered together, Phipps Garden Apartments, Sunnyside Gardens, and the Aluminaire House would offer "a textbook example of the various design ideologies and massing strategies embraced by modernist architects in the 1920s and 1930s." Gutman added that she thought the proposed housing was "a lovely design."[33]

In January 2014, three months after the public hearing, the Landmarks Preservation Commission voted to reject the Aluminaire House, but approved the new housing in principle; that is, that the architects had to make significant modifications to the design. Landmarks Preservation Commission chairman Robert Tierney privately told Fisher he was just not prepared to go against the local council member on this.[34]

Schwarting and Campani finally found a home for the Aluminaire House. Albert Frey lived and practiced in Palm Springs, California, from 1935 until his death in 1998. The city boasts several buildings by Frey amidst a spectacular ensemble of mid-century modern architecture. During the annual Modernism Week celebration in February 2015, Schwarting and Campani presented the story of the house and their decades-long effort to preserve it. Out of that presentation was born the idea to locate the house on public land across from the Palm Springs Art Museum. Mayor Steve Pougnet enthusiastically embraced the idea and sponsored "An Evening for Aluminaire" at the Palm Springs Visitors Center, a former Tramway Gas Station designed by Frey. The event raised nearly a third of the estimated $600,000 relocation cost. "The Aluminaire House, once it is finally home here in Palm Springs, will be a year-round attraction that is perfectly in line with our thriving architectural tourism focus," said Mayor Pougnet. "If you have a product, that is an incredible product, people want to be a part of it . . . we'll be having a heck of a party in downtown Palm Springs."[35]

The adoption of the house by Palm Springs confirms that the house did not have to be in Sunnyside. Fisher concluded that "there were other places where you could legitimately make the argument that that's where it ought to go." Putting the house in Sunnyside "was a marriage of convenience and not a marriage of choice," and that was "part of the reason why it was perceived as a weak idea."[36]

In truth, Palm Springs is a more fitting and appropriate home for the Aluminaire House than Sunnyside would have been, but that is not to say that it would have been inappropriate to site the house in the historic district. In terms of both the history of architecture and the history of planning, and even in terms of the preservation ethos, many legitimate arguments supported the idea. But the marriage would have been too awkward for its neighbors. How blessed that Aluminaire, after such a peripatetic history, should finally find its soul mate in Palm Springs.

There is a coda. In 2016 the city council allocated funds to purchase the long vacant lot for a playground.[37]

A Second Century for
the Garden Suburb

HOW IS A GARDEN SUBURB to survive into its second century?

It is hard to deny that Sunnyside Gardens has fallen from grace. To the knowing eye, it is a degraded landscape. Its arcadian age lasted but four decades, the years when the original covenants were in place and enforced by the residents themselves. Once the easements lapsed, architectural elements were lost, yes; but more than that, a way of thinking vanished as well. The value system that had respected the ideas animating the plan diminished over time, and with it the zeal of the residents to maintain it. This did not happen all at once, nor did all abandon the ideal, but the diminishment is evident.

The first phase of the erosion of the unified vision began suddenly. The expiration of the covenants freed the place from all controls except the city's building code and zoning. In the absence of any enforceable regulatory regime, the visual unity of the Sunnyside experience was soon compromised. Where a minimalist architectural language is employed, the loss of any detail is telling, far more so than in a neighborhood hosting a variety of styles.

A study of planned communities from the 1930s recognized this threat: "It may be a platitude to state that the more distinctive and unique the layout and architecture of a community, the less is required to throw the whole composition off balance, thus obtaining not only a less pleasing result by the introduction of incongruous elements but an actual shock and disappointment to the observer when the promise of a culminating feature or a harmonious pattern is suddenly dissipated."[1] For decades Sunnyside Gardens was protected from such a fate, but when the shield was removed, both plan and architecture were imperiled.

Once lost, the governing principle was all but impossible to reestablish. The Special Planned Community Preservation District zoning effectively stemmed the erosion of the plan, and at the same time reinforced public recognition of the value of the place. Official protection by the city of New York also encouraged Sunnysiders to forge anew a community identity and to work together to preserve what distinguished Sunnyside Gardens from other blocks of row houses in Queens.

With the loss of an appreciation for the values that underlay the protections came the loss of the ethos that emphasized modesty and uniformity over individuality and ostentation. While the special zoning protected the original plan and prevented further incursions into the walkways and gardens, it did not regulate design. Historic district designation would do that, but no one expected that it would come at the cost of losing the protections of the special zoning that had served the community so well for thirty-three years. After designation, the only standard henceforward applied to proposed changes would be a vague and variously defined concept of "appropriateness" as applied by the Landmarks Preservation Commission. In practice, appropriateness has been defined as much as a matter of individual taste as a matter of precedent, let alone history.

Through all negative changes over the decades, the bones of the planned community remained, and the potential for a restoration of its original features is ever possible. With each new homeowner who arrives with little or no understanding of or appreciation of the history of the place or the values that once breathed life into it, there is increased distance between the ideal of the past and the realities of the present. "The common" generally refers to the central green in the middle of each court, a space neither completely public nor purely private. But we might also mean an approach to living in Sunnyside that is shared in common and appreciated in common. It is the idea that no resident has the right to diminish his neighbor's enjoyment of home and garden. It is an acceptance of design guidelines that emphasize a common palette of colors and materials and a respect for a uniform public face over personal taste. Sunnyside Gardens, if its history is to mean anything at all, must remain the exception, a place where venerable community standards take precedence over individual preferences.

It is dismaying to realize that so few homeowners understand what the common means. They just know they don't really use the courtyard, and that they pay taxes on the portion that is theirs. How long can that situation persist? Indeed, with the elimination of the Special Planned Community Preservation District zoning, is it even legal? The only protection remaining is the Landmarks Preservation Commission's power to grant or deny permits, and that power is exercised by commissioners and staff who interpret the regulations on a case-by-case basis. Furthermore, the commission lacks the power to compel anyone to correct work done without permits.

The wonder is why someone would purchase a home in Sunnyside Gardens, a historic community and a historic district, only to ignore, or at least stretch, all rules and standards. No doubt some want the protection and security offered by preservation regulations, but not everyone embraces the obligation to conform to them. No mechanism exists to compel homeowners to restore their property to the 1920s appearance, nor is there any way to force the removal of parking pads or fences privatizing the interior courtyards. Over time, however, it can only be hoped that positive changes will gradually predominate.

Sunnyside Gardens has survived only because it has been subject to architectural and zoning controls for nearly the entire course of its first century. The English garden suburbs—Hampstead, Letchworth, and Welwyn—and Forest Hills Gardens, not to mention Radburn, have endured because each is governed by a body empowered to enforce design standards. That was never the case at Sunnyside, where controls were embedded in the very deeds. That structure was lost, and now all authority rests in the city government. Only when Sunnysiders again take responsibility for the maintenance of their community can true restoration commence.

Still, there is no denying that the experiment that is Sunnyside Gardens remains an example of urban potential, a rebuke to towers in the park, inefficient neighborhood design, and suburban sprawl, places that deaden the senses and provide a minimal sense of community. Sunnyside's planners emphasized human scale, greenspace, walkability, and public and semi-public spaces to foster a sense of neighborliness. As Ada Louise Huxtable wrote, Clarence Stein, Henry Wright, Lewis Mumford, and their circle "endorsed a kind of sensitive and humane physical planning that was part of the climate of the 1920s and 1930s, when the answer to many of the ills of society seemed to be a better place to live." Their "rational, compassionate and somewhat simplistic philosophy" was certainly a product of their time.[2] But it remains a question as to whether it is no more than a historical artifact or whether it might be an expression of universal values awaiting rediscovery in our own time. "In the cities of the future," wrote Lewis Mumford in 1954, "ribbons of green must run through every quarter, forming a continuous web of garden and mall, widening at the edge of the city into protective greenbelts, so that landscape and garden will become an integral part of urban no less than rural life."[3] How he must have despaired at seeing those aspirations swept aside.

The ideal of the human-scale garden suburb was in eclipse by the mid–twentieth century. Rather than a compact, discrete community, new construction resulted in undifferentiated, anonymous places.[4] In the early twentieth century, garden city advocates were responding to the unhealthy environment most city-dwellers endured. Toward the end of the century, architects, planners, and urbanists expressed concern about sprawl, the antithesis of congestion. Their critique coalesced into New Urbanism. Beginning at opposite poles—congestion on the one hand and sprawl on the other—the garden city advocates and the New Urbanists found common ground.[5] While the social motives that inspired the planners of Sunnyside Gardens and Radburn may have faded over the decades, the design principles endure to a surprising degree.

In 1981, Andres Duany and Elizabeth Plater-Zyberk designed Seaside, the first New Urbanist community, on the Florida panhandle. They sought to apply traditional architectural forms and planning principles to build greater social cohesion among residents. In essence, New Urbanism rediscovered the virtues espoused by Clarence Stein, Henry Wright, and the other members of the Regional Planning Association of America in the 1920s.[6] Emily Talen, a historian of New Urbanism, wrote that Seaside was "a place designed—as a matter of principle—for social inclusion; a place built on the premise that a quality public realm lifts all boats." The planning "was motivated by a progressive social ideal. Seaside was never about stoking the engine of capitalism." What she admired about Seaside was precisely what Stein and Wright poured into their design for Sunnyside: "With its awesome public realm, its mix of unit types, its walkability, and its attention to communal functionality . . . it obliges us to concede a basic malfunction in American city planning and find ways to overcome it." Seaside harked back to the Progressive Era, reviving "the temporarily mislaid, optimistic tradition that postulated the importance of civic design and proclaimed its relation to social goals."[7]

Seaside, along with every New Urbanist place, shares with Sunnyside Gardens the goal of a more respectful, human-scaled environment. Each was the result of a single, unified vision, and from the start each was governed by strict zoning controls and design standards. That the New Urbanists struck a nerve with their throwback design principles and emphasis upon the public realm only demonstrates how far suburban design had

Walkway through rear gardens at Seaside, 2017. (Author's photograph.)

diverged from garden city ideals. Like the generation of Stein, Wright, and company, the New Urbanists believe that sound design could advance societal goals. The Charter for the New Urbanism adopted in 1996 proclaimed "that physical solutions by themselves will not solve social and economic problems, but neither can economic vitality, community stability, and environmental health be sustained without a coherent and supportive physical framework."[8]

If that is indeed the case, then surely we must examine with a more critical and disapproving eye the direction of urban growth in the twenty-first century. Completed in 2019, Hudson Yards, with its towering luxury residences and its relentlessly upscale shopping mall, is the very antithesis of the human-scale city, the livable city. What social goals does that mega-project advance, and how does its physical form shape the people who experience it? Beyond New York, what kind of urbanism is to be found in the new megacities in Asia? To suggest a respect for human scale or the necessity of green space and a generous public realm, or to even bewail the quality of life such places offer is to introduce concerns from generations past that might be counted as luxuries today.

In the first decades of the twenty-first century, western Queens experienced phenomenal growth. Long fallow industrial blocks near the Sunnyside Railroad Yard and the Long Island City waterfront began sprouting glass residential towers. In a way, this was a repetition of the growth spurt of a century before, when Queens was transformed from a rural county into an urban borough. There is a crucial difference, however. In the 1910s and 1920s, thoughtful architects and planners asked what kind of city we wanted to build, and what kind of places would most benefit the inhabitants. These questions became part of a larger discussion, influencing both municipal policy and the design of new communities. Sunnyside Gardens came out of that social, intellectual, and architectural ferment.

Few are asking such questions today, and if they are, the conversations have not percolated into the public discourse. As far as public policy is concerned, concerns over the quality of life are almost completely absent. Mayor Michael Bloomberg's 2007 plan for the future city, PlaNYC, sought to prepare the city for an estimated population of 10 million by 2030, up from 8 million in 2000.[9] The question was where these people would live, not how they would live. Mayor Bill de Blasio, Bloomberg's successor, embraced the policy of hyper-development, but inserted an additional emphasis on affordable housing. But the city would not actually build such housing, of course. Rather, his administration's two initiatives, Mandatory Inclusionary Housing and Zoning for Quality and Affordability, would rely upon real estate developers to include such units in their projects, based on generous zoning incentives.[10] Furthermore, the city demanded only a minimal provision for the public realm. The resulting residential towers would be indistinguishable from other luxury housing, each rising as an individual presence, scarcely integrated into the city outside its lobby. These political solutions are a far cry from the world of Stein and Wright.

The housing experiments of the early decades of the twentieth century were only possible because land values were low. That economic reality fostered the development of Jackson Heights, Sunnyside Gardens, and the various model tenements built around the city. As Henry Wright understood, without inexpensive land, efforts to create affordable housing are doomed. The wonder is that with land prices within reach, investors a century ago willingly accepted a lower rate of return to support the building of innovative affordable housing.

The Garden City was only possible in the context of substantial and inexpensive tracts of land. In the context of suburban sprawl, that is simply not possible in the United States. But urbanization is proceeding at an unprecedented pace in Africa, the Middle East, Asia, and South America. Millions upon millions are deserting the countryside for cities, precisely what Ebenezer Howard observed in England at the end of the nineteenth century. The megacities of the twenty-first century lack the infrastructure to house them, protect them, provide them with adequate water and sanitation, or to educate their children. This is the sprawl of slums, or more politely, informal housing. In the face of such pressures, governments believe that they do not enjoy the luxury of considering the quality of life the new residents might enjoy. Where new housing is built, it is in the form of alienating towers, with little provision for a robust public realm. Could the Garden City offer a viable alternative?

The foremost concern of the builders of Sunnyside Gardens was the creation of an environment that would enhance the health and social needs of the inhabitants. They believed that opportunities for casual communion with nature were essential, and they saw as their mission the improvement of the urban life.

That spirit has faded to near invisibility.

A century ago, far-sighted and socially conscious architects and planners sought to build communities, not merely buildings. They considered the experience of place—how residents would interact—and the setting—how the buildings would interact—to be questions of the first order. Judging by what is being built a century later, those questions are not only not being asked, but they are irrelevant. The only relevant question in twenty-first-century New York is how to squeeze a maximum number of units into the allowable zoning, and increasingly what is allowed under the zoning is not an upper limit, but the baseline for negotiating a variance to build something bigger. Here is a profound misreading of Jane Jacob's paean to urban density. When density is the only yardstick by which to measure success, we should not be surprised by the new city rising around us.

In 2001, the city rezoned downtown Brooklyn and part of Long Island City near Queensboro Plaza to foster the growth of new business districts. The Municipal Art Society examined the actual result of the rezoning in 2018. What they found was that "the expected boom in commercial development never materialized. Instead, these neighborhoods were transformed by an explosion of high-end, high-rise residential development, fueled 'unintentionally' by the City's zoning changes." In Long Island City, the plan anticipated a maximum of 300 new residential units, about 300,000 square feet; what resulted was an extraordinary 10,000 units totaling 8.74 million square feet. In Brooklyn the rezoning was expected to bring fewer than 1,000 units by 2013, but three times that many were built, with 5,000 more by 2018.[11]

The explosion in residential construction was predictable, for the city had substituted zoning for planning. The upzonings came with no provision for open space, schools, or any other public amenities beyond those

Residential buildings erected after the 2001 rezoning of Long Island City, 2019. (Author's photograph.)

voluntarily provided by the private developers. Now, the city must catch up to the residential growth and will always fall short. Above all, these new places lack a vibrant public realm. Yes, there are shops and restaurants where residents mingle, but the city's planners neglected to provide any public spaces.

The outcome in Long Island City might be seen as the anti-Sunnyside Gardens. Where Stein and Wright designed a community, the twenty-first century developers erected buildings. Where Sunnyside had private, semi-private, and public spaces, the new residential towers turn inward, providing assorted amenities for residents within; most buildings have private gyms. Sunnyside offered abundant greenspace and walkways through landscaped courtyards; the new buildings rise from the property line and open directly onto the sidewalk, with no connection to even minimal greenery. Stein and Wright designed a place for neighborly interaction. What the new residents of Long Island City find today is an enclosed and aggressively private environment.

A century ago housing reformers asked what we would build if we could build the city anew. They concentrated on the living conditions of the working poor and the lower middle class, believing that income should not determine whether one enjoyed a healthy and uplifting environment. It was their fundamental belief that urban design can and must contribute to the betterment of the citizens of the city.

It was a different time.

If it is a matter of the emulation of specific form, then we have to accept that Sunnyside Gardens fostered few imitators. But the goals of the founders, and the principles that guided their design, can inspire still.

ACKNOWLEDGMENTS

I HAVE BENEFITED FROM advice and assistance from many thoughtful men and women. First, I must thank my colleagues at the Lloyd Sealy Library at John Jay College of Criminal Justice. I could go to them for all manner of assistance, and they could always find an answer (hey, they're librarians). Chief Librarian Larry Sullivan has been ever encouraging and generous with advice, suggestions, and support.

Fredric Nachbaur of Fordham University Press guided my work from manuscript to publication, and I greatly appreciate his keen attention to detail. The comments from the anonymous readers were on the mark and most helpful. I would be remiss if I did not thank the many scholars who have plowed this field before me; their works are cited with sincere appreciation in the bibliography. In particular, I acknowledge the contributions of David Schuyler, of Franklin and Marshall College, who sadly passed away as this book neared completion.

I thank the archivists and librarians who have guided me through their collections: Erik Huber of the Archives at Queens Public Library; Heather Isbell Schumacher of the Architectural Archives of the Stuart Weitzman School of Design at the University of Pennsylvania; the staff of the Columbia University Archives; and the staff of the Division of Rare and Manuscript Collections at Cornell University, where the Clarence Stein Papers are housed.

Special thanks go to Jane Blackburn, the former manager of the Hampstead Garden Suburb Trust, who guided us through the Suburb and

203

generously shared a wealth of materials. Elizabeth Plater-Zyberk of the University of Miami joined us for a presentation titled "From Sunnyside to Seaside" at the AIA National Conference in 2017. Thanks to Michael Schwarting and Frances Campani of the New York Institute of Technology, not the least for their unceasing efforts to save the Aluminaire House. Alex Garvin of Yale University, who sees in cities what many of us overlook, shared advice. On the preservation side, I appreciate the insights and encouragement I received from Anthony C. Wood; Simeon Bankoff, executive director of the Historic Districts Council and an early supporter of the campaign to designate Sunnyside Gardens, who has provided a platform for my preservation musings; and Kevin and Alexandra Wolfe, who bring together architecture, preservation, and friendship. I also thank the members of the Seminar on the City at Columbia University, for an ongoing discussion of the many strands of urban history, especially New York City, and in particular, Kenneth T. Jackson (with whom I heartily disagree on preservation), and longtime chair Lisa Keller.

Above all, I thank my wife, Laura Heim, who has been with me every step of the way.

NOTES

Introduction. Sunnyside Gardens and the Garden City Idea: A Cityscape for Urban Reform

1. See Robert A. M. Stern, David Fishman, and Jacob Tilove, *Paradise Planned: The Garden Suburb and the Modern City* (New York: Monacelli Press, 2013).

2. Lewis Mumford, "Beginnings of Urban Integration," in *The Urban Prospect* (New York: Harcourt, Brace and World, Inc., 1968), 144.

3. Lewis Mumford, "Regions—To Live In," in *Planning the Fourth Migration: The Neglected Vision of the Regional Planning Association of America*, ed. Carl Sussman (Cambridge, Mass.: MIT Press, 1976), 89–93; Lewis Mumford, *The Culture of Cities* (New York: Harcourt, Brace and Company, 1938), 9.

4. Frank E. Manuel and Fritzie P. Manuel, *Utopian Thought in the Western World* (Cambridge, Mass.: The Belknap Press of Harvard University Press, 1979), 759–772.

5. Stephen V. Ward, "Ebenezer Howard: His Life and Times," in *From Garden City to Green City: The Legacy of Ebenezer Howard*, ed. Kermit C. Parsons and David Schuyler (Baltimore: Johns Hopkins University Press, 2002), 17–20.

6. Lewis Mumford, *The Brown Decades: A Study of the Arts in America, 1865–1895* (New York: Dover Publications, Inc., 1971 [1931]), 22.

7. Mumford, "Regions—To Live In."

8. Frederic C. Howe, "The Garden Cities of England," in *The Urban Community: Housing and Planning in the Progressive Era*, ed. Roy Lubove (Englewood Cliffs, NJ: Prentice-Hall, Inc., 1967), 74–77.

9. Michael Kwartler, "Zoning," in *Encyclopedia of New York City*, 2nd edition, ed. Kenneth T. Jackson (New Haven: Yale University Press, 2010), 1432.

10. Samuel Zipp, "The Roots and Routes of Urban Renewal," *Journal of Urban History* 39, no. 3 (2012): 366–391.

11. Nathan Glazer, *From a Cause to a Style: Modernist Architecture's Encounter with the American City* (Princeton: Princeton University Press, 2007), 170.

12. An example of such a critique is Richard J. Whalen, *A City Destroying Itself: An Angry View of New York* (New York: William Morrow and Co., 1965).

13. Emily Talen, *New Urbanism and American Planning: The Conflict of Cultures* (New York: Routledge, 2005), 51, 277.

14. Donald L. Miller, *Lewis Mumford: A Life* (Pittsburgh: University of Pittsburgh Press, 1989), 493–494.

15. Glazer, *Cause to a Style*, 165; see especially chapters 7 and 11.

16. Lewis Mumford, "Mother Jacobs' Home Remedies," in *The Urban Prospect* (New York: Harcourt, Brace and World, Inc., 1968), 182–207.

17. Jane Jacobs, *The Death and Life of Great American Cities* (New York: Random House, 1961), 1.

18. Joseph J. Salvo and Arun Peter Lobo, "Population," in *Encyclopedia of New York City*, 2nd edition, ed. Kenneth T. Jackson (New Haven: Yale University Press, 2010), 1049.

19. Mumford, "Home Remedies," 202–203.

20. Mumford, "Home Remedies," 190–191.

21. Jacobs, *Death and Life*, 17–18.

22. Daniel Schaffer, "The American Garden City: Lost Ideals," in *The Garden City: Past, Present, and Future*, ed. Steven V. Ward (London: E & FN Spon, 1992), 127–145; Robert Fishman, "The American Garden City: Still Relevant?," in *The Garden City: Past, Present, and Future*, ed. Steven V. Ward (London: E & FN Spon, 1992), 146–164.

23. Jacobs, *Death and Life*, 18–19.

24. Mumford, "Home Remedies," 188–189.

25. Jacobs, *Death and Life*, 19–20.

26. Carl Sussman, ed., *Planning the Fourth Migration: The Neglected Vision of the Regional Planning Association of America* (Cambridge, Mass.: MIT Press, 1976), x. It was to counter such assertions that Sussman compiled this collection of writings by members of the Regional Planning Association of America, including essays from the May 1925 issue of the *Survey Graphic*, the Regional Planning Number, edited by Mumford.

27. Roberta Gratz is the author of *The Living City* (1989), *Cities Back from the Edge: New Life for Downtown* (1998), and *The Battle for Gotham: New York in the Shadow of Robert Moses and Jane Jacobs* (2010).

28. Comment made to the author, March 2007.

29. Ada Louise Huxtable, "Clarence Stein—The Champion of the Neighborhood," *New York Times*, January 16, 1977.

30. Anthony Flint, *Wrestling with Moses* (New York: Random House, 2009), 24–25.

31. Jacobs, *Death and Life*, 20–21.

32. Mumford, "Home Remedies," 188–189, 197–198.

33. Jacobs, *Death and Life*, 21–23; Flint, *Wrestling with Moses*, 18–24.

34. Jacobs, *Death and Life*, 25.

35. Whalen, *City Destroying Itself*, 13–16, 21, 36–37, 52–54, 60.

36. See for example Roberta Brandes Gratz, *The Battle for Gotham: New York in the Shadow of Robert Moses and Jane Jacobs* (New York: Nation Books, 2010).

37. Robert Fishman, "The Bounded City," in *From Garden City to Green City: The Legacy of Ebenezer Howard*, ed. Kermit C. Parsons and David Schuyler (Baltimore: Johns Hopkins University Press, 2002), 66.

38. Charles Ascher, "The Radburn Story," oral history interview by F. C. McMullen, December 7, 1970, Ascher Papers, Columbia University, Box 25, Radburn folder 1: 30.

39. Stern, et al., *Paradise Planned*, 11; Judith Kenney, "New Urbanism," in *Encyclopedia of American Urban History Vol. 2*, ed. David Goldfield (Thousand Oaks, Calif.: SAGE Reference, 2007), 539–541; Witold Rybczynski, *Mysteries of the Mall and Other Essays* (New York: Farrar, Straus and Giroux, 2015), 42–45; Celebration, http://www.celebration.fl.us/.

40. William Fulton, *The New Urbanism: Hope or Hype for American Communities?* (Cambridge, Mass.: Lincoln Institute of Land Policy, 1996); John A. Dutton, *New American Urbanism: Re-forming the Suburban Metropolis* (Milan, Italy: Skira editore, 2000).

1. The Garden City and the Garden Suburb in Great Britain

1. Raymond Unwin, *Town Planning in Practice: An Introduction to the Art of Designing Cities and Suburbs* (New York: Benjamin Blom, Inc., 1971 [London: 1909; second edition 1934]), 10.

2. Unwin, *Town Planning*, 2.

3. Unwin, *Town Planning*, 12–13.

4. Ebenezer Howard, *Garden Cities of To-Morrow* (Cambridge, Mass.: MIT Press, 1965).

5. Robert A. M. Stern, David Fishman, and Jacob Tilove, *Paradise Planned: The Garden Suburb and the Modern City* (New York: Monacelli Press, 2013), 202–213.

6. The British government did in fact embark on a program of building new towns along garden city principles after World War II. See Carol E. Heim, "The Treasury as Developer-Capitalist? British New Town Building in the 1950s," *Journal of Economic History* 50, no. 4 (December 1990): 903–924.

7. C. B. Purdom, "New Towns for Old: What They Are and How They Work," *in Planning the Fourth Migration: The Neglected Vision of the Regional Planning Association of America*, ed. Carl Sussman (Cambridge, Mass.: MIT Press, 1976), 129–133.

8. Lewis Mumford, "Beginnings of Urban Integration," in *The Urban Prospect* (New York: Harcourt, Brace and World, Inc., 1968), 142–152.

9. Frederick H. A. Aalen, "English Origins," in *The Garden City: Past, Present, and Future*, ed. Steven V. Ward (London: E & FN Spon, 1992), 28–51.

10. Stern, et al., *Paradise Planned*, 220–228.

11. Clarence S. Stein and Kermit C. Parsons, *The Writings of Clarence S. Stein: Architect of the Planned Community* (Baltimore: Johns Hopkins University Press, 1998), 52–53.

12. Dugald MacFadyen, *Sir Ebenezer Howard and the Town Planning Movement* (Cambridge, Mass.: The MIT Press, 1970), 40–43, 69–71; Stephen V. Ward, "Ebenezer Howard: His Life and Times," in *From Garden City to Green City: The Legacy of Ebenezer Howard*, ed. Kermit C. Parsons and David Schuyler (Baltimore: Johns Hopkins University Press, 2002), 28–31; Frederic J. Osborn, *Green-Belt Cities* (New York: Shocken Books, 1969 [1946]), 107, 183.

13. Stern, et al., *Paradise Planned*, 213–220, 230–235.

14. Stern, et al., *Paradise Planned*, 230–235.

15. Welwyn Garden City Heritage Trust, http://www.welwyngarden-heritage.org/history/item/123-history.

16. Osborn, *Green-Belt Cities*, 1–6, 183.

17. Osborn, *Green-Belt Cities*, 183.

18. MacFayden, *Town Planning Movement*, 119–127, 138–140; Welwyn Garden City Heritage Trust, http://welwyngarden-heritage.org/garden-city-heritage/garden-city-history

/203-history; Our Welwyn Garden City, http://www.ourwelwyngardencity.org.uk/; Stern, et al., *Paradise Planned*, 236–238.

19. Mumford, "Urban Integration," 142–152.

20. Alexander Garvin, *The American City, What Works, What Doesn't* (New York: McGraw Hill, 1996), 320; Mumford, "Urban Integration," 142–152.

21. Aalen, "English Origins," 28–51.

22. Mervyn Miller, *Hampstead Garden Suburb* (Chalford, Great Britain: The Chalford Publishing Co., 1995), 7.

23. Hampstead Garden Suburb Development Company, *Town Planning and Modern Architecture in the Hampstead Garden Suburb*, (Hampstead: Garden Suburb Development Company [1909]), 11, 33; Unwin, *Town Planning in Practice*, 391.

24. Hampstead Garden Suburb Development Company, *Town Planning and Modern Architecture in the Hampstead Garden Suburb*, 5–7, 11.

25. Hampstead Garden Suburb Development Company, *Town Planning and Modern Architecture in the Hampstead Garden Suburb*, 7–8; emphasis in original.

26. Hampstead Garden Suburb Development Company, *Town Planning and Modern Architecture in the Hampstead Garden Suburb*, 7, 13, 17.

27. Unwin, Preface, Hampstead Garden Suburb Development Company, *Town Planning and Modern Architecture in the Hampstead Garden Suburb*, 3.

28. Unwin, Preface, Hampstead Garden Suburb Development Company, *Town Planning and Modern Architecture in the Hampstead Garden Suburb*, 3–4.

29. Miller, *Hampstead Garden Suburb*, 8, 48–55.

30. Stern, et al., *Paradise Planned*, 713–717, 721–727.

31. Frederick L. Ackerman, "War-Time Housing—England's Most Urgent Civic Lesson for America," *American City* 18, no. 2 (February 1918): 97–100.

32. Michael H. Lang, "The Design of Yorkship Garden Village: Product of Progressive Planning, Architecture, and Housing Reform Movements," in *Planning the Twentieth-Century American City*, ed. Mary Corbin Sies and Christopher Silver (Baltimore: Johns Hopkins University Press, 1996), 127.

33. Gazetteer for Scotland, https://www.scottish-places.info/; Stern, et al., *Paradise Planned*, 724–726.

34. Frederick L. Ackerman, "The Significance of England's Program of Building Workmen's Houses," *Journal of the American Institute of Architects*, Vol. V, no. 11 (November 1917): 538–540; Daniel T. Rodgers, *Atlantic Crossings: Social Politics in a Progressive Age* (Cambridge, Mass.: The Belknap Press of Harvard University Press, 1998), 287–288.

35. "Eastriggs: An Industrial Town Built by the British Government," *Journal of the American Institute of Architects*, Vol. V, no. 10 (October 1917): 499–514; "Gretna," *Journal of the American Institute of Architects*, Vol. VI, no. 2 (February 1918): 71–76; Willie Miller Urban Design, "Raymond Unwin: The Art of Designing Cities and Suburbs," https://www.williemiller.com/raymond-unwin-and-gretna.htm.

36. Louis H. Pink, *The New Day in Housing* (New York: Arno Press, 1974 [1928]), 76–77.

2. The Garden Suburb in New York

1. Richard Plunz, *A History of Housing in New York City: Dwelling Type and Social Change in the American Metropolis* (New York: Columbia University Press, 1990), 120.

2. Jacob A. Riis, *How the Other Half Lives: Studies Among the Tenements of New York* (New

York: Dover Publications, Inc., 1971 [1890]), 231–233; Ritchie S. King and Graham Roberts, "Manhattan's Population Density, Past and Present," *New York Times*, March 1, 2012.

3. Joel Schwartz, "Tenements," in *The Encyclopedia of New York City*, 2nd edition, ed. Kenneth T. Jackson (New Haven: Yale University Press, 2010), 1289–1291.

4. Jacob A. Riis, *The Making of an American* (New York: 1920 [1901]), 284–90, 437. The Riis house was torn down in 1973, despite its being listed on the National Register of Historic Places.

5. Robert G. Barrows, "Beyond the Tenement: Patterns of American Urban Housing, 1879–1930," *Journal of Urban History* 9, no. 4 (August 1983): 395–420.

6. Jeffrey A. Kroessler, "Bridges and the Urban Landscape," *Long Island Historical Journal* 2, no. 1 (September 1989): 104–117; Clifton Hood, *722 Miles: The Building of the Subways and How They Transformed New York* (New York: Simon & Schuster, 1993), chap. 6; Robert W. Snyder, *Crossing Broadway: Washington Heights and the Promise of New York City* (Ithaca: Cornell University Press, 2015), 14–17.

7. "Five Years of Home Building in Queens," *Queensborough*, October 1929, 439; Franklin J. Sherman, *Building Up Greater Queens Borough: An Estimate of Its Development and the Outlook* (New York: The Brooklyn Biographical Society, 1929), 38–41.

8. J. Charles Laue, "Americans Becoming a Home-Owning Nation," *New York Times*, December 26, 1926, XX12.

9. Thomas Cogan, "Mathews Model Flats Rebuilt Borough's Landscape," *Queens Gazette*, January 6, 2016. https://www.qgazette.com/articles/mathews-model-flats-rebuilt-boroughs -landscape/.

10. Robert A. M. Stern, *The Anglo-American Suburb* (London: Architectural Design, 1981), 42–3; Robert A. M. Stern, *Pride of Place* (Boston: Houghton Mifflin, 1986), chap. 4; Daniel Karatzas, *Jackson Heights: A Garden in the City* (Jackson Heights Beautification Group, 1990); Robert A. M. Stern, David Fishman, and Jacob Tilove, *Paradise Planned: The Garden Suburb and the Modern City* (New York: Monacelli Press, 2013), 140–144, 188–192.

11. Stern, *Pride of Place*, 142–143.

12. *Forest Hills Gardens: The Suburban Land Development of the Russell Sage Foundation* (New York: The Sage Foundation Homes Co., 1911), 8.

13. *Forest Hills Gardens*, 7; F. A. Austin, "Development of Forest Hills Gardens," *The Real Estate Magazine*, vol. 2, no. 4 (April 1913): 12–18; Alexander Garvin, *The American City: What Works, What Doesn't* (New York: McGraw Hill, 1996), 269.

14. Lewis Mumford, introduction to *Toward New Towns for America*, by Clarence S. Stein (Cambridge, Mass.: MIT Press, 1966 [1957]), 17; Louis H. Pink, *The New Day in Housing* (New York: Arno Press, 1974 [1928]), 78–81.

15. The Sage Foundation Homes Company, *Forest Hills Gardens*, pamphlet No. 1, February 1911; "Forest Hills Gardens, Preliminary Information for Buyers," April 1913; "Declaration of Restrictions, Etc., Affecting Property Known as Forest Hills Gardens," April 1913.

16. Plunz, *History of Housing*, 117–120.

17. Garvin, *American City*, 269–270.

18. Garvin, 269–270.

19. Karatzas, *Jackson Heights*, 12–13.

20. *Newtown Register*, July 22, 1920.

21. Karatzas, *Jackson Heights*, chap. 3 and 4; Jason D. Antos and Constantine E. Theodosiou, *Images of America: Jackson Heights* (Charleston: Arcadia Publishing, 2013), 10.

22. Walter Stabler, "Lack of Building Funds. Mortgage Money Unable to Compete with Tax-Free Government Bonds," *New York Times*, February 15, 1920.

23. Pink, *New Day in Housing*, viii.

24. Rosalie Genevro, "Clarence Stein," in *The Encyclopedia of New York City*, 2nd Edition, ed. Kenneth T. Jackson (New Haven: Yale University Press, 2010), 1241; Roy Lubove, *Community Planning in the 1920s: The Contribution of the Regional Planning Association of America* (Pittsburgh: University of Pittsburgh Press, 1963), 31–33.

25. Clarence S. Stein, "Draft Report of the Housing Committee of the New York State Reconstruction Commission," 1919, in *The Writings of Clarence S. Stein*, ed. Kermit Carlyle Parsons (Baltimore: Johns Hopkins University Press, 1998), 97–98.

26. "Statement of the City Planning Committee of the City Club," Draft Report, March 22, 1920, in *The Writings of Clarence S. Stein*, ed. Kermit Carlyle Parsons (Baltimore: Johns Hopkins University Press, 1998), 110–111.

27. Clarence S. Stein, "Reconstruction Commission of the State of New York," Draft Report, March 22, 1920, in *The Writings of Clarence S. Stein*, ed. Kermit Carlyle Parsons (Baltimore: Johns Hopkins University Press, 1998), 111–112; Clarence S. Stein, "Address to Members of the Advisory Council of the Commission of Housing and Regional Planning, December 27, 1923," in *The Writings of Clarence S. Stein*, ed. Kermit Carlyle Parsons (Baltimore: Johns Hopkins University Press, 1998), 120–123.

28. Kristin E. Larsen, *Community Architect: The Life and Vision of Clarence S. Stein* (Ithaca, N.Y.: Cornell University Press, 2016), 10–11, 65; Elgin R. L. Gould, "The Housing Problem in Great Cities," *Quarterly Review of Economics* 14 (1899–1900): 378–393; Landmarks Preservation Commission, April 24, 1990, Designation List, City and Suburban Homes Company, First Avenue Estate.

29. "Finds Rent Laws Bar Housing Relief," *New York Times*, September 7, 1920; "Summary Ejectment Cases Barred in Supreme Court by New Housing Law; Measures to Check Evictions on Oct. 1," *New York Times*, September 25, 1920; "Vote Tax Exemption for New Dwellings," *New York Times*, February 16, 1921.

30. Vincent F. Seyfried, *300 Years of Long Island City: 1630–1930* (New York: Edgian Press, 1984), 146–156; Lubove, *Community Planning*, 50–53; Karatzas, *Jackson Heights*, 48–49; "Plans Block of $9 a Month Rooms," *New York Times*, February 23, 1922; "Metropolitan Life Insurance Company Finances Huge Building Operations in Queens," *New York Times*, March 12, 1922.

31. "Metropolitan Life Lets Contract for Apartment Experiment in Long Island City," *Queensborough*, June–July 1922, 348–350.

32. *Queensborough*, August 1922, 392.

3. Planning and Building Sunnyside Gardens

1. Frederick L. Ackerman, "War-Time Housing—England's Most Urgent Civic Lesson for America," *American City* 18, no. 2 (February 1918): 97–100.

2. Frederick L. Ackerman, "Houses and Ships," *American City* 19, no. 2 (August 1918): 85–86.

3. Lewis Mumford, "Frederick Lee Ackerman, F.A.I.A., 1878–1950," *Journal of the American Institute of Architects*, Vol. XIV, no. 6 (December 1950): 249–254.

4. Roy Lubove, "Homes and 'A Few Well Placed Fruit Trees': An Object Lesson in Federal Housing," *Social Research* 27, no. 4 (Winter 1960): 469–486.

5. Frederic Law Olmsted, "Lessons from Housing Developments of the United States Housing Corporation," *Monthly Labor Review* 8 (May 1919): 27–38.

6. Olmsted, "Lessons from Housing Developments," 27–38.

7. Ackerman, "War-Time Housing," 97–100; Kristin M. Szylvian, "Industrial Housing Reform and the Emergency Fleet Corporation," *Journal of Urban History* 25, no. 5 (July 1999): 647–689; Michael H. Lang, "The Design of Yorkship Garden Village: Product of Progressive Planning, Architecture, and Housing Reform Movements," in *Planning the Twentieth-Century American City*, ed. Mary Corbin Sies and Christopher Silver (Baltimore: Johns Hopkins University Press, 1996).

8. Kristin Larsen, "Wright, Henry," in *Encyclopedia of American Urban History* Vol. 2, ed. David Goldfield, (Thousand Oaks, Calif.: SAGE Reference, 2007), 901.

9. Robert A. M. Stern, David Fishman, and Jacob Tilove, *Paradise Planned: The Garden Suburb and the Modern City* (New York: Monacelli Press, 2013), 861–863, 882–883; Colonial Terraces Design Guidelines, City of Newburgh, www.cityofnewburgh-ny.gov/ . . . /colonial -terrace-design-district-guidelines.

10. Henry Wright, "The Autobiography of Another Idea," *The Western Architect* 39, no. 9 (September 1930): 137–141, 153.

11. Mumford, "Frederick Lee Ackerman, F.A.I.A., 1878–1950," 249–254; Stern, et al., *Paradise Planned*, 861–863.

12. Jon A. Peterson, *The Birth of City Planning in the United States, 1848–1917* (Baltimore: Johns Hopkins University Press, 2003), 319.

13. Stern, et al., *Paradise Planned*, 849–851.

14. The American Institute of Architects, *Report of the Committee on Community Planning (to the Fifty-Eighth Annual Convention, 1925)*, reprinted in Roy Lubove, *The Urban Community* (Englewood Cliffs, N.J.: Prentice-Hall, Inc., 1967), 116–144; Kristin Larsen, "Cities to Come: Clarence Stein's Postwar Regionalism," *Journal of Planning History* 4, no. 1 (February 2005): 36.

15. Clarence S. Stein, *Toward New Towns for America* (Cambridge, Mass.: MIT Press, 1966 [1957]), 15; Roy Lubove, *Community Planning in the 1920's: The Contribution of the Regional Planning Association* (Pittsburgh: University of Pittsburgh Press, 1963), Ch. 3; Kristin E. Larsen, *Community Architect: The Life and Vision of Clarence S. Stein* (Ithaca, N.Y.: Cornell University Press, 2016), 67–72.

16. "The Tenement House Commission," *New York Times*, January 27, 1885; "For the Benefit of Tenants," *New York Times*, May 8, 1885; United States Bureau of Labor and E.R.L. Gould, *The Housing of the Working People* (Washington, D.C., Government Printing Office, 1895), 196–200; Amie Klempnauer, "Ethical Culture Society of New York," in *The Encyclopedia of New York City*, 2nd edition, ed. Kenneth T. Jackson(New Haven: Yale University Press, 2010), 422; Richard Schwartz, "Ethical Culture Fieldston School," *Encyclopedia of New York City*, 2nd edition, ed. Kenneth T. Jackson (New Haven: Yale University Press, 2010), 422; Jane Allen, "Adler, Felix," *Encyclopedia of New York City*, 2nd edition, ed. Kenneth T. Jackson (New Haven: Yale University Press, 2010), 7.

17. Charles S. Ascher, "The Radburn Story," oral history interview by F. C. McMullen, December 7, 1970 (Ascher Papers, Columbia University, Box 25, Radburn folder 1); Oral History Interview with Charles Ascher, 1972, interviewed by Tom Hogan, The Columbia Center for Oral History (New York: Trustees of Columbia University, 1982), 232.

18. Frederick L. Ackerman, "The Architectural Side of City Planning," in *Proceedings of the Seventh National Conference on City Planning* (Boston: National Conference on City Planning, 1915), 107–128.

19. Frederick L. Ackerman, "Where Goes the City Planning Movement?," *Journal of the American Institute of Architects* (December 1919): 518–520.

20. Lewis Mumford, "Statement for the Ribicoff Committee on governmental expenditures, presented at a public hearing in Washington, D.C., April 21, 1967," in *The Urban Prospect* (New York, Harcourt, Brace & World, Inc., 1968), 210; Donald L. Miller, *Lewis Mumford: A Life* (Pittsburgh: University of Pittsburgh Press, 1989), 497–499.

21. Lubove, *Community Planning in the 1920's*, 72.

22. Lubove, *Community Planning in the 1920's*, 49, 55–57; Larsen, *Community Architect*, 72–74.

23. City Housing Corporation, *Sunnyside Gardens, A Home Community* (ca. 1926).

24. City Housing Corporation, *Sunnyside Gardens, A Home Community*; *Queensborough*, July-August 1924: 388; March 1924: 148; July 1926: 442; January 1929: 53; "Homes at Low Cost Praised at Meeting," *New York Times*, February 1, 1926; Larsen, *Community Architect*, 74–77, 281; Louis H. Pink, *The New Day in Housing* (New York: Arno Press, 1974 [1928]), 87; Oral History Interview with Charles Ascher, 182.

25. James C. Young, "Home Building Put on Low Profit Basis," *New York Times*, January 31, 1926.

26. "First Unit of Sunnyside Colony Is Completed," *Queensborough*, September 1924, 480.

27. "Much New Building, Record Totals $24,192,210," *Queensborough*, April 1925: 224; Stein, *Toward New Towns*, 34. Catherine Bauer effusively praised Romerstadt in her 1934 book, *Modern Housing*.

28. "Research Planned for Better Housing," *New York Times*, November 5, 1926. See Susan Henderson, *Building Culture: Ernst May and the New Frankfurt Initiative* (New York: Peter Lang Publishing, 2013).

29. Stein, *Toward New Towns*, 21; Henry Wright, "Another Idea," 137–141, 153.

30. Lewis Mumford, Introduction to *Toward New Towns for America* (Cambridge, Mass.: MIT Press, 1966 [1957]), 12.

31. "Four Hundred Families Now Live at Sunnyside," *Queensborough*, July 1926: 442; Stein, *Toward New Towns*, 34; Lewis Mumford, *Green Memories: The Story of Geddes Mumford* (New York: Harcourt Brace, 1947), 26–31.

32. Stein, *Toward New Towns*, 16–19; Lubove, *Community Planning in the 1920's*, 49, 55–57.

33. "Dinner for Delegates," *New York Times*, April 20, 1925; "Open Conference on City Planning," *New York Times*, April 21, 1925; "Our Architecture is Called Distinct," *New York Times*, April 22, 1925; "Vienna Gets Next City Plan Meeting," *New York Times*, April 25, 1925; "Bing Represents America," *New York Times*, December 14, 1926; Carl Sussman, editor, *Planning the Fourth Migration: the Neglected Vision of the Regional Planning Association of America* (Cambridge, Massachusetts: The MIT Press, 1976); Richard Plunz, *A History of Housing in New York City: Dwelling Type and Social Change in the American Metropolis* (New York: Columbia University Press, 1990), 147.

34. Stein, *Toward New Towns*, 21; City Housing Corporation, *Sunnyside Gardens, A Home Community*.

35. "First Unit of Sunnyside Colony is Completed," *Queensborough*, September 1924: 480.

36. Percival Mullikin, "Survey Shows Fewest Vacant Apartments in Queens," *Queensborough*, February 1925: 86, 94; Percival Mullikin, "Home Building," *Queensborough*, April 1925: 222; "Home Ownership in Queens," *Queensborough*, April 1925: 224.

37. Stein, *Toward New Towns*, 24.

38. Oral History Interview with Charles Ascher, 166–167.

39. Robert A. M. Stern, with John Montague Massengale, *The Anglo-American Suburb*

(London: Architectural Design, 1981), 46; Alexander Garvin, *The American City: What Works, What Doesn't* (New York: McGraw Hill, 1996), 271.

40. Stein, *Toward New Towns*, 24.

41. Oral History Interview with Charles Ascher, 166; James C. Young, "Home Building Put on Low Profit Basis," *New York Times*, January 31, 1926.

42. G.X. Mathews Company, "Mathews Model Flats, Solving the Housing Problem."

43. Henry Wright, "The Sad Story of American Housing," in Lewis Mumford, ed., *Roots of Contemporary American Architecture* (New York: Dover Publications, 1972 [1952]), 332–334.

44. Mumford, *Green Memories*, 27.

45. *Queensborough*, September 1924: 469; Stein, *Toward New Towns*, 28.

46. Stein, *Toward New Towns*, 24.

47. Lewis Mumford, "Neighborhood and Neighborhood Unit," *Town Planning Review*, January 1954, in *The Urban Prospect* (New York: Harcourt, Brace & World, 1968), 88.

48. Henry Wright, "Another Idea," 137–141, 153.

49. Stein, *Toward New Towns*, 27, 44; Stern, *The Anglo-American Suburb*, 84.

50. "Sunnyside Gardens. New Long Island City Unit is nearly Sold Out." *New York Times*, June 3, 1928; "Sunnyside Gardens Showing Activity," *New York Times*, September 28, 1930.

51. Richard T. Ely, "The City Housing Corporation and 'Sunnyside,'" *The Journal of Land & Public Utilities*, Vol. 2, No. 2 (April 1926): 172–185.

52. "Community Gets $50,000. City Housing Corporation Makes New Sunnyside Gardens Grant." *New York Times*, June 20, 1930; Alexander Garvin, *The American City*, 271.

53. Louis H. Pink, *The New Day in Housing*, 89.

54. Mumford, *Green Memories*, 28–31.

4. Design and Community: Architecture and Landscape as a Social Good

1. Elliot Willensky and Norval White, *The AIA Guide to New York City*, Third Edition (New York: Harcourt Brace Jovanovich, 1988), 743; First Edition, (New York: The Macmillan Company, 1968), 357–358; Oral History Interview with Charles Ascher, 1972, interviewed by Tom Hogan, The Columbia Center for Oral History (New York: Trustees of Columbia University in the City of New York, 1982), 166–167.

2. Louis H. Pink, *The New Day in Housing* (New York: Arno Press, 1974 [1928]), 86.

3. Lewis Mumford, "Neighborhood and Neighborhood Unit," in *The Urban Prospect* (New York: Harcourt, Brace & World, 1968), 67–77.

4. Lewis Mumford, *The Brown Decades: A Study of the Arts in America, 1865–1895* (New York: Dover Publications, Inc., 1971 [1931]), 79, 82.

5. Mumford, *Brown Decades*, 82.

6. Henry Wright, "The Road to Good Houses," *Planning the Fourth Migration: the Neglected Vision of the Regional Planning Association of America*, ed. Carl Sussman (Cambridge, Mass.: MIT Press, 1976), 121–128.

7. Henry Wright, *Rehousing Urban America* (New York: Columbia University Press, 1935), 40.

8. Clarence S. Stein, *Toward New Towns for America* (Cambridge, Mass.: MIT Press, 1966 [1957]), 31.

9. Henry Wright, "The Autobiography of Another Idea," *The Western Architect* 39, no. 9 (September 1930): 137–141, 153.

10. Thaisa Way, *Unbounded Practice: Women and Landscape Architecture in the Early Twentieth Century* (Charlottesville: University of Virginia Press, 2009), 167–168; 227–237.

11. Ruth Horowitz, "Sycamore Trees and Courtyards," 2016, Queens Memory Collection at the Archives at the Queens Library. Ruth and her older brother David were the children of communists who moved to Sunnyside in 1940.

12. Franklin Havelick and Michael Kwartler, "Sunnyside Gardens: Whose Land Is It Anyway?" *New York Affairs* 7, no. 2 (1982): 72–73; Abraham Goldfeld, *Toward Fuller Living Through Public Housing and Leisure Time Activities* (New York: The National Public Housing Conference, 1934), 23.

13. Oral History Interview with Charles Ascher, 177, 192.

14. City Housing Corporation, *Sunnyside Gardens, A Home Community* (ca. 1926).

15. Lewis Mumford, *Green Memories: The Story of Geddes Mumford* (New York: Harcourt Brace, 1947), 26–31; "Sophie Mumford: Green Memories," *The Sunnyside Gardener*, Vol. III, no. 1 (Winter/Spring 1984).

16. Oral History Interview with Charles Ascher, 158, 164–165, 189, 194, 198.

17. Oral History Interview with Charles Ascher, 280.

18. Mumford, "Neighborhood Unit," 75.

19. Goldfeld, *Toward Fuller Living*, 17, 25; Mumford, *Green Memories*, 28–29.

20. "Adds to Sunnyside Park," *New York Times*, January 31, 1929.

21. Oral History Interview with Charles Ascher, 1972, 189; Goldfeld, *Toward Fuller Living*, 19, 23, 27–29; "Sophie Mumford: Green Memories."

5. Building on Success: Radburn and Phipps Garden Apartments

1. "Four Hundred Families Now Live at Sunnyside," *Queensborough* (July 1926).

2. Clarence S. Stein, "Notes on the New Town Planned for the City Housing Corporation," in *The Writings of Clarence S. Stein: Architect of the Planned Community*, ed. Kermit Carlyle Parsons (Baltimore: Johns Hopkins University Press, 1998), 150–151.

3. Charles S. Ascher, "Remarks on the Designation of Radburn as a Historic Landmark, 4 October 1975" (Ascher Papers, Columbia University, Box 25, Radburn folder 1).

4. City Housing Corporation, "Regarding Radburn," 1928; Henry Wright, "The Autobiography of Another Idea," *The Western Architect* 39, no. 9 (September 1930): 137–141, 153.

5. Wright, "Another Idea," 137–141, 153. Mumford's critique of the Regional Plan and a response appeared in the *New Republic* in June and July, 1932. The pieces were reprinted in Carl Sussman, editor, *Planning the Fourth Migration* (Cambridge, Mass.: MIT Press, 1976), 221–267.

6. Clarence S. Stein, *Toward New Towns for America* (Cambridge, Mass.: MIT Press, 1966 [1957]), 37–74; Robert A. M. Stern, David Fishman, and Jacob Tilove, *Paradise Planned: The Garden Suburb and the Modern City* (New York: Monacelli Press, 2013), 275–280.

7. "Rockefeller to Help Finance Radburn, N.J.," *New York Times*, February 19, 1929; "Model Town of Radburn," *New York Times*, March 17, 1929.

8. Clarence S. Stein, "The Architect's Limitations," in *The Writings of Clarence S. Stein: Architect of the Planned Community*, ed. Kermit Carlyle Parsons (Baltimore: Johns Hopkins University Press, 1998), 135–137.

9. Wright, "Another Idea," 137–141, 153.

10. Stein, "New Town Planned," 150–151; Alexander Garvin, *The American City: What Works, What Doesn't* (New York: McGraw Hill, 1996), 273–275.

11. Stein, *Toward New Towns*, Ch. 8.

12. Clarence S. Stein, "New Towns for the Needs of a New Age," *New York Times*, October 8, 1933.

13. Marjorie Sewell Cautley, "Planting at Radburn," *Landscape Architecture*, Vol. XXI, no. 1 (October 1930): 23–29; Thaisa Way, *Unbounded Practice: Women and Landscape Architecture in the Early Twentieth Century* (Charlottesville: University of Virginia Press, 2009), 246–250.

14. Charles S. Ascher, "Private Covenants in Urban Redevelopment," in *Urban Redevelopment: Problems and Practices*, ed. Coleman Woodbury (Chicago: University of Chicago Press, 1953), 228, 232–234, 281; Ascher, "Radburn as a Historic Landmark"; Ascher, "The Extra-Municipal Administration of Radburn: An Experiment in Government by Contract," *National Municipal Review* (July 1929): 442–446.

15. Lewis Mumford, "Mass-Production and Housing," in *City Development: Studies in Disintegration and Renewal* (London: Secker & Warburg, 1946; originally published in *Architectural Record*, January-February 1930), 64–69.

16. Philip Johnson and Henry-Russell Hitchcock, *Modern Architecture, International Exhibition* (New York: Museum of Modern Art, 1932), 194–195.

17. Tracy B. Auger, "Radburn—The Challenge of a New Town," City Housing Corporation (1931), reprinted from *Michigan Municipal Review*, February and March 1931; Stern, et al., *Paradise Planned*, 280–283; Eugenie Ladner Birch, "Radburn and the American Planning Movement: The Persistence of an Idea," *Journal of the American Planning Association* 46, no. 4 (October 1980): 424–439.

18. "Model Town of Radburn," *New York Times*, March 17, 1929; Daniel Schaffer, *Garden Cities for America: The Radburn Experience* (Philadelphia: Temple University Press, 1982), 191–193; Edith B. Wallace and Paula S. Reed, National Historic Landmark Nomination, June 2004, 5 [National Park Service, www.nps.gov/nhl/find/statelists/nj/Radburn.pdf.].

19. "Workers' Housing Planned in Queens," *New York Times*, May 28, 1930; James Mooney, "Atterbury, Grosvenor," in *Encyclopedia of New York City*, 2nd edition, ed. Kenneth T. Jackson (New Haven: Yale University Press, 2010), 75; Eric W. Allison, "Phipps Houses," in *Encyclopedia of New York City*, 2nd edition, ed. Kenneth T. Jackson (New Haven: Yale University Press, 2010), 994.

20. Christopher Gray, "Streetscapes/Henry Phipps and Phipps Houses: Millionaire's Effort to Improve Housing for the Poor," *New York Times*, November 23, 2003; Norval White and Elliot Willensky, *The AIA Guide to New York City*, third edition (New York: Harcourt, Brace &Company, 1988), 298.

21. "Workers' Housing Planned in Queens," *New York Times*, May 28, 1930; "Phipps Houses Started," *New York Times*, October 19, 1930.

22. Kristin E. Larsen, *Community Architect: The Life and Vision of Clarence S. Stein* (Ithaca, N.Y.: Cornell University Press, 2016), 171.

23. "Phipps Garden Apartments in Queens to House 344 Families," *New York Times*, May 10, 1931; "Renting Is Active in Phipps Houses," *New York Times*, August 23, 1931; "Moderate Priced Apartments and Small Homes Feature Queens Building," *Queensborough* (October 1931): 433.

24. Way, *Unbounded Practice*, 2, 241–243.

25. White and Willensky, *AIA Guide*, 743.

26. "Moderate Priced Apartments and Small Homes Feature Queens Building," *Queensborough* (October 1931): 433; White and Willensky, *AIA Guide* 742–743; Robert A. M. Stern, Gregory Gilmartin, and Thomas Mellins, *New York 1930* (New York: Rizzoli International Publications, Inc., 1987), 486–490.

27. "Metropolitan Life Lets Contract for Apartment Experiment in Long Island City," *Queensborough* (June–July 1922): 348–350.

28. Henry Wright, *Rehousing Urban America* (New York: Columbia University Press, 1935), 6–9.

29. Stein, *Toward New Towns*, chap. 3; Buhl Foundation's Chatham Village Photographs, Senator John Heinz History Center, https://www.heinzhistorycenter.org/detre-library-archives/collection-highlights/buhl-foundation-chatham-village-photographs.

30. Stein, *Toward New Towns*, chap. 3.

31. Clarence S. Stein, Letter to Aline Stein, March 29, 1932, in *The Writings of Clarence S. Stein: Architect of the Planned Community*, ed. Kermit Carlyle Parsons (Baltimore: Johns Hopkins University Press, 1998), 211.

32. Clarence Stein, Letter to Aline Stein, August 9, 1933, in *The Writings of Clarence S. Stein: Architect of the Planned Community*, ed. Kermit Carlyle Parsons (Baltimore: Johns Hopkins University Press, 1998), 229.

6. Foreclosure: The Great Depression and the End of a Dream

1. Nathaniel S. Keith, *Politics and the Housing Crisis Since 1930* (New York: Universe Books, 1973), 13–19.

2. *Mathews Bulletin for 1928*; Franklin J. Sherman, *Building Up Greater Queens Borough: An Estimate of Its Development and the Outlook* (New York: The Brooklyn Biographical Society, 1929), 18–20; Percival Mullikin, "Report Shows 102,000 Apartments Vacant in New York City," *Queensborough* (July 1929): 350.

3. V. H. Vreeland, "President, Real Estate Board Says Future Is Bright," *Queensborough* (September 1929): 404.

4. "New Building Cost below Last Year," *Queensborough* (December 1933): 333; Keith, *Politics and the Housing Crisis*, 25.

5. "300,000 Families in Queens Own Their Own Homes," *Queensborough* (September 1932): 288; "Doubts Inflation Aids Home Owner," *New York Times*, April 23, 1933; Keith, *Housing Crisis*, 24.

6. Daniel Schaffer, *Garden Cities for America: The Radburn Experience* (Philadelphia: Temple University Press, 1982), 193.

7. Clarence S. Stein, *Toward New Towns for America* (Cambridge, Mass.: MIT Press, 1966 [1957]), 35.

8. "First Unit of Sunnyside Colony Is Completed," *Queensborough* (September 1924): 480; Daniel Pearlstein, "Sweeping Six Percent Philanthropy Away: The New Deal in Sunnyside Gardens," *Journal of Planning History* 9, no. 3 (2010): 171–172.

9. "Sunnyside Gardens Showing Activity," *New York Times*, September 28, 1930; Schaffer, *Garden Cities for America*, 191–193.

10. "Owners Seek Reduction," *New York Times*, February 26, 1933; "Seeks Mortgage Change," *New York Times*, February 28, 1933.

11. "Home Owners' Group Lost Half of Income," *New York Times*, March 27, 1933; "Home Owners Ask Relief," *New York Times*, April 6, 1933; Pearlstein, "Sweeping Six Percent," 172.

12. Franklin Delano Roosevelt, Acceptance Speech, Democratic National Convention in Chicago, July 2, 1932.

13. "Asks Aid to Home Owners," *New York Times*, July 17, 1933; "Mortgage Relief Urged on Lehman," *New York Times*, August 2, 1933; "Legislature Quits; Liquor Bills Pass; Recovery,

Mortgage Relief, and Anti-Gangster Measures Approved in Stormy Close," *New York Times*, August 25, 1933; Pearlstein, "Sweeping Six Percent," 174–175.

14. "Housing Group in Bankruptcy," *New York Times*, August 2, 1934; Schaffer, *Garden Cities for America*, 196–197; Pearlstein, "Sweeping Six Percent," 175. The bankruptcy papers of the City Housing Corporation are in the archives of the U.S. District Court for the Southern District of New York, National Archives, Northeast Region.

15. "Sunnyside Begins 'Mortgage Strike,'" *New York Times*, April 17, 1933; Schaffer, *Garden Cities for America*, 196–199.

16. Mark Naison, "From Eviction Resistance to Rent Control: Tenant Activism in the Great Depression," in *The Tenant Movement in New York City, 1904–1984*, ed. Ronald Lawson (New Brunswick, N.J.: Rutgers University Press, 1986), 94–133.

17. *The Communist Election Platform, 1936* (Workers Library Publishers, 1936).

18. David Horowitz, *Radical Son: A Journey Through Our Times* (New York: Free Press, 1997), 36–39; Ruth Horowitz, "Sycamore Trees and Courtyards," 2016, Queens Memory Collection at the Archives at the Queens Library.

19. Schaffer, *Garden Cities for America*, 197–198.

20. Loula Lasker, "Sunnyside Up and Down," *Survey Graphic* 25 (July 1936); "Mortgage Strike Is Voted in Queens," *New York Times*, March 25, 1935.

21. "Meets Sunnyside Group," *New York Times*, March 31, 1935; Pearlstein, "Sweeping Six Percent," 173; Kenneth T. Jackson, *Crabgrass Frontier: The Suburbanization of the United States* (New York: Oxford University Press, 1985), 196–203.

22. "Sophie Mumford: Green Memories," *The Sunnyside Gardener*, vol. III, no. 1 (Winter/Spring 1984); Donald L. Miller, *Lewis Mumford: A Life* (Pittsburgh: University of Pittsburgh Press, 1989), 376–377. Oddly, Miller makes no mention of the mortgage strike, even as he discussed Mumford's reaction to the Great Depression and his sympathies toward radical approaches to the crisis (chapter 15).

23. "Mortgage 'Strike' Answered by Suits," *New York Times*, April 11, 1935; Pearlstein, "Sweeping Six Percent," 175–176.

24. "Sunnyside Homes Face More Suits," *New York Times*, April 15, 1935.

25. "Mortgage 'Strike' Answered by Suits," *New York Times*, April 11, 1935.

26. "Mortgage Strikers Rebuffed in Court," *New York Times*, April 16, 1935; "Seeks Sunnyside Plan," *New York Times*, April 30, 1935; Schaffer, *Garden Cities for America*, 199.

27. "Sunnyside Group of Home Owners Asks Lehman Aid," *Long Island Daily Star*, October 21, 1935.

28. "Picket Insurance Office," *New York Times*, November 10, 1935; "269 Owners Sue Housing Company," *New York Times*, November 15, 1935; "Summons Is Served," *New York Times*, December 4, 1935.

29. "Sunnyside Residents Sing and Dance with Brooms to Protest Foreclosures," *New York Times*, December 20, 1935.

30. "City Official Holds 'Wake' for Home in Sunnyside," *New York Times*, August 10, 1936; "1,000 at 'Funeral' of Sunnyside Home," *New York Times*, August 11, 1936.

31. "Mortgage Fight Pushed," *New York Times*, April 12, 1935; Judith Steele, "A Family of Caring Neighbors," *Newsday*, March 18, 1979.

32. "2 Sunnyside Homes Sold," *New York Times*, February 6, 1936; "Notables 'Invited' to Queens Eviction," *New York Times*, February 10, 1936; "Sunnyside Writ Studied," *New York Times*, March 10, 1936; "Sunnyside Crowd Jeers at Eviction," *New York Times*, March 11, 1936.

33. *Gilleeny v. Bing*, 256 A.D. 951, February 28, 1939.

34. "Stay of Eviction Sought," *New York Times*, January 13, 1936; "Sunnyside Eviction Delayed," *New York Times*, January 14, 1936; "6 Seized Fighting Eviction of Family," *New York Times*, January 26, 1936; "Sunnyside Owners Seek Eviction Stay," *New York Times*, January 27, 1936; Pearlstein, "Sweeping Six Percent," 176–178.

35. "Sunnyside Group Loses," *New York Times*, January 15, 1936; "Lehman Keeps Aloof from Sunnyside Case," *New York Times*, January 29, 1936.

36. "10 Lose Sunnyside Homes," *New York Times*, March 13, 1936 "Sunnyside Writ Issued," *New York Times*, June 24, 1936; Schaffer, *Garden Cities for America*, 200–201.

37. "Sunnyside Owners Get 40% Cut Offer," *New York Times*, May 1, 1936; Pearlstein, "Sweeping Six Percent," 178.

38. "Sunnyside Families Picket the Equitable," *New York Times*, July 31, 1936.

39. Oral History Interview with Charles Ascher, 1972, interviewed by Tom Hogan. The Columbia Center for Oral History (New York: Trustees of Columbia University in the City of New York, 1982), 247, 595; Schaffer, *Garden Cities for America*, 202–208. There are no stories in the *New York Times* about foreclosures or evictions in Radburn.

40. Stein, *Toward New Towns*, 35.

7. Envisioning the Future City

1. "Wants Great Funds to Finance Housing," *New York Times*, April 15, 1926, 18.

2. Clarence S. Stein, "New Towns for the Needs of a New Age," *New York Times*, October 8, 1933.

3. Stein, "New Towns."

4. Stein, "New Towns."

5. Stein, "New Towns."

6. Harold L. Ickes, *Back to Work: The Story of the PWA* (New York: Da Capo Press, 1973 [1935]), 182; Howard Gillette, *Civitas by Design: Building Better Communities, from the Garden City to the New Urbanism* (Philadelphia: University of Pennsylvania Press, 2010), Ch. 1.

7. William E. Leuchtenburg, *Franklin D. Roosevelt and the New Deal* (New York: Harper and Row, 1963), 134.

8. Harold L. Ickes, "The Housing Policy of the PWA," *Architectural Forum* (February 1934): 92; Robert D. Kohn, "The Government Housing Program," *Architectural Forum* (February 1934): 88–91; Ickes, *Back to Work*, 183, 190.

9. Frederick L. Ackerman, "Controlling Factors in Slum Clearance and Housing," *Architectural Forum* (February 1934): 94; Ickes, "Housing Policy of the PWA," 92; Kohn, "Government Housing Program," 88–91; "Robert D. Kohn, 83, A Noted Architect," *New York Times*, June 17, 1953.

10. Ickes, *Back to Work*, 190; Gail Radford, *Modern Housing for America: Policy Struggles in the New Deal Era* (Chicago: University of Chicago Press, 1996), chaps. 4 and 6.

11. Clarence S. Stein, Letter to Aline Stein, April 13, 1932; Letter to Lewis Mumford, July 11, 1932, in *The Writings of Clarence S. Stein*, ed. Kermit Carlyle Parsons (Baltimore: Johns Hopkins University Press, 1998), 214, 229; Kristin E. Larsen, *Community Architect: The Life and Vision of Clarence S. Stein* (Ithaca, N.Y.: Cornell University Press, 2016), 11.

12. Stein, Letter to Lewis Mumford, 229.

13. Housing Division, Federal Emergency Administration of Public Works, Bulletin No. 2, "Urban Housing: The Story of the PWA Housing Division, 1933–1936 (Washington, D.C.: Government Printing Office, August 1936), 81; Clarence S. Stein, *Toward New Towns for*

America (Cambridge, Mass.: MIT Press, 1966 [1957]), chap. 5; Robert A. M. Stern, David Fishman, and Jacob Tilove, *Paradise Planned: The Garden Suburb and the Modern City* (New York: Monacelli Press, 2013), 194–196.

14. Cord Meyer Development Company, "Kelvin Apartments in Forest Hills, Long Island," Forest Hills: [1928].

15. Boulevard Gardens Buyers Committee, "Boulevard Gardens," Woodside, Queens, 1991, 4–8, 12–13.

16. Lewis Mumford, "The New Housing," *New Yorker*, December 7, 1935, reprinted in *Sidewalk Critic: Lewis Mumford's Writings on New York*, ed. Robert Wojtowicz (New York: Princeton Architectural Press, 1998), 144–145.

17. *The Boulevard Gardens Beacon*, Vol. 1, No. 1, October 26, 1935.

18. "Governor Opens Hillside Homes," *New York Times*, June 30, 1935; "Hillside Homes 99% Rented," *New York Times*, April 4, 1936.

19. "Governor Opens Hillside Homes," *New York Times*, June 30, 1935.

20. Clarence S. Stein, Speech at the Dedication of Hillside Homes, June 29, 1935, in *The Writings of Clarence S. Stein*, ed. Kermit Carlyle (Baltimore: Johns Hopkins University Press, 1998), 311.

21. Stein, Speech, 311.

22. John Tierney, "The Big City; Coming Closer to a Utopia in the Bronx," *New York Times*, March 18, 2000.

23. Clarence Stein, Letter to Aline Stein, October 24, 1935, in *The Writings of Clarence S. Stein*, ed. Kermit Carlyle Parsons (Baltimore: Johns Hopkins University Press, 1998), 326; Stein, Letter to Aline Stein, 364.

24. Carl Abbott, "*Our Cities* and *The City*: Incompatible Classics?" *Planning Perspectives* 27, no. 1 (January 2012): 103–19; Howard Gillette, "Film as Artifact: *The City* (1939)," *American Studies* 18, no. 2 (1977): 71–85.

25. Lewis Mumford, *The Brown Decades: A Study of the Arts in America, 1865–1895* (New York: Dover Publications, Inc., 1971 [1931]), 36.

26. Clarence S. Stein, "Dinosaur Cities," *Survey Graphic*, May 1925, reprinted in *Planning the Fourth Migration: the Neglected Vision of the Regional Planning Association of America*, ed. Carl Sussman (Cambridge, Mass.: MIT Press, 1976), 65–74.

27. Gillette, "Film as Artifact."

28. Mel Scott, *American City Planning Since 1890* (Berkeley: University of California Press, 1969), 362–363.

29. Kristin E. Larsen, "Cities to Come: Clarence Stein's Postwar Regionalism," *Journal of Planning History* 4, no. 1 (February 2005): 33–51.

8. Preserving the Historic Garden Suburb in London and New York

1. Lewis Mumford, "The Garden City Idea and Modern Planning," in *Garden Cities of To-Morrow* by Ebenezer Howard (Cambridge, Mass.: MIT Press, 1965), 29.

2. Hampstead Garden Suburb Residents Association, "How Lucky We Are To Live Here," n.d.

3. Eric Allison and Lauren Peters, *Historic Preservation and the Livable City* (Hoboken, N.J.: John Wiley & Sons, 2011), 164.

4. Typical of this approach would be Stanley Buder, *Visionaries and Planners: The Garden City Movement and the Modern Community* (New York: Oxford University Press, 1990); and

Daniel Shaffer, *Garden Cities for America: The Radburn Experience* (Philadelphia: Temple University Press, 1982). Even *Paradise Planned: The Garden Suburb and the Modern City* by Robert A. M. Stern, David Fishman, and Jacob Tilove (New York: Monacelli Press, 2013) limits its scope to design and planning, not preservation. An exception is Mary Corbin Sies, Isabelle Gournay, and Robert Freestone, eds., *Iconic Planned Communities and the Challenge of Change* (Philadelphia: University of Pennsylvania Press, 2019).

5. Raymond Unwin, *Town Planning in Practice: An Introduction to the Art of Designing Cities and Suburbs* (New York: Benjamin Blom, Inc., 1971 [London: 1909; second edition 1934]), 364.

6. Frederic J. Osborn, *Green-Belt Cities* (New York: Shocken Books, 1969 [1946]), 74–75, 99–100.

7. Mervyn Miller, *Letchworth: The First Garden City* (Chichester, Sussex: Phillimore & Co. Ltd, 1989).

8. Letchworth Garden City Heritage Foundation, "A Brief History," https://www.letchworth .com/who-we-are/about-us.

9. Letchworth Garden City Heritage Foundation, "Our Objectives," https://www.letchworth .com/who-we-are/about-us.

10. Letchworth Garden City Heritage Foundation, "Strategic Plan, October 2011 to September 2016," www.letchworth.com.

11. Welwyn Hatfield Borough Council, Welwyn Garden City Estate Management Scheme, www.welhat.gov.uk.

12. Susan Hall, "20 million plan to rebuild homes," Our Welwyn Garden City, http://www .ourwelwyngardencity.org.uk/page_id__538_path__0p162p.aspx.

13. Hampstead Garden Suburb Trust, "Hampstead Garden Suburb Conservation Area: Design Guidance," n.d.; Unwin, *Town Planning in Practice*, 364.

14. Leasehold Reform Act 1967, http://www.legislation.gov.uk/ukpga/1967/88/enacted.

15. Hampstead Garden Suburb Scheme of Management, Approved pursuant to the Leasehold Reform Act 1967, by an Order of the Chancery Division of the High Court, dated January 17, 1974, as amended by a further Order dated February 17, 1983.

16. *The Trust Gazette*, 2010.

17. Miller, *Letchworth*.

18. Adam Fergusson, *The Sack of Bath* (London: Persephone Books, 1973).

19. Liverpool Heritage Bureau, *Buildings of Liverpool* (Liverpool: The Bureau, 1978).

20. Mervyn Miller, "English Garden Cities: Challenges of Conservation and Change," in *Iconic Planned Communities and the Challenge of Change*, ed. Mary Corbin Sies, Isabelle Gournay, and Robert Freestone(Philadelphia: University of Pennsylvania Press, 2019), 61–87; Historic England, https://historicengland.org.uk/.

21. Miller, *Letchworth*.

22. Miller, "English Garden Cities," 61–87; Gervase Webb, "Why They Listed This Eden That Is Hampstead's Garden," *Evening Standard* (London), November 29, 1996.

23. Miller, 61–87.

24. *Suburb News*, 2012.

25. Miller, 61–87.

26. Hampstead Garden Suburb Trust, "Report and Accounts for the Year 5 April 2010."

27. Chris Brooke, "Your Gates Must Go; Lawyer Ordered To Remove Barriers Put Up To Protect His Family After Four Robberies at His Luxury Home," *Daily Mail* (London), June 19, 2002.

28. Jane Blackburn, "Trust Wins Landmark Case," *Suburb News* no. 104 (Autumn 2010).

29. Miller, 61–87.

30. Andrew Lainton, "Battle Over the Very First Green Belt at Letchworth," February 25, 2015, https://andrewlainton.wordpress.com/2015/02/25/battle-over-the-very-first-green-belt-at-letchworth/.

31. Lainton, "First Green Belt at Letchworth."

32. Anthony C. Wood, "'Preserving the Patrimony of the People': Albert S. Bard and the Landmarks Law," *City Courant* (Spring 2015): 6–15. For a complete account of preservation efforts before passage of the law, see Anthony C. Wood, *Preserving New York: Winning the Right to Protect a City's Landmarks* (New York: Routledge, 2008).

33. Robert A. M. Stern, *The Anglo-American Suburb* (London: Architectural Design, 1981), 34.

34. Forest Hills Gardens Corporation, "Architecture and Construction Procedures and Guidelines" (Forest Hills: The Corporation, 2002), 3; Charles S. Ascher, "Private Covenants in Urban Redevelopment," in *Urban Redevelopment: Problems and Practices*, ed. Coleman Woodbury (Chicago: University of Chicago Press, 1953), 232.

35. Forest Hills Gardens Corporation, http://foresthillsgardens.org/.

36. Forest Hills Gardens Corporation, "Architecture and Construction Procedures and Guidelines" (Forest Hills: The Corporation, 2002), 4, 6, 12, 16.

37. New York City Landmarks Preservation Commission, http://www1.nyc.gov/site/lpc/about/about-lpc.page.

38. Barry Lewis, *Kew Gardens: Urban Village in the Big City* (Kew Gardens: Kew Gardens Council for Recreation and the Arts, 1999), vii, 23, 29–53.

39. Historic Districts Council, 19th Annual Preservation Conference: Preservation Now!, March 2013, http://hdc.org/program-events/19th-annual-conference/presentations/donald-brennan.

40. Daniel Karatzas, *Jackson Heights, A Garden in the City: The History of America's First Garden and Cooperative Community* (Jackson Heights: Jackson Heights Beautification Group, 1990).

41. Robert A. M. Stern, Gregory Gilmartin, and Thomas Mellins, *New York 1930: Architecture and Urbanism Between the Two World Wars* (New York: Rizzoli, 1987), 479–485; Richard Plunz, *A History of Housing in New York City: Dwelling Type and Social Change in the American Metropolis* (New York: Columbia University Press, 1990), 147.

42. Karatzas, *Jackson Heights*, ix; Local Laws for the City of New York for the Year 1980, No. 10, www.nyc.gov/html/dob/downloads/pdf/ll_1080.pdf.

43. Jackson Heights Beautification Group, http://www.jhbg.org/resources/history.

44. New York City Landmarks Preservation Commission, *Jackson Heights Historic District* (New York: the Commission, 1993), http://s-media.nyc.gov/agencies/lpc/lp/1831.pdf.

9. Preserving Sunnyside Gardens

1. Oral History Interview with Charles Ascher, 1972, interviewed by Tom Hogan, the Columbia Center for Oral History (New York: Trustees of Columbia University in the City of New York, 1982), 170–179.

2. Franklin Havelick and Michael Kwartler, "Sunnyside Gardens: Whose Land Is It Anyway?," *New York Affairs* 7, no. 2 (1982): 72–73.

3. Oral History Interview with Charles Ascher, 177–179.

4. Havelick and Kwartler, "Whose Land Is It Anyway?," 73.

5. Havelick and Kwartler, "Whose Land Is It Anyway?," 72–74.

6. Havelick and Kwartler, "Whose Land Is It Anyway?," 76–77.

7. New York City Planning Commission, "Amendment of the Zoning resolution, pursuant to Section 200 of the New York City Charter, relating to Article X, Chapter 3, concerning the establishment of a Special Planned Community Preservation District, CP-22501," June 12, 1974.

8. Pranay Gupte, "Planners Acting on 'Preservation,'" *New York Times*, November 4, 1973.

9. Elliot Willensky and Norval White, *AIA Guide to New York City*, Third Edition (New York: Harcourt Brace Jovanovich, 1988), 539–540, 773; Pranay Gupte, "Planners Acting"; Pranay Gupte, "Planners Seek to Preserve 2 Neighborhoods in Queens," *New York Times*, November 4, 1973; Glenn Fowler, "Planners Back 2 Queens Zones," *New York Times*, June 16, 1974; Robert E. Thomasson, "Ownership Change Unsettles Fresh Meadows," *New York Times*, May 20, 1973; City Planning Commission, CP-22501, June 12, 1974.

10. Gupte, "Planners Acting"; Gupte, "Neighborhoods in Queens."

11. Phyllis Funke, "Preservation Urged by Parkway Village," *New York Times*, December 9, 1973.

12. Gupte, "Neighborhoods in Queens"; George White, "Sunnyside Gardens and Fresh Meadows Residents Are Wary of New Zoning," *New York Times*, September 1, 1974.

13. "Islands of Amenity," *New York Times*, June 26, 1974.

14. White, "Residents Are Wary"; Department of City Planning, City of New York, "Sunnyside Gardens: A Fact Sheet for Residents," [1975]; Havelick and Kwartler, "Whose Land Is It Anyway?," 75–76.

15. "A Curb Cut Stirs Dispute," *New York Times*, September 8, 1991; Clarie Serant, "Park by House? No (Drive) Way," *Daily News*, April 1, 1993; "Again, an Illegal Driveway Touches Nerves," *New York Times*, October 2, 1994.

16. Tom Robbins, "The Democratic Vision of Sunnyside Gardens," *City Limits*, Vol. X, no. 3 (March 1985): 16.

17. Robbins, "Democratic Vision," 19.

18. Bernard Rabin, "Conservancy Gets Award of Parks Council," *Daily News*, October 9, 1983; Robbins, "Democratic Vision," 18.

19. *Sunnyside Gardener*, Spring 1986.

20. Janet Diehl and Thomas S. Barrett, *The Conservation Easement Handbook: Managing Land Conservation and Historic Preservation Easement Programs* (San Francisco: Trust for Public Land, 1988), 5. The Sunnyside Foundation's program was cited in Andrew Dana and Michael Ramsey, "Conservation Easements and the Common Law," *Stanford Environmental Law Journal* 8 (1989): 5.

21. *Sunnyside Gardener*, Spring 1986; Havelick and Kwartler, "Whose Land Is It Anyway?," 76–79.

22. Nina Rappaport, "Excerpts from National Register Application," *Sunnyside Gardener*, Winter/Spring 1984; National Register Digital Assets, National Park Service, U.S. Department of the Interior, http://focus.nps.gov/AssetDetail/NRIS/84002919.

23. Rabin, "Conservancy Gets Award," 3; Havelick and Kwartler, "Whose Land Is It Anyway?," 78; Jeffrey A. Kroessler and Nina Rappaport, *Historic Preservation in Queens* (Queensborough Preservation League, 1988), 22. The six designations turned back under Manes were: Loew's Triboro Theatre, Astoria, 1974; Jamaica Savings Bank, Jamaica, 1974; Steinway Historic District, 1975; Congregation Derech Emunoh Synagogue, Rockaway, 1978; First Reformed Church, Jamaica, 1979; LaLance & Grosjean Historic District, Woodhaven, 1981.

24. Robbins, "Democratic Vision," 18–19.

25. Robbins, "Democratic Vision," 16–17.

26. Charles S. Ascher, "Remarks on the Designation of Radburn as a Historic Landmark, 4 October, 1975," http://www.alnnj.org/Radburn.html; Daniel Schaffer, *Garden Cities for America: The Radburn Experience* (Philadelphia: Temple University Press, 1982), 151.

27. Linda Flint McClelland, Paula S. Reed, and Edith B. Wallace, "Revisiting Radburn: 'Where Art and Nature Combine To Make Good Living Conditions,'" *New Jersey History* 123, no. 1–2 (Spring–Summer 2005).

28. City Housing Corporation, "Declaration of Restrictions No. 1 Affecting Radburn, Property of the City Housing Corporation, in the Borough of Fair Lawn, Bergen County, New Jersey. Dated March 15, 1929," ([New York]: City Housing Corporation, 1929), http://www .alnnj.org/Radburn.html; Edith B. Wallace and Paula S. Reed, National Historic Landmark Nomination, June 2004; National Park Service, www.nps.gov/nhl/find/statelists/nj/Radburn.pdf.

29. Schaffer, *Garden Cities for America*, 177–187.

30. Charles S. Ascher, "The Extra-Municipal Administration of Radburn: An Experiment in Government by Contract," *National Municipal Review*, July 1929, 442–446.

31. City Housing Corporation, "Declaration of Restrictions No. 1 Affecting Radburn," 5–6.

32. City Housing Corporation, "Declaration of Restrictions No. 1 Affecting Radburn," 12.

33. Clarence S. Stein, *Toward New Towns for America* (Cambridge, Mass.: MIT Press, 1966 [1957]), 73.

34. Ascher, "Remarks on the Designation of Radburn."

35. Charles S. Ascher, "Private Covenants in Urban Redevelopment," in *Urban Redevelopment: Problems and Practices*, ed. Coleman Woodbury (Chicago: University of Chicago Press, 1953), 293–295; Schaffer, *Garden Cities for America*, 183–184.

36. Ascher, "Private Covenants in Urban Redevelopment," 293–295; Charles Ascher, "Reflections on the Art of Administering Deed Restrictions." *The Journal of Land & Public Utility Economics* 8, no. 4 (1932): 373–377; Charles Ascher, "The Radburn Story," oral history interview by F. C. McMullen, Dec. 7, 1970, Ascher Papers, Columbia University, Box 25, Radburn folder 1.

37. The Radburn Association, http://www.radburn.org/; Wallace and Reed, National Historic Landmark Nomination.

38. Robert C. Cooper, "It's 'historic' Radburn," *The Sunday Record*, October 5, 1975.

10. The Fight for the Historic District

1. Marc Ferris, "Trouble in Paradise," *Newsday*, November 4, 2003.

2. Sunnyside Gardens Preservation Alliance, http://sunnysidegardens.us/; Historic Districts Council, http://hdc.org/.

3. Elliot Willensky and Norval White, *AIA Guide to New York City*, Third Edition (New York: Harcourt Brace Jovanovich, 1988), 743.

4. Preserve Sunnyside Gardens, "Frequently Unanswered Questions about Landmarking Sunnyside Gardens," 2007; Ellen Barry, "Area of Sunnyside, Queens, Is Given Landmark Status," *New York Times*, June 27, 2007; Tom Cogan, "Sunnyside Gardens' Status Gets Mixed Reaction," *Queens Gazette*, July 25, 2007; *Brian Lehrer Show*, WNYC, "Cloud Over Sunnyside?," March 7, 2007, http://www.wnyc.org/story/24643-cloud-over-sunnyside/; Jennifer Polland, "First Step Made in Hot Landmark Case," *Queens Tribune*, March 1, 2007; Tom

Angotti, "Sunnyside Fights Over What to Preserve," *Gotham Gazette*, April 11, 2007, http://www
.gothamgazette.com/index.php/development/3525-sunnyside-fights-over-what-to-preserve.

5. Preserve Sunnyside Gardens, "Frequently Unanswered Questions about Landmarking;"
Angotti, "Sunnyside Fights."

6. Tom Angotti, "The Real Estate Market in the United States: Progressive Strategies,"
Unpublished paper, December 1999, Google Scholar, accessed November 2, 2015.

7. Angotti, "Sunnyside Fights."

8. Erin Durkin, "Historic Vote for Queens Neighborhood," *New York Sun*, June 27, 2007.

9. Angotti, "Sunnyside Fights."

10. WNYC radio host Brian Lehrer hosted a discussion with Susan Turner-Meiklejohn
and Jeffrey Kroessler. "Cloud Over Sunnyside?" Warren Lehrer, an outspoken opponent of
designation, was Brian's brother.

11. See for example Suleiman Osman, *The Invention of Brownstone Brooklyn: Gentrification
and the Search for Authenticity in Postwar New York* (New York: Oxford University Press,
2012).

12. Angotti, "Sunnyside Fights."

13. Preserve Sunnyside Gardens, "Frequently Unanswered Questions about Landmarking."

14. Angotti, "Sunnyside Fights."

15. Polland, "First Step Made in Hot Landmark Case"; Jeff Vandam, "Brick Houses,
Windings Paths and Unexpected Sharp Elbows," *New York Times*, December 31, 2006; Ellen
Barry, "Area of Sunnyside, Queens, Is Given Landmark Status," *New York Times*, June 27, 2007;
Tom Topousis, "Tiff Clouds Sunnyside," *New York Post*, March 12, 2007, http://hdc.org/queens
-2/some-more-sunnyside-press.

16. Nik Kovac, "Two (Sunny)Sides to Every Story," *Glendale Register*, March 22, 2007.

17. Adam Pincus, "Landmarks Set Hearing Date for Sunnyside Gardens," *Times-Ledger*,
March 8, 2007; New York City Landmarks Preservation Commission, *Sunnyside Gardens
Historic District Designation* (New York: the Commission, 2007), http://www.nyc.gov/html/lpc
/downloads/pdf/reports/SunnysideGardens.pdf.

18. Jennifer Manley, "Sunnyside's Garden City Earns Designation," *Queens Chronicle*,
June 28, 2007.

19. Manley, "Sunnyside's Garden City"; Magdalene Perez, "A Landmark Approval,"
Newsday, June 27, 2007.

20. Kovac, "Two (Sunny)Sides to Every Story."

21. "Trading on Long Island, City Housing Corporation Sells Blockfront at Sunnyside," *New
York Times*, May 11, 1931.

22. http://www.realtor.com/realestateandhomes-search/11104; *Corcoran Report*, "Sunnyside,
Q2 2019 Market Report," 2019.

23. Statement of the Historic Districts Council Before the City Council Subcommittee on
Zoning and Franchises Regarding the Proposed Change to the Sunnyside Gardens Special
Planned Community District Zoning," June 2, 2009, http://hdc.org/uncategorized/hdc-on-the
-proposed-sunnyside-gardens-rezoning.

24. Landmarks Preservation Commission, *Sunnyside Gardens Historic District Designation*.

25. Landmarks Preservation Commission, "Proposed Alterations and New Construction
of Storefronts in the Jackson Heights Historic District" (New York: the Commission, n.d.),
https://www1.nyc.gov/assets/lpc/downloads/pdf/pubs/JH_English.pdf; Landmarks Preservation
Commission, "District Master Plan for the Douglaston Historic District" (New York: the
Commission, n.d.), https://www1.nyc.gov/assets/lpc/downloads/pdf/pubs/douglaston.pdf.

26. Landmarks Preservation Commission, "Doing Work in Sunnyside Gardens: A Homeowners Guide to the Landmarks Preservation Commission Rules" (New York: the Commission, 2009), 1. https://www1.nyc.gov/assets/lpc/downloads/pdf/pubs/ssg_manual _september_09.pdf.

27. Landmarks Preservation Commission, "Doing Work in Sunnyside Gardens," 4–5.

28. Landmarks Preservation Commission, "Doing Work in Sunnyside Gardens," 9.

29. Municipal Archives, New York City Department of Records and Information Services, https://www1.nyc.gov/site/records/about/municipal-archives.page.

30. Laura Heim Architect, http://heimarchitect.com/hamilton-court-dormer-sunnyside/.

31. Laura Heim Architect, http://heimarchitect.com/sunnyside-porches/.

32. Laura Heim Architect, http://heimarchitect.com/skillman-avenue-residence-sunnyside/.

11. A Question of Appropriateness: The Aluminaire House Controversy

1. Francoise Astorg Bollack, "Defining Appropriateness," in *Saving Place: 50 Years of New York City Landmarks*, ed. Donald Albrecht, Andrew S. Dolkart, and Seri Worden (New York: Monacelli Press, 2015), 125–126.

2. "Empire State Wins Architects' Award," *New York Times*, April 22, 1931.

3. Paul Goldberger, "Icon of Modernism Poised for Extinction," *New York Times*, March 8, 1987.

4. Lewis Mumford, "Mass-Production and Housing," *Architectural Record* (January-February 1930), reprinted in *City Development: Studies in Disintegration and Renewal* (London: Secker & Warburg, 1946), 58–59.

5. Mumford, "Mass-Production and Housing," 59–61, 64.

6. Frederick P. Keppel and R. L. Duffus, *The Arts in American Life* (New York: McGraw-Hill Book Company, Inc., 1933), 111–112.

7. "Landscape Medal Goes to G. D. Clarke," *New York Times*, April 23, 1931.

8. Edward Alden Jewell, "Panorama of Current Week of Art in New York: A Stir Is Caused by Secessionists Who Have Put on a 'Rejected Architects' Show," *New York Times*, April 26, 1931.

9. The Aluminaire Foundation, http://www.aluminaire.org/history/.

10. Keppel and Duffus, *Arts in American Life*, 90–93, 103.

11. Keppel and Duffus, *Arts in American Life*, 110–111.

12. Keppel and Duffus, *Arts in American Life*, 112.

13. The Aluminaire Foundation, History; Goldberger, "Icon of Modernism."

14. The Aluminaire Foundation, History; Goldberger, "Icon of Modernism."

15. The Aluminaire Foundation, History; Goldberger, "Icon of Modernism."

16. The Aluminaire Foundation, History.

17. Real Estate Board of New York, *An Analysis of Landmarked Properties in Manhattan* (New York: REBNY, June 2013), 1–2.

18. Kenneth K. Fisher, Interview by Jeffrey A. Kroessler, October 15, 2015.

19. Fisher interview.

20. Fisher interview.

21. "243 Broome Street and 97–99 Ludlow Street," *Architectural Record*, n.d., http:// archrecord.construction.com/projects/bts/archives/multifamhousing/10_Ludlow_Lofts/.

22. Fisher interview.

23. Clare Trapasso, "Metal of Dishonor, Steel House Relocation Postponed," *New York Daily News*, June 21, 2013.

24. Christian Murray, "Van Bramer to Block Phipps' 210 Unit Development Plan, Essentially Kills Proposal," *Sunnyside Post*, May 31, 2016, https://sunnysidepost.com/van-bramer-to-block-phipps-210-unit-development-plan-essentially-kills-proposal.

25. David Dunlap, "In Queens, Now May Not Be Time for an Old House of the Future," *New York Times*, September 18, 2013.

26. Thaisa Way and Michael Gotkin, "Threat to Rare Progressive-Era Playground Is Big Threat to Valuable Open Space," The Cultural Landscape Foundation, October 11, 2013, http://tclf.org/landslides/vote-determine-fate-of-progressive-era-playground.

27. Emily Nonko, "Sunnyside Gardens Residents Air Complaints about Aluminaire House Proposal," *Brownstoner Queens*, September 13, 2013, http://queens.brownstoner.com/2013/09/sunnyside-gardens-residents-air-complaints-about-aluminaire-house-proposal/.

28. Gabby Warshawer, "Dispute Takes Shine Off Aluminaire House," *Wall Street Journal*, October 9, 2013.

29. Christian Murray, "Aluminaire House Is Wanted: Mayor of Palm Springs Plans to Bring It There," *Sunnyside Post*, February 19, 2015, http://sunnysidepost.com/2015/02/19/aluminaire-house-is-wanted-mayor-of-palm-springs-plans-to-bring-it-there/.

30. The author and his wife, Laura Heim, testified in favor of locating the Aluminaire House in Sunnyside.

31. Historic Districts Council, E-Bulletin: Aluminaire House Testimony, October 11, 2013, http://hdc.org/blog/e-bulletin-aluminaire-house-testimony.

32. Historic Districts Council, E-Bulletin: Aluminaire House Testimony.

33. Andrew Scott Dolkart, Letter to LPC Chair Robert Tierney, June 1, 2013; Marta Gutman, Testimony, August 25, 2013.

34. Fisher interview; Christian Murray, "Landmarks Commission Rejects Aluminaire House Proposal," *Sunnyside Post*, January 17, 2014, http://sunnysidepost.com/2014/01/17/landmarks-commission-rejects-aluminaire-house-proposal/.

35. Aluminaire Foundation; "Palm Springs Becomes Home to Albert Frey's 1931 Aluminaire House," *Palm Springs Life*, March 2015, http://www.palmspringslife.com/Palm-Springs-Life/Desert-Guide/March-2015/Palm-Springs-Becomes-Home-to-Albert-Freys-1931-Aluminaire-House/; Murray, "Aluminaire House Is Wanted.

36. Fisher interview.

37. "Former Phipps Playground Expected to Become City Park, Van Bramer Says," *Sunnyside Post*, June 14, 2016, https://sunnysidepost.com/former-phipps-playground-expected-to-become-city-park-van-bramer-says.

Conclusion: A Second Century for the Garden Suburb

1. Arthur C. Comey and Max S. Wehrly, "A Study of Planned Communities," (Department of Regional Planning of Harvard University, November 1936), quoted in *Paradise Planned: The Garden Suburb and the Modern City*, ed. Robert A. M. Stern, David Fishman, and Jacob Tilove (New York: Monacelli Press, 2013), 867.

2. Ada Louise Huxtable, "Clarence Stein: The Champion of the Neighborhood," *New York Times*, January 16, 1977.

3. Lewis Mumford, "Neighborhood and Neighborhood Unit," *Town Planning Review*, January 1954, reprinted in *The Urban Prospect* (New York: Harcourt, Brace & World, 1968), 91.

4. Robert A. M. Stern, David Fishman, and Jacob Tilove, *Paradise Planned: The Garden Suburb and the Modern City* (New York: Monacelli Press, 2013), 941–961.

5. Emily Talen, *New Urbanism & American Planning: The Conflict of Cultures* (New York: Routledge, 2005), 11; Emily Talen, "Beyond the Front Porch: Regionalist Ideals in the New Urbanist Movement," *Journal of Planning History* 7, no. 1, February 2008, 20–47.

6. Stern, et al., *Paradise Planned*, 11; Andres Duany, Elizabeth Plater-Zyberk, and Jeff Speck, *Suburban Nation: The Rise of Sprawl and the Decline of the American Dream* (New York: North Point Press, 2000). Robert Fishman makes the same point in "The Bounded City," in *From Garden City to Green City*, ed. Kermit C. Parsons and David Schuyler (Baltimore: Johns Hopkins University Press, 2002), 66.

7. Emily Talen, "Just Seaside," in *Views of Seaside: Commentaries and Observations on a City of Ideas*, ed. Andres Duany, et al. (New York: Rizzoli, 2008), 177–179.

8. The Charter for the New Urbanism, 1996; William Fulton, *The New Urbanism: Hope or Hype for American Communities* (Cambridge, Mass.: Lincoln Institute of Land Policy, 1996), 1–3; John A. Dutton, *New American Urbanism: Re-forming the Suburban Metropolis* (Milan, Italy: Skira editore, 2000), 16–17.

9. *PlaNYC: A Greener, Greater New York* (New York: City of New York, 2007), http://www.nyc.gov/html/planyc/downloads/pdf/publications/full_report_2007.pdf.

10. Department of City Planning, Mandatory Inclusionary Housing, New York, 2016, https://www1.nyc.gov/site/planning/plans/mih/mandatory-inclusionary-housing.page; Department of City Planning, Zoning for Quality and Affordability, New York, 2016, https://www1.nyc.gov/site/planning/plans/zqa/zoning-for-quality-and-affordability.page.

11. Municipal Art Society, *A Tale of Two Rezonings: Taking a Harder Look at CEQR* (New York: The Society, 2018) https://www.mas.org/wp-content/uploads/2018/11/ceqr-report-2018.pdf.

BIBLIOGRAPHY

Books

Albrecht, Donald, Andrew S. Dolkart, and Seri Worden, eds. *Saving Place: 50 Years of New York City Landmarks*. New York: Monacelli Press, 2015.

Allison, Eric, and Lauren Peters, *Historic Preservation and the Livable City*. Hoboken, N.J.: John Wiley & Sons, 2011.

Bauer, Catherine. *Modern Housing*. Boston, N.Y.: Houghton Mifflin Company, 1934.

Buder, Stanley. *Visionaries and Planners: The Garden City Movement and the Modern Community*. New York: Oxford University Press, 1990.

Byers, Pam. *Small Town in the Big City: A History of Sunnyside and Woodside*. Sunnyside Community Center, 1976.

Christensen, Carol A. *The American Garden City and the New Towns Movement*. Ann Arbor, Mich.: UMI Research Press, 1986.

Diehl, Janet, and Thomas S. Barrett. *The Conservation Easement Handbook: Managing Land Conservation and Historic Preservation Easement Programs*. San Francisco: Trust for Public Land, 1988.

Duany, Andres, et al. *Views of Seaside: Commentaries and Observations on a City of Ideas*. New York: Rizzoli, 2008.

Duany, Andres, Elizabeth Plater-Zyberk, and Jeff Speck. *Suburban Nation: The Rise of Sprawl and the Decline of the American Dream*. New York: North Point Press, 2000.

Dutton, John A. *New American Urbanism: Re-forming the Suburban Metropolis*. Milan, Italy: Skira editore, 2000.

Evans, Hazel, ed. *New Towns: The British Experience*. New York: John Wiley & Sons, 1972.

Fergusson, Adam. *The Sack of Bath*. London: Persephone Books, 1973.

Flint, Anthony. *Wrestling with Moses: How Jane Jacobs Took on New York's Master Builder and Transformed the American City*. New York: Random House, 2009.

Fulton, William. *The New Urbanism: Hope or Hype for American Communities?* Cambridge, Mass.: Lincoln Institute of Land Policy, 1996.

Garvin, Alexander. *The American City: What Works, What Doesn't.* New York: McGraw-Hill Education, 2014 [1996].

———. *What Makes a Great City.* Washington, D.C.: Island Press, 2016.

Gillette, Howard, Jr. *Civitas by Design: Building Better Communities, from the Garden City to the New Urbanism.* Philadelphia: University of Pennsylvania Press, 2010.

Glazer, Nathan. *From a Cause to a Style: Modernist Architecture's Encounter with the American City.* Princeton, N.J.: Princeton University Press, 2007.

Goldfeld, Abraham. *Toward Fuller Living Through Public Housing and Leisure Time Activities.* New York: The National Public Housing Conference, 1934.

Goldfield, David, ed. *Encyclopedia of American Urban History*, Vol. 2. Thousand Oaks, Calf.: SAGE Reference, 2007.

Goldsmith, Stephen A., and Lynne Elizabeth, eds. *What We See: Advancing the Observations of Jane Jacobs.* Oakland, Calif.: New Village Press, 2010.

Gratz, Roberta Brandes. *The Battle for Gotham: New York in the Shadow of Robert Moses and Jane Jacobs.* New York: Nation Books, 2010.

Henderson, Susan. *Building Culture: Ernst May and the New Frankfurt Initiative, 1926–1931.* New York: Peter Lang Publishing, 2013.

Hood, Clifton. *722 Miles: The Building of the Subways and How They Transformed New York.* New York: Simon & Schuster, 1993.

Horowitz, David. *Radical Son: A Journey Through Our Times.* New York: Free Press, 1997.

Howard, Ebenezer. *Garden Cities of To-Morrow.* Cambridge, Mass.: MIT Press, 1965.

Jackson, Kenneth T. *Crabgrass Frontier: The Suburbanization of the United States.* New York: Oxford University Press, 1985.

Jackson, Kenneth T., ed. *The Encyclopedia of New York City.* New Haven: Yale University Press, 2010.

Jacobs, Jane. *The Death and Life of Great American Cities.* New York: Random House, 1961.

Johnson, Philip, and Henry-Russell Hitchcock, Jr. *Modern Architecture, International Exhibition.* New York: Museum of Modern Art, 1932.

Karatzas, Daniel. *Jackson Heights, A Garden in the City: the History of America's First Garden and Cooperative Community.* Jackson Heights: Jackson Heights Beautification Group, 1990.

Keppel, Frederick P., and R. L. Duffus. *The Arts in American Life.* New York: McGraw-Hill Book Company, Inc., 1933.

Keith, Nathaniel S. *Politics and the Housing Crisis Since 1930.* New York: Universe Books, 1973.

Kroessler, Jeffrey A., and Nina Rappaport. *Historic Preservation in Queens.* Sunnyside: Queensborough Preservation League, 1990.

Larsen, Kristin E. *Community Architect: The Life and Vision of Clarence S. Stein.* Ithaca, N.Y.: Cornell University Press, 2016.

Lawson, Ronald. *The Tenant Movement in New York City, 1904–1984.* New Brunswick: Rutgers University Press, 1986.

Leuchtenburg, William E. *Franklin D. Roosevelt and the New Deal.* New York: Harper and Row, 1963.

Lewis, Barry. *Kew Gardens: Urban Village in the Big City.* Kew Gardens: Kew Gardens Council for Recreation and the Arts, 1999.

Liverpool Heritage Bureau. *Buildings of Liverpool.* Liverpool: The Bureau, 1978.

Lovejoy, Thomas J. *The History of Jamaica Estates, 1929–1969*. Jamaica, N.Y.: Jamaica Estates Association, 1969.

Lubove, Roy. *Community Planning in the 1920s: The Contribution of the Regional Planning Association of America*. Pittsburgh: University of Pittsburgh Press, 1963.

———. *The Urban Community*. Englewood Cliffs, N.J.: Prentice-Hall, Inc., 1967.

MacFayden, Dugald. *Sir Ebenezer Howard and the Town Planning Movement*. Cambridge, Mass.: MIT Press, 1970.

MacKay, Robert B., ed. *Gardens of Eden: Long Island's Early-Twentieth-Century Planned Communities*, New York: W. W. Norton, 2015.

Manuel, Frank E., and Fritzie P. Manuel. *Utopian Thought in the Western World*. Cambridge, Mass.: Belknap Press of Harvard University Press, 1979.

Miller, Donald L. *Lewis Mumford: A Life*. Pittsburgh: University of Pittsburgh Press, 1992 (originally published New York: Weidenfeld and Nicolson, 1989).

Miller, Mervyn. *Hampstead Garden Suburb*. The Archive Photographs Series. Chalford: Chalford Publishing, 1995.

———. *Letchworth: The First Garden City*. Chichester, Sussex: Phillimore, 1989.

Mumford, Lewis. *The Brown Decades: A Study of the Arts in America, 1865–1895*. New York: Dover, 1971 (1931).

———. *City Development: Studies in Disintegration and Renewal*. London: Secker & Warburg, 1946.

———. *The Culture of Cities*. New York: Harcourt, Brace, 1938.

———. *Green Memories: The Story of Geddes Mumford*. New York: Harcourt, Brace, 1947.

———. *Sketches from Life: The Autobiography of Lewis Mumford, The Early Years*, New York: Dial Press, 1982.

———. *The Urban Prospect*. New York: Harcourt, Brace, 1968.

Osborn, Frederic J. *Green-Belt Cities*. New York: Shocken Books, 1969 (1946).

Osman, Suleiman. *The Invention of Brownstone Brooklyn: Gentrification and the Search for Authenticity in Postwar New York*. New York: Oxford University Press, 2012.

Parsons, Kermit C., ed. *The Writings of Clarence S. Stein: Architect of the Planned Community*. Baltimore: Johns Hopkins University Press, 1998.

Parsons, Kermit C., and David Schuyler. *From Garden City to Green City: The Legacy of Ebenezer Howard*. Baltimore: Johns Hopkins University Press, 2002.

Peterson, Jon A. *The Birth of City Planning in the United States, 1848–1917*. Baltimore: Johns Hopkins University Press, 2003.

Pink, Louis H. *The New Day in Housing*. Metropolitan America. New York: Arno Press, 1974 (1928).

Plunz, Richard. *A History of Housing in New York City: Dwelling Type and Social Change in the American Metropolis*. New York: Columbia University Press, 1990.

Radford, Gail. *Modern Housing for America: Policy Struggles in the New Deal Era*. Chicago: University of Chicago Press, 1996.

Rodgers, Daniel T. *Atlantic Crossings: Social Politics in a Progressive Age*. Cambridge, Mass.: Belknap Press of Harvard University Press, 1998.

Rosenwaike, Ira. *Population History of New York City*. Syracuse, N.Y.: Syracuse University Press, 1972.

Rybczynski, Witold. *Mysteries of the Mall and Other Essays*. New York: Farrar, Straus and Giroux, 2015.

Schaffer, Daniel. *Garden Cities for America: The Radburn Experience*. Philadelphia: Temple University Press, 1982.

Scott, Mel. *American City Planning Since 1890*. Berkeley: University of California Press, 1969.

Sherman, Franklin J. *Building Up Greater Queens Borough: An Estimate of Its Development and the Outlook*. New York: Brooklyn Biographical Society, 1929.

Sies, Mary Corbin, Isabelle Gournay, and Robert Freestone, eds. *Iconic Planned Communities and the Challenge of Change*. Philadelphia: University of Pennsylvania Press, 2019.

Sies, Mary Corbin, and Christopher Silver, eds. *Planning the Twentieth-Century American City*. Baltimore: Johns Hopkins University Press, 1996.

Snyder, Robert W. *Crossing Broadway: Washington Heights and the Promise of New York City*. Ithaca, N.Y.: Cornell University Press, 2015.

Stein, Clarence S. *Toward New Towns for America*. Cambridge, Mass.: MIT Press, 1966 (1957).

Stern, Robert A. M. *The Anglo-American Suburb*. London: Architectural Design, 1981.

Stern, Robert A. M., David Fishman, and Jacob Tilove. *Paradise Planned: The Garden Suburb and the Modern City*. New York: Monacelli Press, 2013.

Stern, Robert A. M., Gregory Gilmartin, and Thomas Mellins, *New York 1930: Architecture and Urbanism Between the Two World Wars*. New York: Rizzoli, 1987.

Sussman, Carl, ed. *Planning the Fourth Migration: The Neglected Vision of the Regional Planning Association of America*. Cambridge, Mass.: MIT Press, 1976.

Talen, Emily. *New Urbanism & American Planning: The Conflict of Cultures*. New York: Routledge, 2005.

Unwin, Sir Raymond. *Town Planning in Practice: An Introduction to the Art of Designing Cities and Suburbs*. New York: Benjamin Blom, Inc., 1971 (London: 1909; second edition, 1934).

Ward, Steven V., ed. *The Garden City: Past, Present, and Future*. London: E & FN Spon, 1992.

Warner, Sam Bass. *The Urban Wilderness: A History of the American City*. New York: Harper & Row, 1972.

Way, Thaisa. *Unbounded Practice: Women and Landscape Architecture in the Early Twentieth Century*. Charlottesville: University of Virginia Press, 2009.

Whalen, Richard J. *A City Destroying Itself: An Angry View of New York*. New York: William Morrow, 1965.

Whitaker, Charles H., Edith Elmer Wood, Richard S. Childs, and Frederick L. Ackerman. *The Housing Problem in War and Peace*. Washington, D.C.: Journal of the American Institute of Architects, 1918.

White, Norval, and Elliot Willensky. *The AIA Guide to New York City*. 1st ed. New York: Macmillan, 1968.

Willensky, Elliot, and Norval White. *The AIA Guide to New York City*. 3rd ed. San Diego: Harcourt Brace Jovanovich, 1988.

Wojtowicz, Robert, ed. *Sidewalk Critic: Lewis Mumford's Writings on New York*. New York: Princeton Architectural Press, 1998.

Wood, Anthony C. *Preserving New York: Winning the Right to Protect a City's Landmarks*. New York: Routledge, 2008.

Woodbury, Coleman, ed. *Urban Redevelopment: Problems and Practices*. Chicago: University of Chicago Press, 1953.

Wright, Henry. *Rehousing Urban America*. New York: Columbia University Press, 1935.

Articles, Chapters, and Papers

Abbott, Carl. "*Our Cities* and *The City*: Incompatible Classics?" *Planning Perspectives* 27, no. 1 (January 2012).

Ackerman, Frederick L. "The Architectural Side of City Planning." *Proceedings of the Seventh National Conference on City Planning*. Boston: National Conference on City Planning, 1915.
———. "From Our Special Correspondent in England." *Journal of the American Institute of Architects*, Vol. V, no. 11 (November 1917).
———. "The Significance of England's Program of Building Workmen's Houses." *Journal of the American Institute of Architects*, Vol. V, no. 11 (November 1917).
———. "Where Goes the City-Planning Movement?" *Journal of the American Institute of Architects*, Vol. VII, no. 12 (December 1919).

Angotti, Tom. "The Real Estate Market in the United States: Progressive Strategies." Unpublished paper, December 1999 [Google Scholar, accessed November 2, 2015].

Ascher, Charles S. "The Extra-Municipal Administration of Radburn: An Experiment in Government by Contract." *National Municipal Review* (July 1929).
———. "Private Covenants in Urban Redevelopment." In *Urban Redevelopment: Problems and Practices*, edited by Coleman Woodbury. Chicago: University of Chicago Press, 1953.
———. "Reflections on the Art of Administering Deed Restrictions." *The Journal of Land & Public Utility Economics* 8, no. 4 (1932).

Auger, Tracy B. "Radburn—the Challenge of a New Town." City Housing Corporation (1931?), reprinted from *Michigan Municipal Review*, February and March 1931.

Barrows, Robert G. "Beyond the Tenement: Patterns of American Urban Housing, 1879–1930." *Journal of Urban History* 9, no. 4 (August 1983).

Birch, Eugenie Ladner. "Radburn and the American Planning Movement: The Persistence of an Idea." *Journal of the American Planning Association* 46, no. 4 (October 1980).

Bollack, Francoise Astorg. "Defining Appropriateness." In *Saving Place: 50 Years of New York City Landmarks*, edited by Donald Albrecht, Andrew S. Dolkart, and Seri Worden. New York: Monacelli Press, 2015.

Cautley, Marjorie Sewell. "Planting at Radburn." *Landscape Architecture*, Vol. XXI, no. 1 (October 1930).

Culpin, Ewart G. "The Remarkable Application of Town-Planning Principles to the War-Time Necessities of England." *Journal of the American Institute of Architects* 5, no. 4 (April 1917).

Dana, Andrew, and Michael Ramsey. "Conservation Easements and the Common Law." *Stanford Environmental Law Journal* 8 (1989).

Ely, Richard T. "The City Housing Corporation and 'Sunnyside.'" *Journal of Land & Public Utility Economics* 2, no. 2 (April 1926): 172–185.

Emmerich, Herbert. "The Problem of Low-Priced Cooperative Apartments: An Experiment at Sunnyside Gardens." *Journal of Land & Public Utility Economics* 4, no. 3 (August 1928): 225–234.

Fishman, Robert. "The Bounded City." In *From Garden City to Green City: The Legacy of Ebenezer Howard*, edited by Kermit C. Parsons and David Schuyler. Baltimore: Johns Hopkins University Press, 2002.

Gillette, Howard, Jr. "Film as Artifact: *The City* (1939)." *American Studies* 18, no. 2 (1977).

Gould, Elgin R. L. "The Housing Problem in Great Cities." *Quarterly Review of Economics* 14 (1899–1900): 378–393.

"Government Housing Scheme." *Journal of the American Institute of Architects*, Vol. V, no. 9 (September 1917).

Havelick, Franklin, and Michael Kwartler. "Sunnyside Gardens: Whose Land Is It Anyway?" *New York Affairs* 7, no. 2 (1982).

Heim, Carol E. "The Treasury as Developer-Capitalist? British New Town Building in the 1950s." *Journal of Economic History* 50, no. 4 (December 1990).

Horowitz, Ruth, "Sycamore Trees and Courtyards," 2016, Queens Memory Collection at the Archives of the Queens Library.

Kenney, Judith. "New Urbanism." *Encyclopedia of American Urban History*. Edited by David Goldfield. Vol. 2. Thousand Oaks, Calif.: SAGE Reference, 2007.

Larsen, Kristen E. "*Cities to Come*: Clarence Stein's Postwar Regionalism." *Journal of Planning History* 4, no. 1 (February 2005).

———. "Planning and Public-Private Partnerships: Essential Links in Early Federal Housing Policy." *Journal of Planning History* 15, no. 1 (2016): 68–81.

———. "Research in Progress: The Radburn Idea As An Emergent Concept: Henry Wright's Regional City." *Planning Perspectives* 23 (July 2008): 381–395.

Lubove, Roy. "Homes and 'A Few Well Placed Fruit Trees': An Object Lesson In Federal Housing," *Social Research* 27, no. 4 (Winter 1960).

McClelland, Linda Flint, Paula S. Reed, and Edith B. Wallace. "Revisiting Radburn: 'Where Art And Nature Combine To Make Good Living Conditions.'" *New Jersey History* 12, nos.1–2 (Spring-Summer 2005).

Mumford, Lewis. "Frederick Lee Ackerman, F.A.I.A., 1878–1950." *Journal of the American Institute of Architects*, Vol. XIV, no. 6 (December 1950).

———. Introduction to "The Garden City Idea and Modern Planning." In *Garden Cities of To-Morrow*, by Ebenezer Howard. Cambridge, Mass.: MIT Press, 1965.

Olmsted, Frederick Law, Jr. "Lessons from Housing Developments of the United States Housing Corporation." *Monthly Labor Review* 8 (May 1919).

Pearlstein, Daniel. "Sweeping Six Percent Philanthropy Away: The New Deal in Sunnyside Gardens." *Journal of Planning History* 9, no. (3): 170–182.

Stein, Clarence S. "Housing and Reconstruction." *Journal of the American Institute of Architects*, Vol. VI, no. 10 (October 1918).

Szylvian, Kristin M. "Industrial Housing Reform and the Emergency Fleet Corporation." *Journal of Urban History* 25, no. 5 (July 1999).

Talen, Emily. "Beyond the Front Porch: Regionalist Ideals in the New Urbanist Movement." *Journal of Planning History* 7, no. 1 (February 2008).

Tough, Rosalind. "II. Building Costs and Total Costs at Sunnyside Gardens, L.I." *Journal of Land & Public Utility Economics* 8, no. 2 (May 1932): 43–54.

———. "Production Costs of Urban Land in Sunnyside, Long Island." *Journal of Land & Public Utility Economics* 8, no. 1 (February, 1932): 164–174.

Wood, Anthony C. "Preserving the Patrimony of the People: Albert S. Bard and the Landmarks Law," *City Courant* (Spring 2015).

Wright, Henry. "The Autobiography of Another Idea." *Western Architect* 39, no. 9 (September 1930).

Young, Robert F. "Garden Cities and the Urban Future." In *From Garden City to Green City: The Legacy of Ebenezer Howard*, edited by Kermit C. Parsons and David Schuyler. Baltimore: Johns Hopkins University Press, 2002.

Zipp, Samuel. "The Roots and Routes of Urban Renewal." *Journal of Urban History* 39, no. 3 (2012): 366–391.

Newspapers, Magazines, and Digital Publications

Ackerman, Frederick L. "Houses and Ships." *American City* 19, no. 2 (August 1918).

———. "War-Time Housing—England's Most Urgent Civic Lesson for America." *American City* 18, no. 2 (February 1918).

Brooke, Chris. "Your Gates Must Go; Lawyer Ordered To Remove Barriers Put Up To Protect His Family After Four Robberies At His Luxury Home." *Daily Mail* (London), June 19, 2002.

Goldberger, Paul. "Icon of Modernism Poised for Extinction." *New York Times*, March 8, 1987.

Gray, Christopher. "Streetscapes/Henry Phipps and Phipps Houses: Millionaire's Effort to Improve Housing for the Poor." *New York Times*, November 23, 2003.

Howe, Frederic C. "The Garden Cities of England." *Scribner's Magazine* 52, no. 1 (July 1912).

Lainton, Andrew. "Battle Over the Very First Green Belt at Letchworth," February 25, 2015. https://andrewlainton.wordpress.com/2015/02/25/battle-over-the-very-first-green-belt-at-letchworth/.

Lasker, Loula. "Sunnyside Up and Down." *Survey Graphic* 25, July 1936.

Murray, Christian. "Landmarks Commission Rejects Aluminaire House Proposal." *Sunnyside Post*, January 17. http://sunnysidepost.com/2014/01/17/landmarks-commission-rejects-aluminaire-house-proposal/.

Nonko, Emily. "Sunnyside Gardens Residents Air Complaints About Aluminaire House Proposal." *Brownstoner Queens*. http://queens.brownstoner.com/2013/09/sunnyside-gardens-residents-air-complaints-about-aluminaire-house-proposal/.

Robbins, Tom. "The Democratic Vision of Sunnyside Gardens." *City Limits*, Vol. X, no. 3 (March 1985).

Rosa, Joseph. "A. Lawrence Kocher, Albert Frey, The Aluminaire House, 1930–31." *Assemblage* 11 (April 1990).

Spaziani, Rose. "Modern Artifact: The Story of the Aluminaire House," *NYIT Magazine* (2013). http://www.nyit.edu/magazine/modern_artifact/.

Stein, Clarence S. "New Towns for the Needs of a New Age: An Architect Pictures the Coordinated Community of the Future." *New York Times*, October 8, 1933.

Strickland, Julie. "Aluminum House Plan Gets Chilly Reception in Sunnyside." *The Real Deal*. http://therealdeal.com/blog/2013/10/16/aluminum-house-plan-gets-chilly-reception-in-sunnyside/.

Velsey, Kim. "Is the Aluminaire House Proposal About Historic Preservation or New Development? And Does It Matter?" *New York Observer*, September 6, 2013. http://observer.com/2013/09/is-aluminaire-house-proposal-about-historic-preservation-or-new-development/.

Warshawer, Gabby. "Dispute Takes Shine Off Aluminaire House." *Wall Street Journal*, October 9, 2013.

Webb, Gervase. "Why They Listed This Eden That Is Hampstead's Garden." *Evening Standard* (London), November 29, 1996.

Interviews

Ascher, Charles S. "The Radburn Story." Oral history interview by F. C. McMullen, December 7, 1970. Ascher Papers, Columbia University, Box 25, Radburn folder 1.
Oral History Interview with Charles Ascher, 1972, interviewed by Tom Hogan. The Columbia Center for Oral History. New York: Trustees of Columbia University in the City of New York, 1982.
Fisher, Kenneth K.. Interview by Jeffrey A. Kroessler, October 15, 2015.
Vengoechea, Pablo. Interview by Jeffrey A. Kroessler, November 24, 2015.

Websites

Aluminaire Foundation, http://www.aluminaire.org/.
Architects League of Northern New Jersey, Radburn Historical Documents, http://www.alnnj.org/Radburn.html.
Buhl Foundation's Chatham Village Photographs, Senator John Heinz History Center, https://www.heinzhistorycenter.org/detre-library-archives/collection-highlights/buhl-foundation-chatham-village-photographs.
Celebration, Florida, http://www.celebration.fl.us/.
Congress for the New Urbanism, https://www.cnu.org/.
English Heritage, https://www.english-heritage.org.uk/.
Forest Hills Gardens Corporation, http://foresthillsgardens.org/.
Gazetteer for Scotland, https://www.scottish-places.info/
Historic Districts Council, www.hdc.org.
Historic England, https://historicengland.org.uk/.
Jackson Heights Beautification Group, http://www.jhbg.org/resources/history.
Landmarks Preservation Commission, City of New York. https://www1.nyc.gov/site/lpc/index.page.
Laura Heim Architect PLLC, http://heimarchitect.com/.
Letchworth Garden City Heritage Foundation, www.letchworth.com.
Municipal Archives, New York City Department of Records and Information Services. https://www1.nyc.gov/site/records/about/municipal-archives.page.
National Register Digital Assets, National Park Service, United States Department of the Interior. http://focus.nps.gov/AssetDetail/NRIS/84002919.
Our Welwyn Garden City, http://www.ourwelwyngardencity.org.uk/.
Realtor.com, http://www.realtor.com/.
Sunnyside Gardens Preservation Alliance, http://sunnysidegardens.us/.
Willie Miller Urban Design, https://www.williemiller.com/raymond-unwin-and-gretna.htm.
Yorkship Village, http://www.yorkshipvillage.com/.

Organizational Documents and Publications

Blackburn, Jane. "Trust Wins Landmark Case." Suburb News, Issue 104 (Autumn 2010).
Ascher, Charles S. "Remarks on the Designation of Radburn as a Historic Landmark," October 4, 1975. http://www.alnnj.org/Radburn.html.
City Housing Corporation, "Declaration of Restrictions No. 1 Affecting Radburn, Property of the City Housing Corporation, in the Borough of Fair Lawn, Bergen County, New Jersey. Dated March 15, 1929." [New York]: City Housing Corporation, 1929.

Forest Hills Gardens Corporation. "Architecture and Construction Procedures and Guidelines," May 2002. http://foresthillsgardens.org/architecture/.

Hall, Susan. "20 Million Plan To Rebuild Homes." Our Welwyn Garden City. http://www.our welwyngardencity.org.uk/page_id__538_path__0p162p.aspx.

Hampstead Garden Suburb Development Company, Ltd. *Town Planning & Modern Architecture in the Hampstead Garden Suburb*. Hampstead: Garden Suburb Development Company, Ltd., [1909].

Hampstead Garden Suburb Residents Association, Brochure, n.d.

Hampstead Garden Suburb Scheme of Management, Approved Pursuant to the Leasehold Reform Act 1967, by an Order of the Chancery Division of the High Court, dated 17th January 1974, as amended by a further Order dated 17th February 1983.

Hampstead Garden Suburb Scheme of Management, Issue 8, September 2010.

Hampstead Garden Suburb Trust. "Hampstead Garden Suburb Conservation Area: Design Guidance." n.d.

Hampstead Garden Suburb Trust. "An Introduction to the Role, Procedures, and Operations of the Trust." n.d.

Hampstead Garden Suburb Trust. "Report and Accounts for the Year 5 April 2010."

Letchworth Garden City Heritage Foundation. "A Brief History." http://www.letchworth.com /heritage-foundation/letchworth-garden-city/a-brief-history.

Letchworth Garden City Heritage Foundation. "Our Objectives." http://www.letchworth.com /heritage-foundation/about-us/our-objectives.

Letchworth Garden City Heritage Foundation. "Strategic Plan, October 2011 to September 2016." www.letchworth.com.

Municipal Art Society. *A Tale of Two Rezonings: Taking a Harder Look at CEQR*. New York: The Society, 2018. https://www.mas.org/wp-content/uploads/2018/11/ceqr-report-2018.pdf.

Real Estate Board of New York. *An Analysis of Landmarked Properties in Manhattan*. New York: REBNY, June 2013.

Wallace, Edith B., and Paula S. Reed. National Historic Landmark Nomination, June 2004. www .nps.gov/nhl/find/statelists/nj/Radburn.pdf.

Welwyn Hatfield Borough Council, Welwyn Garden City Estate Management Scheme. www .welhat.gov.uk.

Government Documents and Publications

City of New York, Local Law No. 10, 1980. http://www.nyc.gov/html/dob/downloads/pdf/ll_1080 .pdf.

Colonial Terraces Design Guidelines, City of Newburgh. www.cityofnewburgh-ny.gov/ . . . /colonial-terrace-design-district-guidelines.

Department of City Planning, City of New York. "Amendment of the Zoning Resolution, Pursuant to Section 200 of the New York City Charter, Relating to Article X Chapter 3 Concerning the Establishment of a Special Planned Community Preservation District," CP-22501, June 12, 1974.

Department of City Planning, City of New York. "Sunnyside Gardens: A Fact Sheet for Residents." n.d.

Housing Division, Federal Emergency Administration of Public Works, Bulletin No. 2. "Urban Housing: The Story of the PWA Housing Division, 1933–1936." Washington, D.C.: Government Printing Office, August 1936.

Landmarks Preservation Commission, City of New York. "District Master Plan for the Douglaston Historic District." New York: the Commission, n.d.

Landmarks Preservation Commission, City of New York. "Doing Work in Sunnyside Gardens: A Homeowners Guide to the Landmarks Preservation Commission Rules." New York: the Commission, 2009.

Landmarks Preservation Commission, City of New York. *Jackson Heights Historic District.* New York: the Commission, 1993. http://www.nyc.gov/html/lpc/downloads/pdf/reports/JACKSON _HEIGHTS_HISTORIC_DISTRICT.pdf.

Landmarks Preservation Commission, City of New York. "Proposed Alterations and New Construction of Storefronts in the Jackson Heights Historic District." New York: the Commission, n.d.

Landmarks Preservation Commission, City of New York. *Sunnyside Gardens Historic District Designation.* New York: the Commission, 2007. http://www.nyc.gov/html/lpc/downloads/pdf /reports/SunnysideGardens.pdf.

Leasehold Reform Act, 1967. http://www.legislation.gov.uk/ukpga/1967/88/enacted.

United States Bureau of Labor and Gould, E.R.L. *The Housing of the Working People.* Washington, D.C.: Government Printing Office, 1895.

Newspapers, Magazines, and Digital Publications

Architectural Record

Brownstoner Queens, https://twitter.com/brownstonerqns.

Daily Mail (London)

Evening Standard (London)

Nation

New York Institute of Technology Magazine

New York Observer

New York Times

New Yorker

Newsday

Real Deal, http://therealdeal.com/.

Suburb News

Sunnyside Gardener

Sunnyside Post, http://sunnysidepost.com/.

Survey Graphic

Trust Gazette

Wall Street Journal

INDEX

Jeffrey A. Kroessler is a Professor at the Lloyd Sealy Library, John Jay College of Criminal Justice, CUNY, and author of *The Greater New York Sports Chronology*; *New York, Year by Year: A Chronology of the Great Metropolis*; *Historic Preservation in Queens*; and other works.

EMPIRE STATE EDITIONS SELECT TITLES FROM EMPIRE STATE EDITIONS

Tom Glynn, *Reading Publics: New York City's Public Libraries, 1754–1911*

Craig Saper, *The Amazing Adventures of Bob Brown: A Real-Life Zelig Who Wrote His Way Through the 20th Century*

R. Scott Hanson, *City of Gods: Religious Freedom, Immigration, and Pluralism in Flushing, Queens.* Foreword by Martin E. Marty

Dorothy Day and the Catholic Worker: The Miracle of Our Continuance. Edited, with an Introduction and Additional Text by Kate Hennessy, Photographs by Vivian Cherry, Text by Dorothy Day

Mark Naison and Bob Gumbs, *Before the Fires: An Oral History of African American Life in the Bronx from the 1930s to the 1960s*

Robert Weldon Whalen, *Murder, Inc., and the Moral Life: Gangsters and Gangbusters in La Guardia's New York*

Joanne Witty and Henrik Krogius, *Brooklyn Bridge Park: A Dying Waterfront Transformed*

Sharon Egretta Sutton, *When Ivory Towers Were Black: A Story about Race in America's Cities and Universities*

Pamela Hanlon, *A Wordly Affair: New York, the United Nations, and the Story Behind Their Unlikely Bond*

Britt Haas, *Fighting Authoritarianism: American Youth Activism in the 1930s*

David J. Goodwin, *Left Bank of the Hudson: Jersey City and the Artists of 111 1st Street.* Foreword by DW Gibson

Nandini Bagchee, *Counter Institution: Activist Estates of the Lower East Side*

Susan Celia Greenfield (ed.), *Sacred Shelter: Thirteen Journeys of Homelessness and Healing*

Elizabeth Macaulay-Lewis and Matthew M. McGowan (eds.), *Classical New York: Discovering Greece and Rome in Gotham*

Susan Opotow and Zachary Baron Shemtob (eds.), *New York after 9/11*

Andrew Feffer, *Bad Faith: Teachers, Liberalism, and the Origins of McCarthyism*

Colin Davey with Thomas A. Lesser, *The American Museum of Natural History and How It Got That Way.* Forewords by Kermit Roosevelt III and Neil deGrasse Tyson

Wendy Jean Katz, *Humbug: The Politics of Art Criticism in New York City's Penny Press*

Lolita Buckner Inniss, *The Princeton Fugitive Slave: The Trials of James Collins Johnson*

Mike Jaccarino, *America's Last Great Newspaper War: The Death of Print in a Two-Tabloid Town*

Angel Garcia, *The Kingdom Began in Puerto Rico: Neil Connolly's Priesthood in the South Bronx*

Jim Mackin, *Notable New Yorkers of Manhattan's Upper West Side: Bloomingdale–Morningside Heights*

Matthew Spady, *The Neighborhood Manhattan Forgot: Audubon Park and the Families Who Shaped It*

Robert O. Binnewies, *Palisades: The People's Park*

Marilyn S. Greenwald and Yun Li, *Eunice Hunton Carter: A Lifelong Fight for Social Justice*

Elizabeth Macaulay-Lewis, *Antiquity in Gotham: The Ancient Architecture of New York City*

For a complete list, visit www.fordhampress.com/empire-state-editions.